Life's Greatest Lesson

The Message Jesus Intended for Us

Dwight Nichols

Copyright © 2002 by Dwight Nichols. All rights reserved. Printed in the United States of America. No part of this book may be reproduced in any manner without written permission from the publisher, except by a reviewer, who may quote brief passages in a review.

Library of Congress Control Number 2002092516

ISBN 0-9624064-4-9

The information offered in this book is not a substitute for professional consultation. Matters regarding physical and mental health require the services of qualified doctors and or therapists. The publisher and author disclaim all liability with the use of the information contained in this book.

For information, address: New Era Training, P. O. Box 9895, Knoxville, TN   37940-0895

Other books by the author:

Listening to Ourselves: The Key to Everything that Matters
Contents

	Caution - Read This First: How To Get The Most Out Of This Book	1
	Foreword - How This Book Was Written	4
1.	Introduction	6
2.	Fear - The Devil Within Us	10
3.	The Masks We Wear	20
4.	Why We Are The Way We Are	29
5.	How To Change The Way We Are	63
6.	How To Tame Your Mind	86
7.	Discovering Ourselves	98
8.	How To Get What You Want	128
9.	How To Have Peace of Mind	153
10.	How To Love and Be Loved	167
11.	Relationships That Work	185
12.	The Secret Of Sexual Fulfillment	220
13.	How To Be Healthy and Happy	248
14.	Breakthrough to Awareness	271
15.	The Truth That Sets Us Free	301
16.	Summary	318
	Appendix - A 30-Day Program For Changing Your Life	320

Discover Truth and Be Free
(A companion booklet to: *Listening to Ourselves*)

Chapter	Contents	Page
1	Introduction	1
2	The Way Things Are	3
3	The Way Things Should Be	6
4	Things That Don't Work	13
5	The Cause of Our Suffering	22
6	The Solution to Mental Suffering	44
7	The Discovery of Truth	55
8	Summary	67

To the many fellow travelers, to those who responded to my previous writings (my first book, *Listening to Ourselves: The Key to Everything that Matters,* and my essays on the Internet), to many special people (especially my family), and to those who might find something in this book that might help them in some manner.

There is no happiness where there is no wisdom. — Sophocles

The beginning of wisdom is to call things by their right names. — Chinese proverb

---

It's logical, reasonable, desirable and possible ... and consistent with what Jesus said:

The way the world *could be* begins with us. The way we *could be* is loving, happy, satisfied, and contented ... deep inside, the way everybody wants to be. When we as a society are the way we *could be*, in due time this world will be the way it *could be* ... safe, loving, peaceful, and harmonious.

Heaven on earth *could be* like the heaven within us— perfect ... if only we understood and embodied the message Jesus intended for us.

When we change, our world changes. It all begins with us. If we do not change, who will? If we do not change now, when will we?

Contents

Caution! Read this first!   i

Introduction   1
Although it has been glossed over, Jesus told us everything we need to know to learn the greatest lesson life has to offer.

1. Our Purpose in Life   7
When we are fulfilling our purpose (which is very simple) we are happy, satisfied, and contented. Jesus told us what our top priority in life is; however, we have glossed over what he said.

2. Why Christianity Isn't Working   18
Learn the truth about false religious teachings that are a stumbling block in our path to the discovery of the truth that sets us free … that impede us from understanding what Jesus said. Learn the one thing that would cause Christianity to flourish.

3. The Truth about What Will Save Us   56
About 2,000 years ago, Jesus told us what will save us. Learn the truth about what saves us … according to what Jesus said.

4. Truth Is the Way   79
The hidden secret of the ages … this must be it! What is truth? Where is truth? How do we discover the truth that sets us free? Learn a simple exercise for discovering the truth.

5. Understanding What Jesus Said   102
Jesus' ministry was about 2,000 years ago, and many Christians don't understand what Jesus said. Learn the truth about the gospel that Jesus preached and why he preached it.

6. The Hidden Cause of Suffering   147
What is Satan? Where is Satan? Learn the truth! Jesus said, "It's done unto us as we believe." Learn the core beliefs that cause us suffering and unhappiness. Learn the truth about the cause of evil and what obliterates it.

7. Why Christians Leave Christianity — 161
It's ironic, but Christians leave Christianity in an effort to learn the basic message Jesus intended for us. From the wisdom in a six-word statement in the New Testament, we know the cause of — and the solution to —the things that trouble us the most (anger, anxiety, depression, hate, jealousy, stress, the break-up of families, etc.). From this six-word statement, we know what will save us. Jesus came not to call the righteous, but sinners to repentance. Who are those who are already saved without the teachings of Jesus? Learn the truth! There are two possibilities.

8. The Power of God — 190
There is only one power, the power of God. Satan has no power. Learn the truth about the power of God and how it works through us according to the way we believe in our hearts.

9. Wisdom and Understanding — 213
Learn the simple secret for being happy. This is it! No superficial stuff that doesn't work! The *secret* has been known for about 3,000 years; it's in the Old Testament. When we are happy, we have peace and joy ... what everyone desires.

10. Prayer that Never Fails — 225
Jesus' prayer is a way of affirming life as it is meant to be ... the kind of life — the kind of world — that Jesus wanted us to enjoy. Learn the truth about a form of prayer that will save us, a form of prayer that never fails.

11. The Essential Teachings of Jesus — 250
The most essential teachings of Jesus (what will save us) are in the Old Testament. Understanding this helps us shift our focus of study from the man Jesus to his message.

12. When Will Suffering and Violence End? — 289
Both Jesus and Isaiah told us when suffering and violence will end. However, what they said has been glossed over and misinterpreted. Jesus made it quite clear.

13. Summary — 316

Caution! Read this first!

This will help you get the most from reading this book. You will find some view points that are inconsistent with the teachings of Christianity; **however, they are consistent with the teachings of Jesus.** Everything here is made abundantly clear in this book.

An understanding of the Holy Scriptures is simplified once we realize that the word "Lord" as used by the spiritual teachers of the Old Testament means the same thing as the word "Father" as used by Jesus. And, whatever we call it (Lord, Father, true self, higher self, spiritual self, sacred self), it is within us.

Further, the sole purpose for Jesus preaching the gospel is that we might have peace and joy ... *now*, not after we are dead. Christians seem to pay only scant attention to several things Jesus said; e.g., "God is not the God of the dead, but of the living."

There are several factors that render the Holy Scriptures elusive to grasp and understand. Two things that cause considerable confusion about what Jesus said are: False beliefs cause us to distort and misinterpret what we read and study. And, a fundamentalist is one who interprets the Bible literally. Jesus used idioms, metaphors, proverbs, parables, and symbolism. We cannot understand some of the things Jesus said if we interpret idioms literally.

An all-knowing, perfect God — with infinite wisdom and intelligence — did not create us and planet earth to be so complicated that we must decipher and understand everything in the Bible to know the truth that sets us free ... which will save us.

Jesus said that his way is simple: "Learn of me ... and ye shall find rest unto your souls. For my yoke is easy, and my burden is light" (Matthew 11:28-30). We find rest unto our souls and we find peace and joy when we discover the truth that sets us free.

The Apostle Paul (who is credited with writing about two-thirds of the New Testament) left us with many great gems of wisdom. However, the misinterpretations and an exaggeration of what the Apostle Paul said have overshadowed what Jesus said.

Many Christians seem to believe that the gospel is the good news about Jesus and that the essence of the gospel is that Jesus died on the cross to save us from our sins. Further, the teachings of Christianity emphasize such things as the birth of Jesus, his death on the cross, his resurrection, and such things as Jesus is our savior, believe on Jesus and be saved, take Christ into your heart, and so on.

These things are not the gospel that Jesus preached and believing these things does not save us. These things do not alter what we must do to be saved, according to what Jesus said. Believing the gospel that Jesus preached — and doing what he said to do — would save us. Remember that Jesus said, "learn of me."

Also, Jesus said to his disciples, "Go ye into all the world and preach the gospel to every creature. ... He that believeth [the gospel] and is baptized shall be saved, but he that believeth not shall be damned" (Mark 16:16-17).

Twenty selected sayings of Jesus are explained in this book ... explained in our language that is easy to understand. If you read this book from beginning to end (reading slowly and pondering as you read), you will know without a doubt that we would be saved if we believed and understood these selected sayings of Jesus (essentials of the gospel that Jesus preached) ... and if we did what Jesus said to do.

Fundamentalists misinterpret some of the Scriptures, making them seem to support what they believe. For example, Jesus is attributed with saying, "I go to prepare a place for you." This could not mean what fundamentalists seem to think it means—that Jesus has gone to prepare a place for Christians to enjoy after they die. This belief is inconsistent with selected sayings of Jesus that are reasonably clear and easy to understand. The selected sayings of Jesus, explained in this book, are more than enough to save us ... if only we believe and comprehend — and do — what Jesus said. In all simplicity, we are saved when we love as both Moses and Jesus commanded us to love: with all our heart, with all our soul, and with all our mind.

If we (as a society) were saved:
- We would not suffer from anxiety, depression, jealousy, anger, hatred, guilt, shame, emotional insecurity, and psychosomatic illnesses. We would not suffer from those tribulations that rob us of peace and joy.
- Families would be peaceful, harmonious, stable, functional, and they would remain together.
- The social problems that plague our society would cease: crime, violence, shootings in the schools; spousal, child, and

drug abuse; rape, murder, road-rage, robberies, the breakup of families, teenage suicide ... the list goes on.
- We would have no need for therapists, astrologers, psychics, tranquilizers, antidepressants, and medication to help us sleep. We would have no need for pain relievers for tension headaches, which plague more than 50 million Americans.
- We would be our own best therapist, psychic, astrologer, physician, savior, and guru.

False beliefs about such significant things as heaven, hell, Satan — and about what Jesus said — have led us astray from the true teachings of Jesus. False teachings have impeded us from finding our way to God, and consequently, have impeded us from enjoying the abundant life Jesus wanted for us.

Christians would do well to ask themselves the following questions and to answer them honestly, truthfully and rationally:
- Will believing and following the teachings of Jesus (not the same thing as the teachings of Christianity) save us?
- Are the teachings of Christianity consistent with the gospel that Jesus preached?
- Do the teachings of Christianity alter what we must do to be saved, according to what Jesus said?
- Jesus said, "The kingdom of God is within you." Do Christians really believe this? Who are the unbelievers?
- Jesus said, "Seek ye first the kingdom of God." Did Jesus expect us do this? If so, where did Jesus expect us to seek? He said, "the kingdom of God is within you."
- Jesus said, "clean the inside of the cup and the platter."
- Jesus said, "Be ye therefore perfect, even as your Father who is in heaven is perfect."

Was Jesus just talking, or did he expect people to believe and do what he said? When we "clean the inside of the cup and the platter," when we cast the devils (Satan) from our heart, when we discover the truth that sets us free, when we are converted and become as little children (same thing as "being born again"), we are as perfect as Jesus told us to be ... and we are saved. When we are saved, we do the will of our Father, a prerequisite for enjoying heaven, according to Jesus ... same thing as letting God reign in our hearts.

We, our families, our society — the very world itself — are in need of a healing. The man Jesus is not our savior; however, the gospel that Jesus preached and that he commanded his disciples to preach to every creature in the world would save us and heal us ... if only we believed — and did — what Jesus said.

Don McAlvany, author of *Storm Warning: The Coming Persecution of Christians and Traditionalists in America*, said:

> The United States of America, the greatest nation in the history of the world up until a few decades ago, is in decline in every way that a nation can be—economic, financial, social, political, moral, spiritual. We lead the world in divorce, violent crime, drug usage, pornography, promiscuity, illegitimate births, homosexuality, abortion, teenage pregnancies, teenage suicide, alcoholism, child abuse, and per capita prison population.
>
> We have the most corrupt government in our history, but the great majority of Americans (including Christians) don't really care, because they feel prosperous, and because the morals of our leaders simply reflect the morals of our people.

The message Jesus intended for us would change all this ... if only we believed and did what Jesus said. If the gospel that Jesus preached and that he commanded his disciples to preach in all the world had been taught during the past 2,000 years (since the death of Jesus), we, our families, our society, our nation — the very world itself — would be characterized by love, peace, and joy. That's the kind of life — that's the kind of world — Jesus wanted for us. If we believed and did what Jesus said, we would enjoy the abundant life that Jesus wanted us to enjoy ... deep inside the soul of us, what everyone wants.

Think about it! Those who believe the gospel "shall be saved" and those who don't believe "shall be damned." Regardless of what we believe about heaven and hell, doesn't it behoove us to believe the gospel that Jesus preached and to be saved now? There are no provisions for being saved after we die. Think about what a difference it would make with our families, our society and us if we were saved and enjoyed peace and joy — if we enjoyed heaven — *now* ... the "abundant life" that Jesus wanted for us.

If we do not discover the truth that sets us free *now*, when will we?

Introduction

We are beginning the twenty-first century (about 2,000 years since Jesus' ministry), and the vast majority of the two billion Christians throughout the world does not understand and abide by the gospel that Jesus preached. Yet, the message that Jesus intended for us is the way to harmony with truth, God, and nature ... deep inside the soul of us what every one of us desires.

The sole purpose for Jesus preaching the gospel is that we might have peace and joy ... that we might enjoy heaven *now.* False teachings about such things as heaven, hell, Satan and about what Jesus taught have led us astray from the true teachings of Jesus.

If we lived in harmony with truth and had peace and joy, we would be happy, peaceful, and contented. Families would be loving, peaceful, harmonious, and stable, and they would stay together. The social problems that plague us (drug, child, and spousal abuse, divorce, teenage suicide, alcoholism, shootings in the schools, rape, murder, violence ... the list goes on) would not exist.

As it is, we (as a society) are stressed, anxious, fatigued, restless, and impatient. We suffer from all sorts of mental suffering and disastrous, deplorable circumstances. Anger, hatred, jealousy, resentment, insecurity, anxiety, depression, guilt, shame, loneliness, tension headaches, obesity, and mental turmoil are commonplace. We take tranquilizers and antidepressants to help us cope. We spend billions of dollars annually on such things as self-help books, therapy, marriage counseling, psychics, and astrologers. We assume that all that negative stuff that robs us of genuine love, joy, peace, and happiness is natural and normal; it is not. All that stuff is because we are out of harmony with truth, God, and nature.

The things we do in an effort to control crime and violence (prisons, police, the FBI, the laws, the courts, punishment) do nothing to correct the underlying cause of the problems. The ultimate solution to mental suffering and the problems that plague us is knowing the truth that sets us free. The only thing that will bring us the love, joy, peace and happiness we insatiably desire is living in harmony with truth, God, and nature ... what everyone wants to do ... all in agreement with what Jesus said.

Without doubt, the church — with its social activities and Christian fellowship — is one of the most popular organizations in our society and provides a great service to humankind. The social benefits derived from the church are numerous; however, they are a pittance in comparison to the potential benefits derived from believing and abiding by the gospel that Jesus preached. Without the churches, our society most likely would have already self-destructed. But, let's face it! Mainline churches are not teaching the gospel that Jesus preached ... or at least not making it clear.

We tend to think that Christianity is derived from the teachings of Jesus. However, if we notice what is being taught — and if we understand what Jesus taught — we realize that teachers of Christianity are not teaching the gospel that Jesus preached ... at least not teaching it in a manner we can believe, understand, and embody. Many Christians are so captivated by the man Jesus (not by what he taught) that they gloss over his most essential teachings.

Many religious teachers are dedicated and have a sincere desire to help people find salvation. However, instead of teaching what Jesus taught, fundamentalists teach what they believe, which is not consistent with the teachings of Jesus. Also, they teach about such things as the birth of Jesus, the resurrection, Jesus dying on the cross to save us from our sins, that Jesus loves us, that Jesus is our savior, that Jesus is returning soon, believe on Jesus and be saved, take Christ into your heart ... and on and on and on. These things are not the gospel that Jesus preached, and believing these things do not save us. Believing the gospel that Jesus preached — and doing what he said to do — would save us (explained clearly in Chapter 3, "The Truth about What Will Save Us").

Fundamentalists believe that the gospel is the good news about Jesus. The gospel is what Jesus preached and what he commanded his disciples to preach to every creature in the world.

Carl Jung, Swiss Psychiatrist, said: "Through pride we are ever deceiving ourselves. But deep below the surface of the average conscience a still, small voice says to us, something is out of tune."

Introduction

Although not aware of it, we wear our masks, pretending to be other than the way we believe and think in our heart ... pretending to be loving, righteous, happy, and contented. In an effort to enhance our self-esteem and to get a superficial sense of satisfaction, we do and say things that seem to make us appear special and important ... things we can gloat over. These things do not bring us peace, joy, and happiness. These things do not satisfy our soul. Thus, we keep seeking and searching for something to make us happier (happier, not happy). All the while, we desire to live the abundant life Jesus wanted for us; we desire peace and joy.

David Gergen, Editor at Large, *U.S. News & World Report* (December 6, 1999), said: "Across the land, Americans are hungering for something more than money and a new car. They are looking for answers that satisfy the soul and restore a sense of belonging to one another."

Jesus' message — if believed, understood and embodied — satisfies our soul. Let's face it! We have missed the message Jesus intended for us! Underlying all the seeking and searching in which people are engaged (trying one religion and then another, moving from one church to another, reading self-help books galore, participating in personal growth groups, practicing yoga and Zen, joining cults and various study groups, seeking guidance from psychics and astrologers, getting help from therapists and psychiatrists ... the list goes on) is the inherent desire to find peace, joy, and happiness ... the inherent desire to express life in harmony with truth ... the inherent desire to unify with God.

Twenty selected sayings of Jesus that are not taught clearly by orthodox teachers are explained clearly in this book. If we master an understanding of any one of those sayings (not all of them, but any one of them), we will be well on our way to understanding the message Jesus intended for us ... well on our way to learning the greatest lesson life has to offer. A clear understanding of most any one of those statements is more than enough to transform the way Christianity is being taught ... all made clear in this book.

Teaching falsely about such things as heaven, hell, and Satan — and not teaching what Jesus taught — is what Jesus alluded to when he said, "Many false prophets shall rise and shall deceive many." From a cursory observation of all the hypocrisy, suffering, and turmoil in our society (a society in which about 90 percent of the families are dysfunctional), many people are deceived.

We are beginning the twenty-first century and many Christians, do not seem to know what Satan is and where it is. Many so-called believers do not seem to believe — or understand — what Jesus said about heaven being within us. Further, many do not seem to know that discovering the truth that sets us free, that "cleaning the inside of the cup and the platter," that casting the devils from our heart, that being as perfect as our Father who is in heaven is perfect, and that purifying our hearts would save us ... that doing any one of these things would save us.

Throughout history, great teachers (Buddha, Mohammed, Aristotle, Spinoza, Emerson, Plato, Socrates, Ernest Holmes, Charles and Myrtle Fillmore, and others) have left us with many great gems of wisdom. However, fundamentalists have ignored or criticized what these people said. Fundamentalists have judged some as being atheist and unbelievers. Fundamentalists do not realize it, but their disagreements are because they do not believe and understand what Jesus said.

A common practice of fundamentalists is to label those who do not agree with their false beliefs as atheists and unbelievers. Thomas Jefferson, the third President of the United States, was criticized because he did not accept the false teachings of the church. Speaking about Jesus and his teachings, Jefferson said: "When, in short, we shall have unlearned everything that has been taught since his day, and got back to the pure and simple doctrines he inculcated, we shall then be truly and worthily his disciples; and my opinion is that if nothing had ever been added to what flowed purely from his lips, the whole world would at this day have been Christian." (*The Gospel According to Jesus* by Stephen Mitchell).

Throughout history there have been those who have been critical of religion and the teachings of Christianity. In the 1700s, Voltaire (historian and philosopher) said: "Nothing can be more contrary to religion and the clergy than reason and common sense. ... For seventeen hundred years the Christian sect has done nothing but harm" (*The Great Quotations,* Compiled by George Seldes).

Introduction

Christianity has the potential to bring us joy, peace, and happiness ... the potential to restore peace, harmony, and stability to our families ... the potential to render our society, our nation — the very world itself — peaceful, safe, and harmonious ... if only teachers of Christianity would teach the gospel of Jesus in a manner we could believe, understand and embody.

Many people believe that it is wrong to disagree with someone's religious beliefs. False, *religious* beliefs are not sacred; they are not holy ... they are not religious. Instead of being religious, false beliefs are a hindrance to understanding the true teachings of Jesus. They constitute the greatest stumbling block known to humankind in our pathway to harmony with God ... which is the ultimate goal of all our seeking and searching.

I have attempted to make the teachings of Jesus so simple and clear that fundamentalists cannot read this book from the beginning to the end and disagree with what I am saying without realizing that they do not agree with what Jesus said. What I am making clear is that it is not my philosophy or my gospel that I am advocating. It is the gospel that Jesus preached and that he commanded his disciples to preach to every creature in the entire world. Fundamentalist will tend to disagree with what I am saying by explaining what they believe. They will have difficulty in explaining that what I am saying is not consistent with the teachings of Jesus, *based on the gospel that Jesus preached.*

I realize that if I simply wrote *just another book*, most likely it would be given the same type of treatment that fundamentalists have given to the writings of others who do not agree with their erroneous beliefs. Thus, I have exposed false religious teachings that hinder us from understanding what Jesus said, and I have explained the essential teachings of Jesus (what will bring us peace and joy; what will save us) in our language that is easy to understand. Understanding what is false helps us understand what is true.

Further, I have attempted to make the message Jesus intended for us so clear that churches will begin incorporating the message of Jesus into their teachings. My thinking is that we do not need another religion, another religious denomination, and we do not need more cults, witches, satanic worshippers, psychics, astrologers, therapists, false teachers ... and on and on and on. What is needed is for the gospel of Jesus to be taught in the churches ... taught in a manner we can understand, believe and embody.

The benefits derived from believing and doing what Jesus said are incomprehensible; they are what everyone wants. The church — with its organization and the infrastructure already in place — is an ideal place for the gospel of Jesus to be taught.

For eons people have searched for, and philosophers have mused over, the truth. We tend to think of truth as being something cloaked in secrecy that only the mystics, masters, saints, and sages could possibly comprehend. Yet, truth is basic to the teachings of both the Buddha and Jesus. Truth ("thus saith the Lord" and "hear ye the word of the Lord") is the essence of the teachings of the writers of the Old Testament. Truth is basic to all the great religions. Truth will save us, according to what Jesus said.

Jesus said, "You shall know the truth, and the truth shall make you free." George Berkeley, Irish philosopher and clergyman, said, "Truth is the cry of all, but the game of the few." In the 1700s, Denis Diderot, essayist and philosopher, said, "I can be expected to look for the truth but not to find it." All the while, for about 3,000 years, the secret to discovering truth has been in the Old Testament. It's simple to understand, if only we read, study, and assimilate what we read ... all made clear in this book.

Deep inside the soul of us (the place inside of us where "we live, and move, and have our being"), there is nothing we want more than to be free to live in harmony with truth. You will find in this book all the guidance you need in order to know what you must do to discover the truth that will set you free. This book takes the mystery out of Jesus' teachings so that we can understand what he said ... so that we can learn the greatest lesson life has to offer, which is the gospel that Jesus preached about 2,000 years ago. The gospel that Jesus preached would save us, if only we understood and believed what he said ... and did what he said to do.

Can you imagine what our families and our society would be like if we were unified with God and had peace and joy? It's the abundant life that Jesus wanted for us. It's what this book is about.

Chapter 1
Our Purpose in Life

Many people get themselves into a quandary when trying to figure out what their purpose is, thinking that they would be happy if only they knew. We would do well to keep simple things simple. Our purpose on planet Earth is to express life in agreement with truth and nature.

When we are expressing life in agreement with truth, we are happy, satisfied, and contented. And we are making a positive contribution to the world and everything in it. It cannot be otherwise. That is the way an all-knowing, all-loving, all-powerful God designed the process to work.

As it is, we as a society are trapped in a rat race. A German Proverb is: "In America, an hour is 40 minutes." The rat race is not bringing us what everyone wants, which is love, joy, peace of mind, and contentment; loving, lasting, satisfying relationships; loving, happy, harmonious, stable, functional families; and a safe, harmonious, sane society ... all of which we would enjoy if we expressed life in agreement with nature ... in agreement with that which is true. Underlying all the efforts that have created the rat race is the inherent desire to express life in agreement with truth and nature.

Living in agreement with truth and nature is the simplest thing we will ever do and the one thing we inherently and insatiably desire to do ... the one thing that assures us a happy, satisfied, and contented life. Unfortunately, paraphrasing Buddha, "People are led astray, thinking delusion is better than truth."

Missing our purpose in life has left us with a void, and we attempt to fill the void by trying all sorts of things. We struggle and strive and try to be happier, but *trying to be happier* is not the same thing as being happy. People strive for more money, more material things, more love, more friends, more recognition, more adulation, more power, more prestige ... and on and on and on, trying to be happier ... trying to get love and approval ... trying to get a feeling of belonging. Trying to impress others, we try to keep up with the Joneses without taking note of the fact that the Joneses are stressed, unhappy, and burdened with debt.

We think our titles, our labels, our houses, our automobiles, our clothing (our wealth and material things) will convey an impression of something other than the way we feel deep inside. And we accumulate more material things, generate more activity, and do and say those things that we think will make us appear special and important ... all misguided efforts to feel the way we would feel if we were simply in agreement with our purpose in life ... if we were in agreement with truth and nature.

We get on an ego kick, trying to help others ... when all the while we are vicariously trying to help ourselves ... trying to appear important and special ... trying to win love and approval ... trying to be happy, satisfied, and contented. We try to change other people without recognizing the faults within ourselves ... without acknowledging our loneliness, isolation, and emptiness.

When we suffer from low self-esteem, we will stop short of nothing to make ourselves appear impressive and important ... to gain attention, recognition, praise, and adulation. To our false ego-self, it is most important to appear special and important ... most important to appear happy, regardless of how empty we feel. We keep up our facade (wearing our mask) projecting an image of the way we hope others see us ... not the way that we really feel.

A vast portion of our thoughts, time, energy, and efforts is useless and wasted when we are trying to demonstrate to other people something about ourselves that we do not really feel ... something about how great we are, how important we are, how intelligent we are, how loving and righteous we are ... and on and on and on. All we need to be happy, satisfied, and contented is to be real ... just letting things be the way they are supposed to be ... which is in agreement with truth and nature.

T. S. Eliot, American-born writer and poet, said, "Half of the harm that is done in this world is due to people who want to feel important."

Ego gratification does not satisfy our soul. We never can get enough of anything that does not satisfy the soul to satisfy us ... thus the search goes on ... the rat race accelerates. For the most

Our Purpose in Life

part, people do not cease their erratic efforts (characteristic of the rat race) long enough to ask the simple questions: What would satisfy me? What would make me happy and contented? What must I do to love and to be loved? The things that matter the most in life — love, peace, and joy — are simple ... and free.

Sometimes we get caught up in achieving those things we can boast about and gloat over ... things desired by the elephantine ego. There is no way to measure the time, energy, and thoughts that evolve from our fearful, false ego-self; however, it is safe to assume a vast majority. Love and truth are so powerful that a comparatively small minority of the population functioning from the center of love and truth is ample to keep our society glued together ... not safe, loving, happy, and harmonious ... just glued together.

Oftentimes we confuse our purpose in life with our selected profession, thinking that our profession is our purpose. Regardless of our profession, we do not have peace and joy if we are not expressing life in harmony with truth. Many teachers emphasize the importance of doing our best. Our best is not our ultimate best if we are not expressing life in harmony with truth.

Can you imagine? Can you comprehend what our life, our families, our society — the very world itself — would be like if whatever we do in life (regardless of our status, regardless of our profession, hobbies), we do it from the center of love and truth? It's incomprehensible what we, our families, our society, our nation — the very world itself — would be like if we did the only thing that will ever make us happy, satisfied, and contented ... which is to express life in harmony with truth, God, and nature.

Let's face it! Much of our life is a fake. We are out of harmony with truth and nature ... out of harmony with God. We simply wear our masks, projecting an image of being different from the way we really are. We keep up our facade, pretending to be different from the way we really believe and think in our heart.

Thus, we are attempting the impossible—trying to prove that a lie is true ... trying to prove something about ourselves that we do not honestly feel. There is not enough time in a lifetime to prove that a lie is true. Thus, we double-time, trying to stay in place ... and the rat race gathers momentum. Almost everyone is in a frenzy.

Stress, struggle, strain, and fatigue characterize our lives. Stress, fatigue, tension headaches, depression, anxiety, and psychosomatic illnesses are so prevalent that we take them for granted, as if they are natural and normal; they are not.

Our false ego-self can keep us busy, doing things we can gloat over and doing things that make us appear special and important. We can do something to gloat over — something that seems to make us appear special and important — and soon we are back to square one, "needing" to do something else to gloat over and make us appear special and important. It is impossible to do enough things to gloat over and that makes us appear special and important to satisfy our soul ... to be genuinely satisfied and contented.

It's little wonder that we are stressed, restless, and discontented. These things do not bring us joy and peace. On the contrary, these things lead to the death of our spirit. Psychological stress (the kind that makes us sick and that leads to death) is a state of mind induced by obscure, insidious fear ... a fear of what might happen or a fear of what might not happen ... but always fear. We are so far alienated from our purpose in life (from being in harmony with truth, nature, and God) that we cannot comprehend the peace, love, joy, happiness, satisfaction, and contentment derived simply from being humble, honest, truthful ... from being real.

For the most part, we are missing our purpose in life, and we are missing our primary goal in life. In trying to be happier (not happy), we are continually setting goals. We have short-term goals, long-term goals, primary goals, secondary goals, career goals, educational goals, financial goals, and on and on and on. These goals are aimed toward survival and toward rendering our lives reasonably comfortable and pleasant. And these goals are worthy.

However, beyond these secondary goals, we inherently have an ultimate goal in life. Usually we do not acknowledge our ultimate goal for what it is; we do not focus on it; and we do not achieve it. And it is by far the most important goal in life.

If only we pause long enough and think about it, we do not like being troubled, stressed, worried, fearful, depressed, anxious, sad, lonely, selfish, greedy, evil, crooked, egotistical, insecure, jealous, possessive, hateful, angry. Let's face it! We do not like disastrous

Our Purpose in Life 11

relationships, troubled marriages, the breakup of families, divorce, and dysfunctional families. We do not like being sick, having tension headaches, taking painkillers, taking tranquilizers, and taking antidepressants.

Let's face it! We are not satisfied with all the things we do to gain attention, praise, recognition, and adulation ... all the things we do to gloat over. We really do not like the hectic life ... always in a frenzy. In brief, we do not like being unhappy, dissatisfied, restless, and discontented. We do not like wearing our masks, pretending to be something we are not ... we do not like living a lie!

Christopher Marlowe said, "There is no sin but ignorance." Instead of all the stuff that robs us of the life of our spirit, there is a way of life that is far simpler and far more satisfying ... there is a simple way of enjoying the "peace that passeth all understanding."

Deep within, we know there is something more and better than what we are experiencing; we know there must be another way. We keep seeking and searching, but our goal is not clear ... we are not focused. Without clarity of our goal, we try all sorts of things, attempting to find a happy, satisfied, and meaningful life. We keep struggling and striving for more of this and more of that, but there never seems to be enough. There is never enough of anything that is not really satisfying to satisfy us; thus the seeking and searching and the struggling and striving continue.

There is an easy way out of the messy morass in which we have found ourselves. Our ultimate goal in life — that for which we keep seeking and searching — is closely related to our purpose in life. Although I am not aware of any mainline churches that make it clear to us, Jesus told us what our ultimate goal is. Underlying all our seeking and searching is the desire to enjoy the abundant life that we would enjoy if we understood the goal that Jesus gave us, and then focused on it and achieved it. Jesus said, "Seek ye first the kingdom of God, and his righteousness; and all these things shall be added unto you."

Think about it! "Seek ye first the kingdom of God!" Once we discover the kingdom of God (the same thing as the kingdom of Heaven), which is within us, according to what Jesus said, what else is there to search for? This is the end of our seeking and searching! This is the end of our suffering!

Thus, Jesus gave us our top priority in life ... our basic, inherent goal in life, which is heaven ... and while we are alive. Naturally we need some of the necessities of life such as food, clothing, and shelter; however, the means for achieving the necessities in life are rather clear-cut. Discovering heaven is not so clear-cut, but should be a top priority. As it is, we as a society have become materialistic-oriented and are missing out on the quality of life that we inherently desire, which is a life characterized by love, joy, health, happiness, peace of mind, and inner serenity.

About 300 BC, Zeno, Greek Philosopher, said, "The goal of life is living in agreement with nature." Often we gloss over statements similar to this without knowing what they mean and, consequently, without realizing the significance of them. Living in agreement with nature is the same thing as living in agreement with truth, which is the same thing as being unified with God, and that is heaven. And life does not get any better than heaven. When we are in harmony with truth, God, and nature — the only thing that will bring us peace, joy, and happiness — we make a positive contribution to planet earth.

Think about it! We can only change the form of something. We cannot add to or take from what God created, which includes everything that we can see, smell, and touch—and some things that we cannot see, smell and touch. Nature is an expression of God. If we study nature sufficiently, we notice that everything designed and created by God is perfect, and it has a purpose. Everything we observe in nature has the capabilities of reproducing, multiplying, and has a means of protection, getting nourishment and surviving.

The means of protection by the many creatures we observe in nature is nothing less than ingenious; e.g., the electric eel with the capability of generating electricity that can deliver an electrical shock, the porcupine with its quills, the skunk with its odor, the honey bee with its stinger, the snake with its fangs and venom, the seemingly helpless-appearing sea wasp jellyfish with its near invisible tentacles that can lash a deadly sting. Some fish use camouflage as a means of protection. When a chameleon becomes frightened,

Our Purpose in Life

the color of its skin changes; perhaps this offers some degree of protection.

There is nothing haphazard or coincidental in nature. It is no coincident that a duck has web feet for swimming and oil to repel water from it feathers, no coincident that a squirrel has teeth designed for eating nuts and feet perfectly designed for climbing trees to get nuts. It is no coincident that a humming bird has a beak for getting nectar from the flowers and that it can hover while getting the nectar.

The ingenuity designed and created in the carnivorous plants is nothing less than amazing; e.g., the leaves of the pitcher plant serve three purposes. The outside of the leaf contains nectar that attracts insects. The inside secretes an enzyme that digests a captured insect. The top of the leaf folds down to form a closure and to keep rainwater out so that it will not interfere with the digestive process.

Although the largest of the carnivorous plants can capture prey as large as frogs, perhaps the Venus flytrap is the most widely known of the carnivorous plants. The inside of the leaf contains sensitive hairs that cause the flytrap to snap shut once an insect makes contact with them. This can happen in about half a second. Then the leaf produces a red sap that digests the insect. Once the insect has been digested and absorbed as a nutrient, then the flytrap opens again, ready for another catch.

Just think! A God that did all this for the carnivorous plant also designed and created our body and every part of it (eyes, ears, nose, liver, lungs, digestive system, heart, brain, and on and on and on) with a skill and ingenuity that is incomprehensible ... all to make life a joy and a blessing.

If only we would live in harmony with truth and nature, which is the same thing as being in harmony with God, then we could (borrowing from the words of Isaiah), "Go forth with joy, and be led forth with peace; the mountains and the hills shall break out before you into singing, and all the trees of the field shall clap their hands" (Isaiah 55:12).

The beauty of the many colors we observe in nature is beyond description. Although the colors are all around us, they never clash. Think about it, the colors of the birds, fish, animals, flowers, fruits, vegetables, butterflies, insects, rainbows, sunsets, leaves in the autumn, and on and on and on ... and they never clash. The greatest of artists cannot improve on the beauty of a rose or a butterfly.

Often we take the beauty of the colors for granted, without any appreciation for what nature has done for us. It could have been otherwise. Can you imagine what it would be like if nature had done what the Army does? The Army colors all military equipment, supplies, and clothing the same color, olive drab.

Have you ever noticed the unity among the various animals, fish, and birds? Whether cattle, horses, buffaloes, sheep, fish in the waters, or birds in the air, they move in unity with one another. In their way they communicate with one another.

It is no coincident that wild geese fly in a v-formation and reap the benefits of the aerodynamics of it, with the leader of the flock encountering the most resistance. When the leader of the flock needs a reprieve, it takes a position in the rear of the formation where the flying is not as tiring as it is in the lead position. If one of the geese experiences some difficulty that forces it to drop out of the formation, another of the geese will also drop out of the formation to be with it.

And there is a balance in nature. Would it not be tragic if there were as many elephants as there are ants, one of the most plentiful creatures on Earth? Nature did not make any such mistake. Nature does not make mistakes. However, people are certainly capable of disturbing nature. It is possible that people — functioning from their false ego-self — might destroy the civilization as we know it, but Mother Earth will survive.

We are the only creatures on Earth that willingly get out of harmony with nature. Animals remain in agreement with nature, unless they are removed from their natural habitat and, consequently, disturbed by humans. And now we know that animals disturbed by humans can become neurotic; e.g., many dogs suffer from separation anxiety.

Everything in nature fits in the ecological system in some manner. No one likes to get bitten by a mosquito. However, bats and martins thrive on mosquitoes as a food supply. Incidentally, if a mosquito has ever bitten you, you got a perfect bite. Similarly, if a

Our Purpose in Life

bee has ever stung you, you got a perfect sting. Everything in nature was created with perfection.

Having worked with bees to a very limited extent and having been stung several times, I thought that I knew something about bees. However, what I knew was a pittance in comparison to what I was to learn. A friend asked me to help him cut a tree that had bees in it so that we could get the bees and put them into a beehive.

When we were getting ready to go into the woods to cut the tree, gathering the things needed for cutting the tree (saw, ax, wedge), I noticed that we had no protective gear that one commonly uses when working with bees (gloves, screened mask, a bee smoker). When I ask about this, my friend replied, "we won't need any." Although I was quite curious, we proceeded to the woods without me asking any more questions.

After we had cut the tree, the bees were quite disturbed. My friend said, "let's let the bees settle for a few minutes." After the bees settled, we cut out a portion of the tree, exposing the bees. Again, the bees were disturbed. And again, my friend said, "let's let the bees settle for a few minutes." After a few minutes, he said, "now the bees are settled." Very gently and easily he sat on the tree next to the bees. With his movements in harmony with the bees, my friend quite easily, gently and calmly scooped up the bees *with his bare hand* and placed them into the hive. Not one bee stung him.

My friend had learned an important lesson about nature, a lesson that many people never learn. He had one of the greatest teachers: Nature! What my friend learned was not from reading books or from classroom instructions. My friend did not know how to read and write.

Our deep-down longing is to live in harmony with truth, God, and nature. Henry David Thoreau, American writer, philosopher, and naturalist, said, "Blessed are they who never read a newspaper, for they shall see Nature, and through her, God. ... We can never have enough of nature. ... Nature is full of genius, full of the divinity, so that not a snowflake escapes its fashioning hand."

Wherever we look in nature that has not been disturbed by human beings, we find beauty, harmony, cleanliness, rhythm, perfection ... the magical, the magnificent, the mysterious, the miraculous. All the beautiful, mystical, magical, magnificent, and miraculous things we observe in nature is the handiwork of an all-knowing, all-perfect, all-powerful God.

Nature has a way of giving us all that we need to be happy, satisfied, peaceful, joyous and contented ... if only we would abide by the inner voice of our true self, rather than acquiescing to our false ego-self. Everything that God created is perfect. *This includes us.* We are perfect; we just don't know it. Thinking that false ways are more satisfying than the ways of truth, we have let our false ego-self lead us astray from our true spiritual self, the self of us that is perfect, created in the image and likeness of God. If we are living in agreement with truth and nature — in agreement with our true spiritual self — we are in harmony with God ... and we are happy, satisfied, and contented.

Jesus said, "Ye ask who are those that draw us to the kingdom, if the kingdom is in Heaven? ... The fowls of the air, and all beasts that are under the earth or upon the earth, and the fishes of the sea, these are they which draw you, and the Kingdom of Heaven is within you" (*New Sayings of Jesus, second saying*, from *Bartlett's Familiar Quotations* by John Bartlett). Note the statement, "... the Kingdom of Heaven is within you." ... more about this later.

From the *The Secret Teachings Of Jesus – Four Gnostic Gospels*, translated by Marvin W. Meyer, we find how Jesus responded to his disciples about heaven. Jesus' disciples asked him, "When will the new world come?" He said to them, "What you look for has already come, but you do not know it."

It is almost unbelievable that we are beginning the twenty-first century and have explored everything from the bottom of the oceans to outer space, except by far the most important thing we can possibly explore, which is our inner selves. The only place we will discover the truth that will set us free is within ourselves. And, most importantly, the only place that we can discover heaven is within us ... which is our ultimate, inherent goal in life ... the goal that is the most desired, but for the most part is not achieved.

To a great extent, we as a society have taken simple concepts and complicated them beyond comprehension and understanding. Following are some of the things we all want most in life (these are

Our Purpose in Life

our secondary goals; these are things that accrue to us easily and naturally when we are in agreement with truth and nature). We desire to love and be love, to be happy, and to have peace and joy. We desire a loving, lasting, satisfying relationship. We desire a loving, happy, harmonious family. Having these, then we have a natural urge to share our life, our love, and our joy with others. Individually and as a family, we desire a sense of belonging, a sense of community for sharing our life, love, and goodness with others ... honestly and truthfully ... just being real ... no false ego-stuff that demands attention, praise, and adulation.

Once we are transformed from being confused to being clear — from being scared to being sacred — there is that something within us that urges us — compels us! — to share our love and goodness with others.

The need to belong explains the popularity of cults and gangs. Somehow it feels better to belong to these than to have no feeling of belonging at all. A satisfying, healthy feeling of belonging begins in a loving, happy, harmonious family environment.

If we miss our top priority in life — which is unification with God, which is heaven — we can spend a lifetime trying to fill the void within with stuff that never fills the void. All the material wealth and all the attention, praise, and adulation that it is possible to gain in a lifetime are never enough to fill the void. What have we gained if we gain the whole world but lose our soul ... if we are alienated from our true self ... if we are alienated from God?

In summary, our purpose in life is to express life in agreement with truth, God and nature. Our inherent goal in life — in our heart of hearts, that for which we keep seeking and searching — is the abundant life that Jesus wanted us to enjoy. The abundant life is heaven ... here and now, not after we are dead and gone ... all consistent with what Jesus taught. Living in agreement with truth, God, and nature is the simplest thing we will ever do and the one thing we inherently and insatiably desire to do ... the one thing that will assure us a happy, satisfied, and contented life. Living in agreement with truth, God and nature is the same thing as being unified with God ... and that is heaven ... our ultimate goal in life.

Chapter 2
Why Christianity Isn't Working

Christianity isn't working primarily because teachers are not teaching the message Jesus intended for us ... at least not teaching what Jesus said in a manner that we believe and understand. In addition, modern-day teachers do not teach in the manner that Jesus taught. Jesus was not reluctant to call a hypocrite a hypocrite.

Many teachers seem to think that religion is a personal matter and that no one should be critical of the religious beliefs of others. One might argue that the "religious" beliefs of many people are not religious. Instead, they are false beliefs that deter one from understanding the true teachings of Jesus. Truth has never harmed — and will never harm — anyone. Telling people the truth has the potential for helping them to discover the truth that sets them free ... has the potential for helping people understand what Jesus said.

Notice how clear and straightforward Jesus spoke to Pharisees, scribes, fools, hypocrites, heathen, blind guides and false teachers: "And when thou prayest, thou shalt not be as the hypocrites are; for they love to pray standing in the synagogues and in the corners of the streets, that they may be seen of men. ... But when ye pray, use not vain repetitions, as the heathen do; for they think that they shall be heard for their much speaking. ... But woe unto you, scribes and Pharisees, hypocrites! for ye shut up the kingdom of heaven against men; for ye neither go in yourselves, neither suffer ye them that are entering to go in. ... Ye fools and blind; for whether is greater, the gold, or the temple that sanctifieth the gold? Ye fools and blind; for whether is greater, the gift, or the altar that sanctifieth the gift? ... Woe unto you, scribes and Pharisees, hypocrites! For ye pay tithe of mint and anise and cummin, and have omitted the weightier matters of the law, judgment, mercy, and faith ... Many false prophets shall rise and shall deceive many. ... Ye blind guides, who strain at a gnat, and swallow a camel. Woe unto you, scribes and Pharisees, hypocrites! For ye make clean the outside of the cup and of the platter, but within they are full of

Why Christianity Isn't Working 19

extortion and excess. Thou blind Pharisee, cleanse first that which is within the cup and platter, that the outside of them may be clean also. ... Ye fools, did not he that made that which is without make that which is within also? ...Woe unto you, scribes and Pharisees, hypocrites! For ye are like unto whited sepulchres, which indeed appear beautiful outward, but are within full of dead men's bones, and of all uncleanness. ... Even so ye also outwardly appear righteous unto men, but within ye are full of hypocrisy and iniquity" (Matthew 23:13-27).

In addition to noting how direct and straightforward Jesus spoke, note also the statement in the above, "for ye shut up the kingdom of heaven against men; for ye neither go in yourselves, neither suffer ye them that are entering to go in." Jesus was speaking about heaven in the present moment ... not a place where the saved go after they die. Note also that Jesus said that false, religious leaders do not enjoy heaven and they hinder others from discovering heaven.

Jesus said, "People honoureth me with their lips, but their heart is far from me. Howbeit in vain do they worship me, teaching for doctrines the commandments of men" (Mark 7:7). Many people praise and worship the man Jesus, but they do not believe and understand what he said. Thus, their heart is far from being in harmony with the true teachings of Jesus ... far from being in harmony with God.

According to Jesus, worshipping him with our lips is in vain. Many people are "holding on to the tradition of men" and "teaching doctrines of men ... rejecting the commandments of God" ... rejecting what Jesus taught.

If we believed and embodied what Jesus said, the way we believe and think in our heart would be in harmony with truth. We would be pure in heart. We would have genuine peace and joy. We could say with honesty, humility, and understanding, "I and my Father are one" ... the same thing as being unified with God.

Many Christian teachers are honorable and have good intentions; by their fruits, we know them. They have a sincere desire to help people find salvation. However, not understanding and believing what Jesus said, many teachers teach what they believe ... not what Jesus taught. A sure way of finding salvation is by believing and doing what Jesus taught.

Many Christian teachers have let the teachings of the Apostle Paul overshadow the true teachings of Jesus. To be saved, they teach such things as believe on the Lord Jesus Christ and take Christ into your heart. Fundamentalists believe that Jesus shed his blood and died on the cross to save us. Some fundamentalists go so far as to say that there is no salvation apart from the cross, and that one cannot be saved without believing in the sacrificial death of Jesus on the cross. Thus, they believe and teach stuff that is not the gospel, and they gloss over what Jesus said will save us.

Jesus told his disciples, "Go ye therefore, and teach all nations ...teaching them to observe all things whatsoever I have commanded you" (Matthew 28:19). Teaching about such things as being washed in the blood, taking Christ into our hearts, believing on Jesus, and Jesus dying on the cross to save us from our sins is not teaching the gospel that Jesus preached. Instead, these teachings are a stumbling block in our path to understanding the true teachings of Jesus. They are a stumbling block in our path to unification with God ... the goal of all great religions.

The things Jesus commanded his disciples to teach include the twenty selected sayings of Jesus explained in the next chapter. These sayings of Jesus have only been mouthed by many Christian teachers; they have not been taught clearly in mainline churches in a manner we can understand and embody. The twenty selected sayings of Jesus — if understood and embodied — are more than enough for people to understand the message that Jesus intended for us ... more than enough for us to find salvation.

What this boils down to is that many Christian teachers teach what they believe, but what they believe is not the gospel of Jesus. Because of differences in beliefs, we have more than 250 denominations in the Protestant religion. Clearly, many false beliefs are being taught.

This will be difficult for fundamentalists to understand and accept, but there are ways of being saved; there are ways to discover the truth that sets us free; there are ways to unify with God had we never heard of the man Jesus.

Why Christianity Isn't Working

Regardless of how fundamentalists misconstrue the Scriptures, the spiritual writers of the Old Testament are a prime example of people being saved without the teachings of Jesus. They were saved long before Jesus shed his blood and died on the cross. What fundamentalists believe and teach about Jesus shedding his blood and dying on the cross does not alter what we must do to be saved.

The Buddha is another prime example of one who discovered truth (a prerequisite for being saved) without the teachings of Jesus. The Buddha, Jesus, and the spiritual teachers of the Old Testament were the personification of truth.

Fundamentalists seem to agree that the spiritual teachers of the Old Testament were saved without the teachings of Jesus. However, they add something to their way of thinking to make the salvation of the spiritual teachers of the Old Testament seem impossible without the death of Jesus on the cross. There are varied explanations; following is one example. Fundamentalists believe that the spiritual teachers of the Old Testament were saved by faith. This is true; however, some fundamentalists add to this, saying that the spiritual teachers of the Old Testament trusted in God, looking for the promise of redemption through the cross that was to come.

Although fundamentalists might twist the Scriptures in an attempt to make this seem true, there is no biblical Scriptures to support this belief. Jesus' death on the cross had no bearing on the spiritual teachers of the Old Testament finding salvation. The word "cross" is not mentioned in the Old Testament. The way the spiritual teachers of the Old Testament found salvation is explained in Chapter 11, "The Essential Teachings of Jesus."

On the surface, it seems that Christianity is based on the teachings of Jesus; however, fundamentalists give undue emphasis to the teachings of the Apostle Paul who wrote almost two-thirds of the New Testament. In addition, they have gone beyond what the Apostle Paul said, exaggerating and adding to what he said. For example, the Apostle Paul said, "Christ died for our sins according to the Scriptures" (1 Corinthians 15:3).

Fundamentalists have taken this statement by the Apostle Paul, twisting it, stretching it, and misinterpreting it and gave it a meaning that is meaningless. What will save us is explained clearly in chapter 3, "The Truth about What Will Save Us." Suffice it here to say that Jesus' death on the cross does not alter what we must do to be saved.

The Apostle Paul's statement about Jesus dying for our sins is true in the sense that we could say the same thing about many truth teachers, whose purpose for teaching was to help people overcome suffering and to find peace and joy ... the same purpose that Jesus preached the gospel. Saint Andrew (one of Jesus' apostles) was crucified on a cross for teaching the gospel, the same reason that Jesus was crucified. In a sense, we could say that Saint Andrew shed his blood, dying on the cross, to save us from our sins. He taught the gospel for the same reason that Jesus taught the gospel ... and he died for the same reason that Jesus died. James, a brother of Jesus and author of "The Letter of James," was executed because he was teaching the gospel.

Other truth teachers were persecuted because they were attempting to do the same thing that Jesus did. In their own way, other truth teachers were teaching people the truth to help them overcome their suffering. Thus, the explanation of why Jesus died is the same explanation of why other teachers of truth were executed, punished, or ostracized.

Most of the apostles of Jesus were punished, imprisoned, or put to death. Those who were executed died for the same reason that Jesus was executed—for teaching the gospel. The Apostle Paul was imprisoned, beaten, and executed by the Romans because he was teaching the gospel. Regardless of the details about John the Baptist being beheaded, he would not have been imprisoned and subsequently beheaded had he not been teaching the gospel.

Some truth teachers were punished by having their tongue cut out. Socrates' most popular saying was "Know thyself" ... the same thing as knowing the truth that sets us free. He was executed by being forced to drink a cup of poison. When we "know thyself," we know the truth that sets us free.

Spinoza was ostracized by orders from authorities, who issued a statement prohibiting anyone from visiting with him or letting him visit with them.

Why Christianity Isn't Working

H. L. Mencken, Journalist, critic, and essayist, said, "For the habitual truth-teller and truth-seeker, indeed, the whole world has very little liking. He is always unpopular, and not infrequently his unpopularity is so excessive that it endangers his life. ... Run your eye back over the list of martyrs, lay and clerical; nine-tenths of them, you will find, stood accused of nothing worse than honest efforts to find out and announce the truth" (From *The Vintage Mencken,* by Alistair Cooke).

Regardless of what the Apostle Paul had in mind when he said that Jesus died for our sins, it does not change what we must do to free ourselves from our sins and our suffering. It does not alter what we must do to free ourselves from our fears, false beliefs, hate, anger, resentment, jealousy, revenge, hypocrisy ... what we must do to rid ourselves of the impurities (the devils) in our mind as alluded to by the Buddha. Regardless of why and how Jesus died, it does not alter what we must do to "clean the inside of the cup and the platter." In brief, it does not alter what we must do to be saved.

Buddha said that it is evil to cling to false doctrine. We know from observation that evil is rampant. If conservatives are clinging to false doctrine (false beliefs about such things as God, heaven, hell, devil, Satan and not believing the gospel of Jesus), then what they are doing is evil. "Evil" is defined by Webster: "Anything that causes harm, pain, misery, disaster." False religious beliefs impede us from embarking on the path to the discovery of the truth that frees us from suffering.

The Apostle Paul was a firm believer in the teachings of Jesus. He wanted the gospel preached in all the churches. He left us with some insightful gems of wisdom bearing on the teachings of Christianity. However, the beliefs that have emerged from misconstruing, misinterpreting, and misunderstanding what he said are not consistent with the gospel of Jesus. The following statements by the apostle Paul are examples of things he said that have been misconstrued: "Believe on the Lord Jesus Christ and thou shall be saved. ... There is none righteous, no not one. ... But God commendeth his love toward us, in that, while we were yet sinners, Christ died for us. Much more then, being now justified by his blood, we shall be saved from wrath through him. For if, when we were enemies, we were reconciled to God by the death of his Son, much more, being reconciled, we shall be saved by his life. And not only so, but we also joy in God through our Lord Jesus Christ, by whom we have now received the atonement."

Let's face it! Some of the Apostle Paul's statements are not clear. If we study and assimilate the teachings of Jesus and those of the spiritual teachers of the Old Testament, we know that we are not unified with God by the death of Jesus. We are unified with God if we believe, understand, and embody the gospel that Jesus preached. And the part, "we shall be saved by his life," is easy for some people to misinterpret. What will save us, according to what Jesus said, is made abundantly clear in Chapter 3, "The Truth about What Will Save Us."

Paul's use of the word "atonement" (mentioned above) is the only time that this word is used in the New Testament. Yet, fundamentalists take this passage from the teachings of the Apostle Paul and give it a meaning that is not consistent with what Jesus said will save us. It seems like Christian teachers focus attention on the teachings of the Apostle Paul, along with a passage from "The First Letter of John," and ignore and gloss over the gospel that Jesus preached. They seem to emphasize the importance of believing on Jesus, yet they do not understand or believe what he said. Their teachings about what will save us seem to come from the teachings of the Apostle Paul. Yet, what Jesus said is quite clear.

John the Baptist said, "But if we walk in the light, as he is in the light, we have fellowship one with another, and the blood of Jesus Christ his Son cleanseth us from all sin. ... If we say that we have no sin, we deceive ourselves, and the truth is not in us. ... If we say that we have not sinned, we make him a liar, and his word is not in us" (1 John 1:7-10).

The Apostle Paul said, "In whom [Jesus] we have redemption through his blood, the forgiveness of sins, according to the riches of his grace" (Ephesians 1:7). Fundamentalists know that the Apostle Paul could not be speaking about the physical blood from the body of Jesus; however, they don't seem to have translated the meaning of the word "blood," which is an idiom, meaning the true teachings of Jesus. Some fundamentalists go so far as to say that sins past and future are covered by his blood as Jesus made atonement for our sins.

Thus, understanding that the word "blood" is an idiom, meaning truth, we realize that truth cleanseth us from all sin and consequently will save us; we realize that we are saved by understanding and embodying the true teachings of Jesus.

It seems that fundamentalists have fabricated false beliefs about sin and sinning based on their misunderstanding of what the Apostle Paul and the Apostle John said. Some of the beliefs are farfetched, confusing, and misleading. Some fundamentalists go so far as to say that everyone sins; everyone is a sinner. This seems to suggest that Christians sin ... that they are sinners. Thus, they seem to suggest that what is true for sinners is true for Christians; e.g., we all sin; we're all sinners; no one is perfect and never will be; only Jesus was perfect. Somehow or another, some Christians believe that Jesus took our sins on him when he died on the cross. It seems that some Christians believe that it is okay to sin; that God forgives and Jesus died on the cross to redeem us from our sins.

I am not clear what Christians believe about sin and sinning. However, Jesus' teachings are strict. Following the teachings of Jesus does not allow for sinning. Remember that Jesus told us to be perfect. When we are expressing life in agreement with our true perfect, spiritual self we are not sinners and we don't sin.

We know from the teachings of Jesus that sinners will not enjoy heaven. We know that Jesus came to call sinners to repentance. We know that we are free from sin when we discover the truth that sets us free, when we "clean the inside of the cup and the platter," when are as perfect as Jesus told us to be, when we cast the devils from our heart, when we are unified with God. We know from the teachings of Jesus that we do not sin if we "do the will of the Father," a prerequisite for enjoying heaven ... according to Jesus.

Fundamentalists seem to give too much emphasis to something that the Apostle Paul said and let it distort their views about sin and sinning. The Apostle Paul, speaking about the Jews and the Gentiles, who did not believe and accept the gospel, said, "They are all under sin; as it is written, there is none righteous, no, not one. There is none that understandeth, there is none that seeketh after

God" (Romans 3:9-11). It seems that fundamentalists focus on the part, "There is none righteous, no, not one," and misconstrue what the Apostle Paul said. Or, they don't believe what Jesus said, "I came not to call the righteous, but sinners to repentance." The righteous are not sinners.

In a troubled, fractured society (a society in which about 90 percent of the families are dysfunctional), it's safe to say that most people sin and are sinners. It's safe to say that few have found the narrow way to life that few find. Consequently, a vast majority is on the broad path to destruction. The purpose for Jesus preaching the gospel is that we would be saved, and consequently, have peace and joy. When we are saved, we are no longer sinners; we do not sin ... and we have peace and joy. What fundamentalists say about sin and sinning is not the gospel that Jesus preached, and it does not alter what we must do to be saved.

Some Christians seem to believe that we were born sinners, because of something that David, the Psalmist, said: "Behold, I was shapen in iniquity; and in sin did my mother conceive me" (Psalms 51:5). There is more about this statement in Chapter 4, "Truth Is the Way," but suffice it here to say that the Psalmist's statement does not mean that we were born sinners. Fundamentalists seemed to have ignored and glossed over what Jesus said:

- "They that are whole have no need of the physician, but they that are sick; I came not to call the righteous, but sinners to repentance" (Mark 2:17). This raises questions about those who are righteous without the teachings of Jesus (explained later in this book).
- "Except ye be converted, and become as little children, ye shall not enter into the kingdom of Heaven" (Matthew 18:3). Little children are not born with sin and evil in their hearts; they are not sinners when they are born. They are born pure in heart, the prerequisite for enjoying heaven.
- "Be ye therefore perfect, even as your Father who is in heaven is perfect" (Matthew 5:48). Note what Jesus said. Do Christians believe that we are to do what Jesus said to do, "Be ye therefore perfect?" Some fundamentalists proclaim that we are not perfect and never will be. When we are as perfect as Jesus told us to be, we

Why Christianity Isn't Working

are not sinners. Instead, we are sinless ... a prerequisite for enjoying heaven.

The beliefs that fundamentalists have concocted seem to free them from the responsibility for doing what they must do to be saved. Christians quote Scriptures and speak about confessing sins. But how often do you hear Christians confess their faults? How often do you hear anyone say something like, "I know my anger, hate, jealousy, or insecurity cause me problems in the work environment, in the family, in my relationships? Instead, don't they usually point a finger at something or someone else?

Christianity seems to offer an easy way out; however, Christianity isn't working. Rather than acknowledge and take responsibility for the messy morass they have created for themselves, Christians (who are really hypocrites) say things like, "I love Jesus, I accept Jesus as my savior, Jesus died for my sins, and so on ... and do nothing about acknowledging and confessing their faults ... do nothing about "cleaning the inside of the cup and the platter." Shakespeare said, "The fault is not in the stars, but in ourselves."

To be saved, we must be free of our faults; we must be as perfect as Jesus told us to be. A prerequisite for enjoying heaven is to be converted and be pure in heart like little children. We will never enjoy heaven with sin and evil in our hearts ... with a heart that is not pure. Jesus should be an example for Christians. Jesus wanted us to be perfect — to be free from sin — so that we will have peace and joy. Jesus said, "These things have I spoken unto you, that my joy might remain in you, and that your joy might be full" (John 15:11). When we are free of our faults, we have peace and joy.

All the following words (some used in religion and some used in psychology and elsewhere) are aspects of the mind: conscious mind, subconscious mind, supra-conscious mind, heart, soul, spirit, Father (as used by Jesus), Lord (as used by spiritual leaders of the Old Testament), devil, demons, Satan, id, ego, superego, true self, false self, spiritual self, sacred self, higher self, and heaven and hell. Regardless of what words we use, these are aspects of something within us, whatever we might call that something.

In addition, many religious teachers have not taken the time to examine some false beliefs that are being passed onto us as the gospel. Let us take a look at some old beliefs that have many people stuck in a messy morass of disbelief, discontent, and confusion. Some of these old false beliefs constitute some very basic, significant definitions.

In *Webster's New Twentieth Century Unabridged Dictionary* we find two definitions for the words "heaven" and "hell", a theological definition that is false and misleading, and we find an understandable definition that is true and actual ... that is in agreement with the teachings of Jesus.

The theological definition of heaven is: "the place where God and his angels are, variously conceived of as the place where the blessed will live after death." This is not in agreement with what Jesus taught.

And then there is a practical definition, which is in agreement with the message Jesus intended for us when he said he came that we might have life and have it more abundantly. Heaven is defined by Webster as: "... a state of great happiness ... a state of bliss; a sublime or exalted condition." That is the condition we experience when we free ourselves from the cause of our suffering, unhappiness, restlessness, and discontent. This practical definition is in agreement with the Apostle Paul's description of heaven. The Apostle Paul said, "The kingdom of God is righteousness, and peace, and joy" (Romans 14:17).

Similarly, there are two definitions of "hell." According to Webster, in Christianity, hell is "the place where fallen angels and devils live and where sinners and unbelievers go after death for torment and eternal punishment." Supposedly, Christianity is derived from the teachings of Jesus, but Jesus did not teach this kind of stuff.

And again there is an understandable, practical definition of hell: "any place or condition of evil, pain, misery, cruelty." There is plenty of hell here on Earth while we are alive. If we study and assimilate what Jesus said and understand the idioms he used, we realize that hell is a troubled, tormented, fearful state of mind.

The theological definition of Satan according to Webster is: "In Christian theology, the great enemy of man and of goodness; the devil; usually identified with Lucifer, the chief of the fallen angels,

Why Christianity Isn't Working 29

cast out of heaven by Michael, according to the Talmud." You may note this theological definition is according to the Talmud, not according to what Jesus said ... not according to the Bible. Satan is explained in Chapter 6, "The Hidden Cause of Suffering."

The way that Christianity is taught might make it somewhat difficult to define the word "Christian." According to definitions in selected dictionaries, a politician could be as crooked as a barrel of fishhooks and make the following statement and it be a true statement: "I am a Christian."

One of the definitions of "Christian" in the *Webster's New Twentieth Century Unabridged Dictionary* is "a person professing belief in Jesus as the Christ or in the religion based on the teachings of Jesus."

You may note the word "professing" ... not the same thing as actually doing as Jesus did or doing as he taught us to do. And also note the part, "religion based on the teachings of Jesus." How many teachers do you know who are teaching the gospel that Jesus taught? How many teachers do you know who teach with clarity what Jesus said about the kingdom of God being within us? How many teachers do you know who really teach us what will save us, according to what Jesus said (explained in the next chapter)?

Here is another definition of "Christian" from the same dictionary: "In a general sense, anyone born of Christian parents." This leaves a lingering question about the Christian parents, particularly in view of the next definition from another dictionary.

According to *Webster's New Collegiate Dictionary*, a Christian is: "One who believes or who *professes or is assumed to believe* in Jesus Christ and the *truth as taught by him*." Italics are added to pique one's thinking. "Professes" and "assumed" are not the same thing as actually believing and actually doing. How many people do you know who understand and believe the truth as taught by Jesus?

I do not think you will find this in any dictionary or learn this in the church; but, strictly speaking, a Christian is one who believes the gospel that Jesus preached and who has been saved. Or to put it simply, a Christian is one who lives in agreement with truth ... or one who has a pure heart ... or one who is unified with God ... or one who has "cleaned the inside of the cup and the platter" ... all the same thing ... all according to the example that Jesus set for us. From a practical standpoint, a Christian does what is right even when no one is paying attention ... just expressing life in agreement with truth, not *needing* to demonstrate anything to anyone ... not *needing* praise and adulation ... not *needing* to appear special and important ... not *needing* love, acceptance, and approval.

A clarification is in order regarding my use of the word "ego." Many and varied meanings exist for the word, depending on various sources such as dictionaries, psychology, psychiatry, and religion. I think of our ego-self as being the false self of us ... the part of us that we think we are but, in fact, are not. Our ego-self is based on everything that is fearful and false. Relative to our overall wellbeing — the way we are, the way we think in our heart — I do not attempt to distinguish between such words as ego, devil, Satan, demons, unclean spirits, and subconscious, fearful, false beliefs. All are aspects of our false ego-self.

Our society is rife with crime, violence, suffering, rape, spousal, child, and drug abuse. About 90 percent of America's families are dysfunctional. Deep inside, everyone wants to have peace and joy and to be happy. No one is genuinely loving, happy, peaceful and contented in a dysfunctional family.

About half of marriages end in divorce; and, according to a noted psychologist, the majority of married couples are basically dissatisfied and unhappy. Stress, fatigue, and psychosomatic illnesses are common complaints. Militia groups are springing up throughout our nation. Restlessness, discontent, crookedness, corruption, and scandals are commonplace. Schools are not a safe place to be. Clearly, Christianity is not working for the masses of the people.

According to the book, *The Day America Told The Truth*, by James Patterson and Peter Kim, of 11 developed countries in the world, the United States is by far the most violent. If we, as a society, understood and embodied what Jesus said, we would not have violence. Instead, we would have peace, joy and harmony.

There is a way of living that everyone insatiably desires—a way that is alien to the vast majority of people. That way of living

Why Christianity Isn't Working

was advocated by Jesus ... that way of living is in harmony with truth, God, and nature.

If we, as a society, comprehended the message Jesus intended for us, love, harmony, and peace would characterize our society. Families would be loving, happy, harmonious, functional, stable, and they would remain together. Our communities and our nation — the very world itself — would be a safe place to live. Quite naturally, we would do unto others was we would have others do unto us. All mental and emotional suffering and all unhappiness would vanish. Crime, violence, rape, drug abuse, child abuse, spousal abuse — all that is ugly and deplorable — would cease.

The essence of Jesus' teachings is truth, peace, and love. This is simple and clear. What is not clear is why religious teachers — many of whom purport to be teaching the gospel — are not teaching the gospel that Jesus commanded his disciples to preach to every creature in all the world ... or at least not making it clear.

The author of an article in the May 22, 1989 issue of *TIME* said: "Not only are the traditional denominations failing to get their message across; they are increasingly unsure just what the message is." If traditional denominations really understood the gospel that Jesus taught, then the gospel would be the message of the churches.

As it is, many orthodox religious teachers believe that the entire Bible is the inspired word of God. And they teach a hodgepodge of stuff and overlook what should be a top priority, which is the message that Jesus intended for us. What greater message could there possibly be than discovering the truth that sets us free ... free from the hidden cause of our mental suffering, restlessness, and discontent and free to enjoy the abundant life ... here and now?

It's tragic how people have used biblical Scripture to justify whatever it is they wish to justify ... mostly what they believe. Often what many people believe is not what Jesus taught, and they miss the important message that Jesus left for us.

In his book, *The Bible Tells Me So: Uses and Abuses of Holy Scripture,* Jim Hill demonstrates how people use the Holy Scriptures to justify their beliefs regarding 34 topics of special interest. It's interesting to note that people have used the Scriptures to justify slavery, and people have used the Scriptures to justify the abolishment of slavery. And it is interesting to note that the same verse of Scripture has been used for both the justification and also for the opposition of the same issue.

What it boils down to is that teachers of Christianity cover a lot of stuff, but they miss the most important teachings of Jesus. Very simply, the message that Jesus intended for us is not being taught ... at least not taught in a manner that we can understand, embrace, and embody.

An article appeared in the October 3-5, 1997, issue of, *USA WEEKEND*, titled "The Debate Over What The Bible Says." This article is a discussion of five contentious issues by two well-known theologians. The theologians did what many religious teachers usually do; they selected verses from throughout the Bible to support their viewpoints. They differed on four of the five contentious issues. And they only referred to the teachings of Jesus one time.

Twenty selected sayings of Jesus are listed in Chapter 3, "The Truth about What Will Save Us." If we understood any one of those statements (not all of them, but any one of them), we would be well on our way to understanding what Jesus taught. The two well-known theologians did not mention one of these significant sayings of Jesus. They only mentioned Jesus in reference to what he said about the camel going through the eye of the needle: "It is easier for a camel to go through the eye of a needle than for a rich man to enter the kingdom of God."

An article appeared in the July 2, 1997, issue of the *The Knoxville News-Sentinel* titled "Church of Christ conservatives ask boycott of Jubilee." The Jubilee is a four-day convention (an annual meeting) of the Church, which according to the article, "... has become a battle between conservative and liberal members who want to change traditional teachings."

Another article, bearing on the differences in religious beliefs, appeared in the April 26, 1998, issue of the *Knoxville News-Sentinel* about fighting between Southern Baptist factions. The article states, "The sides are still miles apart theologically."

Theologians have had about 2,000 years to understand what Jesus said, but it seems as if the arguments could go on and on and on. Regardless of their differences — and regardless of the condi-

Why Christianity Isn't Working

tions in our own nation — religious leaders are hoping to spread the gospel worldwide. With all the different beliefs, it seems that a high priority should be getting clear about what Jesus said and being consistent with the gospel they are spreading. As it is, one might well wonder, "Whose gospel are they spreading?"

The differences in viewpoints, the contentious issues, and the infighting shed light on why Christianity is not working and why religious teachers are teaching a hodgepodge of stuff but not teaching the basic message that Jesus intended for us. Orthodox religious teachers have not bothered to study, assimilate, and understand what Jesus taught. They teach and debate their viewpoints ... not what Jesus said. Thus, we have the many different denominations and all the hodgepodge of stuff that is taught under the guise of Christianity ... and the debates are not abating.

An article appeared in the *The Knoxville News-Sentinel,* June 25, 2000, about the possibility of Texas Baptists severing ties with the conservative Southern Baptist Convention. Differences between the two organizations, regarding something that the Apostle Paul said about women submitting themselves to their husbands, has raised the possibility that the Texas convention will create a new Baptist denomination.

If Christians really understood the message Jesus intended for us, what the Apostle Paul said would not create such a controversy.

There is a simple solution to halt the eternal debates and to clear up all the confusion about Christianity: Simply quit debating and focus attention on the basic teachings of Jesus ... not on the man Jesus, but on his teachings. If we as a society fully understand and believe the gospel as taught by Jesus, in due time the situations that are the subject of contentious issues will simply fade away.

Thus, instead of debating the contentious issues, our time and efforts would reap untold rewards if spent on understanding what Jesus said and then on how to teach the gospel in a manner that people believe and understand.

I am reminded of a response to essays on my Web site from a man who expressed his disillusionment with the impact that Christianity has had on his small nation. He said, "The major cause of all my problems has been the Christian religion. Because of the

Christian religion I will never be able to worship as did my ancestors who once roamed this land. Because of European domination through Christianity I have been stripped of all my beliefs and given a false hope in God. I'm from a small nation that has many social dysfunctions because of Christianity. The only way for my people to adapt to this change has been to become alcoholics and withdraw from society."

Think about it! If we understood and embodied the message Jesus intended for us, we would not have about 20 million alcoholics in our nation; we would not have any. Ninety percent of the families would not be dysfunctional. If 10 percent of the families are functional, the potential exists for all families to be functional. About half of the marriages would not end in divorce; none would end in divorce. We would not have the shootings in the schools, the bombings of abortion clinics, and the crime and violence that characterize our society. Our families and our society would not be plagued with the problems that confront us.

Another way of thinking about all this is that we would not endure all the suffering we endure had we not been led astray from the teachings of Jesus ... led astray by false teachings that impede us from embarking on a path to truth and harmony with God.

Supposedly, we are a Christian nation. But are we really? How can we really be a Christian nation with so many people who really do not understand what Jesus said and who do not do what he taught? It seems that Jesus' teachings are ignored, glossed over, misinterpreted, or concealed.

Are we really a nation of Christians or a nation of hypocrites? If we are a Christian nation, why are so many families dysfunctional (about 90 percent)? Do Christians have dysfunctional families? About 50 percent of marriages end in divorce. It's interesting to note that the states with the highest divorce rate are in the heart of the Bible belt (Alabama, Tennessee, Kentucky, Arkansas and Oklahoma). Do Christians divorce?

If we are a Christian nation, why is America the most violent of all developed countries? Are Christians violent? If we are a Christian nation, why are so many people plagued with anger, hatred, jealousy, anxiety, depression, selfishness, resentment,

Why Christianity Isn't Working 35

restlessness, discontent, stress, tension headaches (which plague more than 50 million Americans), psychosomatic illnesses? Why are so many people taking tranquilizer and antidepressants? Why all the dysfunctional families? Why the break-up of so many families? ... and on and on and on. None of this is characteristic of a true Christian.

Many people think of a Christian as being a person who believes and does as Jesus taught. If we applied that as a definition, this would exclude many people who profess to be Christian. Clearly, many so-called Christians do not really understand what Jesus taught, and consequently, do not do what he said to do.

Jesus said to the scribes, Pharisees, and hypocrites: "Ye blind guides, which strain at a gnat and swallow a camel ... you make clean the outside of the cup and the platter, but within, they are full of extortion and excess. Thou blind Pharisee, cleanse first that which is within the cup and platter that the outside of them may be clean also" (Matthew 23:24-26).

Our families would not be fractured and dysfunctional and we would not have all the crime, violence, suffering, shootings in the schools, bombings of abortion clinics, and on and on and on if we (individually and collectively as a society), did what Jesus said to do, if we "cleaned the inside of the cup and platter."

We have myriad groups aimed at helping people add meaning to their lives; e.g., personal growth groups, special study groups, varied religious groups, Satan worshippers, snake handlers, psychics, astrologers, psychiatrists, counselors, cults, militia groups, and organizations such as Alcoholics Anonymous, the women's liberation movement, the new-age movement ... and on and on and on.

We would not have any of the above groups if we as a society were getting the basic message that Jesus intended for us. Underlying all the efforts of the above-type endeavors is the desire to enjoy inner peace and joy ... the desire to express life in agreement with truth and love ... the same thing as being in harmony with God.

When we stop to think about it, the church is not a *practical* place to get help for many of the problems that plague us, our families, and our society; e.g., help for alcoholism, drug abuse, child abuse, spousal abuse, depression, anger, tension headaches, psychological problems, marital and sexual problems.

Antidepressants, tranquilizers, and pain relievers are among the most widely sold drugs on the market ... and many Christians use them. People who believe and do what Jesus taught — who know the truth that sets them free — do not need antidepressants and tranquilizers.

The worst of all scenarios is that the church is not a practical place to help children who have no choice in their upbringing and are trapped in dysfunctional families that are molding and shaping their destiny in life. To a great extent our future is predestined by our family environment—by the way we have learned to believe and to think in our heart. We do not change the way we believe and think in our heart unless we consciously embark on a method of being transformed. The Apostle Paul said, "Be ye transformed by the renewing of your mind."

Perhaps helping people overcome the problems mentioned above is not the purpose of the church; however, during the past 2,000 years, if the churches had been teaching the gospel that Jesus preached — teaching it in a manner that we understand and embody — we would not have the problems alluded to above.

Sometime ago I attended a church that was different from what I had attended. I was stunned to hear the Minister say, "A question ministers do not usually ask aloud is, 'Are churches helping — or impeding — people find their way to God?' "

This certainly is a thought-provoking question, especially if we are opened-minded and use our common sense and power of reasoning. After all, the ultimate goal in life — the ultimate goal of religion — is unity with God. And while it seems that this is what the churches are all about, they just might be impeding us from unifying with God.

In view of the conditions in our society alluded to above; in view of the fact that very few people are genuinely happy, satisfied, and contented (only wearing their masks pretending to be); in view of all the confusing and contradicting beliefs of many professing Christians; in view of the fact that about 90 percent of America's families are dysfunctional; and especially in view of the fact that

Why Christianity Isn't Working

many Christians do not really understand what Jesus said, then the answer to the question, are churches impeding people from finding their way to God, must be "yes."

Churches are impeding us by misleading us and having us think that they are teaching what Jesus taught (which is the gospel of the kingdom of God ... which is the way to God), when in actuality they are not. Let's face it! A lot of the stuff many people believe is false. False teachers would have us believe that Jesus was sent into this world to save us, so that we might enjoy heaven *after we die*. There is nothing in the teachings of Jesus or in the teachings of the spiritual teachers of the Old Testament to support the belief that heaven is a place where the saved go after they die. Even if heaven were a place for Christians to go after they die, orthodox teachers are not teaching us how to be saved, according to what Jesus said.

In the latter 1800s, Leo Tolstóy, Russian writer and moral philosopher, said: "The true Christian teaching is very simple, clear, and obvious to all, as Jesus said. But it is simple and accessible only when man is freed from the falsehood in which we were all educated, and which is passed off upon us as God's truth. ... When, at the age of fifty, I first began to study the Gospels seriously, I found in them the spirit that animates all who are truly alive. ... When I perceived that only light enables men to live, I sought the source of this light. And I found it in the Gospels, despite the false teachings of the church. And when I reached this source of light, I was dazzled by its splendor, and I found in it answers to all my questions about life." (*The Gospel According to Jesus* by Stephen Mitchell).

During biblical times before Jesus' ministry, people believed in an angry, vengeful God, who kept count of every sin and punished them for their sins by storms, pestilence, and famines. Jesus came along — with viewpoints that were radical during the time of his ministry — teaching that God is love and that the kingdom of Heaven is within us, and teaching such things as, "It is done unto us as we believe," and "You shall know the truth and the truth shall make you free."

However, Jesus had difficulty getting the people to "have ears to hear" what he said. Still today, we find the same thing, people failing to understand what Jesus said.

While I was writing my first book, *Listening to Ourselves: The Key to Everything that Matters* (meditating and pondering on what I was writing), I found myself getting an understanding of what Jesus said that is different from what I had been taught in the church. I went so far as to say such things as "We are our own saviors. We are saved when we are living in harmony with truth. We discover truth by doing what Jesus and Buddha did; they discovered truth within themselves. We discover truth by being still, paying attention, and listening to ourselves."

I included similar comments in my essays on my Web site, and I explained that truth would save us. The responses to my Web site demonstrate in more ways than one the failure of organized religion. I received several varied responses about what will save us, and no one mentioned what Jesus said ... demonstrating that many Christians do not really know what will save us, according to what Jesus said.

Amidst all the confusion and lack of understanding about being saved, Jesus said everything we need to know if only we would pay attention. Responses to my essays motivated me to do an in-depth study of what Jesus said. My essays alluded to things consistent with what Jesus said; however, what I said is different from what fundamentalists teach. I said that truth would save us and that we are our own saviors. I also commented that walking down the aisle of the church and professing to accept the Lord Jesus Christ as our savior (a ritual advocated by many Christians) does not save us. Apparently what Jesus said has been glossed over, or at least not made clear. We are in the twenty-first century, and these varied responses indicate that teachers are not teaching what Jesus said ... or, at least not making it clear.

By far, most of the responses to my Web site were positive and appreciative; however, those who disagreed with what I said, focused on the following:

- "If thou shalt confess with thy mouth the Lord Jesus, and shalt believe in thine heart that God has raised him from the dead, thou

Why Christianity Isn't Working 39

shalt be saved." [Note: It is not necessary to confess with our mouth the Lord Jesus or to believe in our heart that God raised Jesus from the dead in order to be saved. Again, what will save us, according to what Jesus said, is made clear in the next chapter.]
- "For whosoever shall call upon the name of the Lord shall be saved." [Note: This is true, but it does not mean what we have been led to think it means, explained in the next chapter.]
- "For we are saved by hope." [Note: We are not saved by hope. Actually, hope is tainted with fear. When we *hope* that something will happen, we have a vague sense of fear that it won't.]
- "For by grace are ye are saved through faith; and that not of yourselves; it is the gift of God: Not of works, lest any man should boast." [Note: This statement can be misleading if it is not explained. "Works" as alluded to here are products of the false ego-self, something to boast about and to gloat over; something we think will make us appear special and important; something we do that seems to be loving and kind, but we do it to impress others ... to give a false impression of who we are. These kinds of works will never save us. The foregoing statement does not explain what will save us.]
- "Neither is there salvation in any other; for there is none other name under Heaven given among men, whereby we must be saved." [Note: Fundamentalists seem to interpret this to mean that there is no way to be saved, except by Jesus. This statement is useful to us only if we understand it; explained in Chapter 11, "The Essential Teachings of Jesus."]
- "We believe that through the grace of the Lord Jesus Christ we shall be saved." [Note: We could wrangle with this statement and never understand what would save us. What Jesus said is simple and clear.]
- "Believe on the Lord Jesus Christ, and thou shalt be saved, and thy house." [Note: Not a practical, helpful statement for being saved.]

Of all the things the respondents to my Web site cited about what we must do to be saved, no one mentioned what Jesus said that would save us. None of these statements is as clear as what

Jesus said. So, why not focus on what Jesus said ... until we understand and embody what he said?

One respondent to my Web site suggested that it is not necessary to do as Jesus taught or to do as Jesus did in order to be saved. He went so far as to say, "Do not you think that it is interesting that he said 'believes' as opposed to 'lives in accordance with his teaching'"?

One person commented that the word "kingdom" itself contained a clue as to what is required for being saved. He stressed the word "king," stating that Jesus spoke of entering the kingdom of Heaven. He added that in order to enter the kingdom, there must be a king, "king" being part of the word "kingdom." And he said that Jesus is the king.

Another person suggested that heaven is a place to go, a place to enter. His thinking was influenced by the word "enter," based on what Jesus said: "Except ye be converted, and become as little children, ye shall not enter into the kingdom of Heaven."

Another person's response went so far as to state that in order to be saved we must believe in Jesus Christ as being God's only begotten son and to accept him as our personal savior. Then he followed this with, "He that heareth and believeth not is already condemned." It's interesting that he did not quote the passage where Jesus told us what would save us.

All of the confusion about what will save us points to the fact that organized religion has failed us. The churches are not teaching us what Jesus said ... at least not teaching it in a manner we can understand, believe and embody.

The confusion about what will save us reminds me of a dilemma in which I found myself several years ago. My family and I were returning home from a vacation at the beach. As we were driving along on the Interstate, one of my sons (about nine years old) was standing on the floor of the car, in front of the back seat, peering over my shoulder. Like a bolt out of the blue, he ask me straight forward, matter-of-fact, and unequivocally clear, "Daddy, where is heaven?" I was stumped! Never had I been confronted so directly and clearly with this question. Other questions about hell, Jesus, and Satan followed. After pussyfooting around the questions,

Why Christianity Isn't Working

trying to find answers based on my religious teachings, it occurred to me that the only true, honest answer I had for my son is, "I don't know." That's tragic! ... and to think that Jesus' ministry was about 2,000 years ago, and I had attended church quite regularly.

It became clear to me that what I had learned in the church is false. Shortly thereafter I began a relentless search to determine what is false and what is true. All the while, I had a feeling that the teachings of Jesus were sacred, but that we were not getting his message.

One of the most basic, significant things I learned in the church, which is false and misleading, is that Jesus came to save us, so that we would enjoy heaven after we die. After studying the teachings of Jesus, I learned that his sole purpose for preaching the gospel is that we might have peace and joy *now.* Think what a difference it would make if we knew, understood, and embodied what Jesus said ... if we had peace and joy ... if our families and our society were peaceful, joyous, and harmonious. It's incomprehensible. It's what Jesus wanted for us.

I was also confused about the concept of Jesus dying to take away the sins of the world. Clearly, the sins of the world have not been taken away. On the contrary, the sins of the world of ego are mounting. If the gospel that Jesus preached and that he commanded his disciples to preach to every creature in the world had been taught since his death about 2,000 years ago (taught in a manner that we can understand and embody), we, our families, and our society — the very world itself — would be peaceful and harmonious ... we would enjoy the abundant life Jesus wanted for us.

Sometime during my writing and studying, I became aware of the fact that many Christians have glossed over what Jesus said: "The kingdom of God is within you" (Luke 17:21). We are beginning the twenty-first century, and many Christians do not know or understand something as significant as this. To believe that the kingdom of God is within us (what Jesus said) is not consistent with the belief of fundamentalists, who believe that heaven is a place where Christians go after they die. There is no justification in the Bible for this belief. Fundamentalists do not seem to accept the fact that heaven is in everyone, and we enjoy it when we purify our hearts and are unified with God.

Fundamentalists misinterpret some things that Jesus said, which in turn causes them to distort other things that Jesus (and others) said. The following is an example. Jesus said, "In my Father's house are many mansions; if it were not so, I would have told you. I go to prepare a place for you. And if I go and prepare a place for you, I will come again and receive you unto myself, that where I am, there ye may be also" (John 14:2-3). Fundamentalists interpret the phrase, "I go to prepare a place for you," literally. Fundamentalists seem to interpret this to mean that Jesus went to prepare heaven, a place for Christians to go after they die.

Let's face it! What Jesus meant by "I go to prepare a place for you" is not clear. In view of the message that Jesus intended for us, in view of the essentials of the gospel that are clear, and in view of his mission that we might have peace and joy, we know that the statement does not mean what fundamentalists seem to think it means, that Jesus literally went away someplace to prepare heaven for Christians ... a place for the saved to go after they die.

Jesus did not need to go and prepare a place for us. Everything we need is already within us, if only we would do what Jesus and the spiritual teachers of the Old Testament said *and did*. What is important is that we do not let some verse of scripture that we do not understand deter us from the message intended for us.

The belief that Jesus literally went someplace to prepare heaven, a place for the saved to go after they die, is not consistent with other teachings of Jesus. The following are examples of things Jesus said that are not consistent with him going to prepare heaven for Christians and that he is coming again to take Christians to heaven. The following statements by Jesus allude to heaven being within us, not a place that Jesus has gone to prepare.

- If I cast out devils, then the kingdom of God is come unto you (Matthew 12:28) ... meaning the moment the devils are cast out.
- The kingdom of God is within you (Luke 17:21) ... meaning now.
- Blessed are the poor in spirit; for theirs is the kingdom of heaven (Matthew 5:3).

Why Christianity Isn't Working

- But woe unto you, scribes and Pharisees, hypocrites! for ye shut up the kingdom of heaven against men; for ye neither go in yourselves, neither suffer ye them that are entering to go in (Matthew 23:13) ... speaking about the present.
- But I tell you of a truth, there be some standing here, which shall not taste of death, till they see the kingdom of God (Luke 9:27). Clearly, Jesus was speaking about the present.
- Thou art not far from the kingdom of God (Mark 12:34). This alludes to the present, not about a place that Jesus went to prepare.
- Seek ye first the kingdom of God ... and all things will be added unto you (Matthew 6:33). Jesus was speaking about seeking the kingdom of God that is within us, not about seeking a heaven that he has gone to prepare.
- Suffer the little children to come unto me, and forbid them not; for of such is the kingdom of God (Mark 10:14).
- Our Father which art in heaven, Hallowed be thy name. Thy kingdom come; thy will be done in earth, as it is in heaven.

In addition, the statement, "I go to prepare a place for you," is not consistent with something the apostle Paul said: "Eye hath not seen, nor ear heard, neither have entered into the heart of man, the things which God hath prepared for them that love him." Heaven is already within us and is ours to enjoy as soon as we "clean the inside of the cup and the platter" ... and let God rule in our heart.

Let's face it! We are not clear about what Jesus meant by "I go to prepare a place for you." In an effort to avoid contradictions in their statements, some fundamentalists allude to two heavens, one while we are alive on planet earth and an eternal home in heaven after one dies. At least a part of their thinking seems to be based on something the Apostle Paul said: "I knew a man in Christ above fourteen years ago, (whether in the body, I cannot tell; or whether out of the body, I cannot tell: God knoweth;) such an one caught up to the third heaven" (2 Corinthians 12:2).

Let's face it! We are not sure what the Apostle Paul meant by "third heaven." We do know that the word "heaven" is used in more ways than one in the Bible, and we do know that the heaven that Jesus preached about is the heaven that he said is within us. Sometimes he called heaven the "kingdom of God," and sometimes he called it the "kingdom of heaven."

In addition, what fundamentalists believe about Jesus going to prepare a place for Christians and that he will return to take them with him is not consistent with the sole purpose for Jesus teaching the gospel, which is that we might have peace and joy ... here and now.

Note that Jesus said, "In my Father's house." Jesus told us that the "kingdom of God" is within us. And we know the "Father" (our true spiritual self) is within us. Thus, "my Father's house" and all its mansions must be within us. Where else could it be? Remember that when Jesus prayed, he said: "Our Father which art in heaven, Hallowed be thy name. Thy kingdom come; thy will be done in earth, as it is in heaven." ... all within us.

Let us remember that Jesus' teachings (as well as the rest of the Bible) include metaphors, symbolism, proverbs, parables, and idioms, which are not common in our language. In addition, it seems that Jesus did not intend for some people to understand all of his teachings (explained elsewhere in this book).

The part of the foregoing passage by Jesus that is easily understandable is "that where I am, there ye may be also" (John 14:3). Jesus said, "I and my Father are one" ... the same thing as being unified with God. In our language, Jesus was in a state of consciousness of being in harmony with his true spiritual self ... the state of consciousness that brings peace and joy. And that is where he wanted us to be ... in harmony with our true spiritual self, rather than living in the world of the ego, which always brings suffering in one form or another.

Thus, we know from the teachings of Jesus that heaven is within us and that we enjoy it when we obliterate the devils from our subconscious mind ... when we are living in harmony with our true spiritual self (what Jesus called the Father). And from "The Book of Genesis," we know that "In the beginning God created the heaven and the earth."

Fundamentalists try to make the statement, "The kingdom of God is within you," seem like Jesus did not mean what he said. Some fundamentalists attempt to explain away what Jesus said

Why Christianity Isn't Working 45

about the kingdom of God being within us by saying that the Hebrew interpretation of the phrase by Jesus means that heaven is in our midst. If we interpret "in our midst" to mean the reign of God in our hearts, then we understand the essence of the gospel that Jesus preached. Letting God reign in our hearts is the same thing as "doing the will of the Father," as Jesus advocated. We know from the teachings of Jesus, only those who do the will of the Father will enjoy heaven. Letting God reign in our hearts is consistent with what Jesus said about the kingdom of God being within us.

Some fundamentalists say that the "kingdom of God" is not the same thing as the "kingdom of heaven." Their explanations seem to suggest that heaven is not within us. Although they don't say it aloud, it seems that fundamentalists do not believe what Jesus said about heaven being within us. In the following passages, the phrases "kingdom of God" and "kingdom of heaven" are used interchangeably:

- John the Baptist said, "Repent ye; for the kingdom of heaven is at hand" (Matthew 3:2).
- Jesus said, "And as ye go, preach, saying, The kingdom of heaven is at hand" (Matthew 10:7).
- Jesus said, "The time is fulfilled, and the kingdom of God is at hand; repent ye, and believe the gospel" (Mark 1:15).
- Jesus said, "Blessed are the poor in spirit; for theirs is the kingdom of heaven" (Matthew 5:3).
- Jesus said, "Blessed be ye poor; for yours is the kingdom of God" (Luke 6:20).
- Jesus said, "Verily I say unto you, That a rich man shall hardly enter into the kingdom of heaven" (Matthew 19:23).
- Jesus said, "That except your righteousness shall exceed the righteousness of the scribes and Pharisees, ye shall in no case enter into the kingdom of heaven" (Matthew 5:20).
- Jesus said, "Verily I say unto you, That the publicans and the harlots go into the kingdom of God before you" (Matthew 21:31).
- Jesus said, "But seek ye first the kingdom of God, and his righteousness; and all these things shall be added unto you" (Matthew 6:33).

- Jesus said, "Not every one that saith unto me, Lord, Lord, shall enter into the kingdom of heaven; but he that doeth the will of my Father which is in heaven" (Matthew 7:21).
- Jesus said, "Let the dead bury their dead; but go thou and preach the kingdom of God" (Luke 9:60).
- Jesus said, "But I tell you of a truth, there be some standing here, which shall not taste of death, till they see the kingdom of God" (Luke 9:27). Note that Jesus is speaking of people seeing the kingdom of God while they are living.
- Jesus said, "Thou art not far from the kingdom of God" (Mark 12:34). Jesus' comment suggests that the scribe's understanding rendered him close to discovering the kingdom of God. "Not far from the kingdom of God" does not allude to a place where Christians go after they die, a place that Jesus has gone to prepare.

Thus, the phrases "kingdom of heaven" and the "kingdom of God" are synonymous; whether we call it kingdom of God or kingdom of heaven, it is within us. There is nothing in the above passages (or any place in the Bible) to suggest anything about heaven being a place where Christians go after they die.

From a source not in the Bible, Jesus said: "The kingdom of Heaven is within you; and whosoever knoweth himself shall find it." This was discovered in 1903 in a Greek papyrus (*The Home Book of Quotations,* by Burton Stevenson).

Clearly, the statement by Jesus, "The kingdom of God is within you," has been glossed over and misinterpreted. I did a casual type of inquiry (no in-depth study) to confirm what I suspected, that many Christians do not know or understand something as significant as what Jesus said: "The kingdom of God is within you" (Luke 17:21). For example, two devout Christians (very honorable people, with honorable intentions) stopped by my place to talk with me about their church. I casually commented that perhaps we had different beliefs. When one of them ask me what I believe, I replied that I believe what Jesus said: "The kingdom of God is within you." One of them replied, "But what about the verse in 'The book of Genesis'...?" The verse she alluded to was written several hundred years before Jesus' ministry, and it does not

Why Christianity Isn't Working 47

alter what Jesus said. This was her way of using a verse of Scripture to make it seem that Jesus said something other than what he said.

Similarly, I spoke to another devout Christian (very sincere and with good intentions), and I mentioned the subject statement to him. At that particular time, he didn't respond to my specific comments. However, when I was speaking with him about a couple of weeks later, he ask me where in the Bible the statement about the kingdom of God being within us could be found, saying that he had searched the Bible and could not find it. When I told him where to find the verse, he read it, and then he began explaining the parable about the Sower of the seed ... in a sense, questioning what Jesus said about the kingdom of God being within us.

Similarly, I mentioned the verse to a Minister. He did not know that Jesus said, "the kingdom of God is within you." His first impulse was that someone other than Jesus said this; he thought perhaps that it came from the Dead Sea Scrolls that were discovered quite some time after the Bible was written. When I replied that Jesus said it, he asked if the statement is in the King James Version of the Bible. I ended up showing him the verse. As he read it, he paused and asked, "Have you read the rest of this passage? This is about the ascension."

Finally, I ask him how he interpreted that particular statement by Jesus, "The kingdom of God is within you." His reply was: "The kingdom of God is inside all of those who worship God as their sovereign Lord and King." This is not what Jesus said; this is not in the Bible.

For clarification, the word "you" as used by Jesus in the subject statement means everyone. If we really believe and understand the gospel that Jesus preached, we realize that Heaven is within us, and we enjoy it the moment we discover the truth that sets us free ... all in agreement with what Jesus said.

To protect the young minister's privacy, I have no intentions of identifying him. I am only mentioning this to stress a point. Something as significant as what Jesus said, "The kingdom of God is within you," is not being taught clearly in mainline churches. Perhaps the primary explanation is that what Jesus said is contrary to a false belief of many Christian teachers about what heaven is and where it is ... something that Jesus did not teach.

Because of a question that the young minister answered for me, I am deeply indebted to him. I gained an invaluable understanding and a great appreciation for the Old Testament teachings as a result of what he said. I have heard many times that every word in the Bible is the inspired word of God. Yet, to me there seems to be contradictions. I ask the young minister, "What is the basis for the belief that the entire Bible is the inspired word of God?" His answer to me was that it comes from the many uses of the phrases, "Hear ye the word of the Lord" and "Thus, saith the Lord." I learned that these two phrases appear more than a thousand times in the Old Testament.

I was amazed when I searched for these phrases on the computer that has the Bible on it and began to discover a wealth of wisdom that seems to have been glossed over. It became clear to me how and why the word of the Lord is true. It also became clear to me that the word "Lord" as used by the spiritual teachers of the Old Testament means the same thing as the word "Father" as used by Jesus. Further, it became clear to me that Jesus borrowed heavily from the writers of the Old Testament. It also became clear to me that the essential teachings of Jesus — what will save us — are in the Old Testament. And, quite importantly, it became clear to me that whatever we call it (Lord, Father, true self, higher self, spiritual self, sacred self, divine self), it is within us.

Further, we can and we must do what Jesus and the spiritual teachers of the Old Testament did to find wisdom and understanding. We must be still and commune with our innermost being ... our true spiritual self. We must do what David, the Psalmist, said to do: "Commune with your own heart."

Furthermore, with regard to worshipping God (as suggested by the Minister), if you read all this book carefully, pondering as you read, you will realize that when we know the truth that sets us free, naturally we worship our true spiritual self ... not Jesus and not a God up in the sky someplace. This is true and understandable, according to what Jesus said (explained later in this book).

Why Christianity Isn't Working

One person responding to my Web site said, "I ran a search of six Bible versions, and I could not find where Jesus said, "'The kingdom of Heaven is within you.'" The actual verse in the Bible has the phrase "kingdom of God" rather than "kingdom of Heaven." Perhaps, this explains why he did not find it. Perhaps he did not realize that the phrases are used interchangeably.

It's tragic that many people are not aware that the subject statement by Jesus is in the Bible, or they do not understand and accept what Jesus said. We are beginning the twenty-first century and something as significant as this is not being taught clearly in the mainline churches. The verse of scripture, in the King James Version of the Bible, is in "The Gospel According to Luke," 17:21.

The varied misunderstandings about a very significant statement by Jesus (The kingdom of God is within you) demonstrate a failure of the churches. They are not teaching — or at least not making it clear — what Jesus said.

There was a similar pattern in the responses to my essays. People quoted various Scriptures, trying to find a verse to make it seem that Jesus said something other than what he said. What Jesus said is contrary to their deeply held beliefs about such significant things as heaven, hell, Satan, and devils. And the responses demonstrate that those who do not understand and believe what Jesus said, try to twist the Scriptures (including what Jesus said) to make them seem to be consistent with their false beliefs ... impossible! It's little wonder that people keep studying, studying, and studying ... and never arrive at an understanding of the truth that sets them free ... never understand the message Jesus intended for us.

What Jesus said about the kingdom of God being within us is clear. That statement is not a parable and not a metaphor. It is not anything that is difficult to understand ... if only we believe and understand what Jesus said. To understand what Jesus said requires that we study, assimilate, and *believe* what he said.

Many unbelievers (who think that they are believers) of what Jesus said often refer to "The Revelation to John" (The Apocalypse) in an effort to support their false beliefs. Let's face it! In spite of all the study and interpretations, no one really understands all those visions in "The Revelation to John." It is misleading to interpret a vision of John in a manner that seems to support a false belief that is not consistent with the gospel that Jesus preached.

There is a bit of mystery in the teachings of Jesus. He used idioms, metaphors, symbolism, parables, proverbs, and descriptive language that can render his teachings elusive to grasp. However, by far, the greatest hurdle to understanding what Jesus said is having a mind-set of false beliefs. As awesome as the human mind is, we cannot believe opposing beliefs at the same time. We cannot believe what Jesus said about heaven being within us and, at the same time, believe that heaven is a place where the saved go after they die. Jesus and the spiritual teachers of the Old Testament did not teach that heaven is a place where the saved go after they die.

Thus, if we harbor the false belief about heaven, then when we read what Jesus said about heaven being within us, it's like a blur, like "seeing through a glass darkly." We are not sure of what we have read ... our mind is glazed over. Thus, we gloss over what we have read and go on with something else. To use Jesus' expression, we do not have "ears to hear" what Jesus said.

Thus, fundamentalists twist the Scriptures, adding to and taking from them — straining out a gnat and swallowing a camel — trying to make that which is false in agreement with that which is true ... it cannot be done! Thus, they study, study, study, and the debating goes on and on and on. Pitifully and painfully, we miss the message Jesus intended for us.

Regardless of what all the verses of Scriptures mean that people allude to, trying to make what Jesus said to be in agreement with their false beliefs about such things as heaven, hell, and Satan, it hardly takes away from the fact that Jesus said, "The kingdom of God is within you." False beliefs do not alter what we must do to be saved ... what we must do to understand and believe what Jesus said ... what we must do to discover the truth that sets us free ... what we must do to enjoy the abundant life Jesus wanted for us.

A lot of what we get from modern-day religious teachers and from self-help books is hope and inspiration. But hope and inspiration do not save us from our suffering. These do not satisfy our soul. Soon, we are back to square one, looking for something to

Why Christianity Isn't Working 51

inspire us. When we are expressing life in harmony with truth, we are inspired.

Some fundamentalists are confused about what the gospel is. Much of what fundamentalists believe to be the gospel is not what Jesus taught. Instead, it is an exaggeration and elaboration on what the Apostle Paul said. With about 250 different denominations, clearly there is confusion about the gospel. Some fundamentalists think that the gospel is the "good news" about Jesus. They think that the essence of the gospel is that Jesus died for our sins.

The gospel of Jesus is what he taught and what he told his disciples to teach: "Go ye therefore and teach all nations ... teaching them to observe all things whatsoever I have commanded you." Surely this would include the selected sayings of Jesus that I have explained in the next chapter. I am not aware of any mainline churches where these sayings of Jesus are being taught in a manner that people can understand and embody.

When enough teachers begin teaching the meaning of these sayings of Jesus in a manner that we believe, understand and embody, in due time people will be happy, satisfied, and contented ... not wearing their masks pretending to be. Families will be loving, happy, harmonious, functional, stable, and will stay together. Our society will be a peaceful, happy, harmonious, and safe place to live. People will naturally "do unto others as they would have others do unto them."

Some religious teachers emphasize the passages about the ascension and transfiguration. When we realize that a considerable part of these passages is based on visions, we realize that the passages are not particularly significant for understanding what Jesus taught. Visions are of the mind, not reality. In Acts 1:9-10, we find the following language: "... while they beheld, he [Jesus] was taken up; and a cloud received him out of their sight. ... And while they looked steadfastly toward heaven as he went up." Some fundamentalists believe that Jesus literally ascended up into the clouds, even though the people of that time spoke of seeing visions.

We know that the people did not literally see Jesus go up into the clouds into heaven, as stated literally in the Bible: "I see the heavens opened, and the Son of man standing on the right hand of

God." Clearly, this was a vision. No one has ever seen God. And just as Jesus did not literally ascend into the clouds into heaven, he is not going to return to earth.

Regardless of what transpired, one of the most important things we can do is to believe the gospel that Jesus preached and do what he said to do. Regardless of what the passage about the ascension means, it does not alter what we must do to discover the truth that sets us free. It does not alter what we must do to be saved ... according to what Jesus said. In brief, regardless of what transpired, it is not the gospel that Jesus preached. And, as made clear in the next chapter, those who believe the gospel will be saved and those who do not believe will be damned.

To believe and understand the message of Jesus, we need to study what he said, rather than glossing over it and getting diverted to stuff that we do not understand. Those people who think that Jesus went away to prepare heaven for Christians to enjoy after they die seem to gloss over what Jesus said: "God is not the God of the dead, but of the living" (Matthew 22:32). The only time we have for unifying with God — and living in harmony with God — is while we are alive.

Instead of teaching what Jesus taught, false teachers have bombarded us with false teachings about Jesus and about such significant things as heaven, hell, and Satan. False, age-old beliefs have been drummed into us so thoroughly that we believe they are true; it's like we have been brainwashed ... it's like these false, age-old beliefs are etched in stone.

The stuff with which we have been bombarded is confusing, misleading, and some of it is downright false. It is not the gospel that Jesus preached, and it is not consistent with what the spiritual teachers of the Old Testament taught.

The Apostle Paul let us know, "... that no man put a stumbling block or an occasion to fall in his brother's way." There are no greater stumbling blocks than false, misleading teachings. Worse than useless and misleading, false teachings are stumbling blocks in our path to the discovery of the truth that sets us free; they are stumbling blocks in our path to harmony with God.

Why Christianity Isn't Working

Here are some examples of teachings that are meaningless and misleading: Jesus is our savior. Jesus loves you. Jesus is your friend. Trust Jesus. Jesus Christ is the answer. Jesus died for our sins. Jesus is coming soon. Believe on the Lord Jesus Christ and you will be saved. ... and on and on and on. These teachings are not the gospel that Jesus preached.

How could it possibly help suffering people to tell them that Jesus is their friend and that he loves them? He died about two thousand years ago. Although sympathizing and empathizing with someone who is suffering might soothe and pacify them temporarily, this does not "clean the inside of the cup and the platter;" this does not obliterate the devils from their mind ... the hidden cause of their suffering. This does not help them discover the truth that sets them free.

False, age-old beliefs about heaven, hell, and Satan, handed down for generation after generation, have done more to impede us from understanding — have done more to impede us from "having ears to hear" — what Jesus said than anything else in this world.

How many people do you know who actually do as Jesus commanded us to do? Who "turn the other cheek"? Who love as Jesus commanded us to love? Who know the truth that sets them free? Who have "cleaned the inside of the cup and platter"? Who know how to "enter into the closet and *shut the door"?* Who are as humble as a little child? Who forgive — not seven times — but seventy times seven? It seems that people read and hear these things and simply gloss over them.

Jesus' teachings are strict. Either we are saved and unified with God, or we are sinners. Like being wet or dry, we cannot be both at the same time. We cannot love and hate at the same time. We cannot enjoy inner serenity and peace and at the same time harbor anger, hatred, envy, guilt, jealousy, and evil in our heart. We cannot be free in the spirit of truth and harbor insidious, obscure fears and deeply held false beliefs about ourselves. Briefly, we will never enjoy heaven until we are pure in heart—until we are free from sin and evil.

Many people go through life, occasionally doing good deeds and pretending to be Christian. It seems that the beliefs of many

Christians are concocted in such a manner to let them cling to their sinful ways (actually being hypocrites), rather than following the true teachings of Jesus.

Jesus said, "No man, having put his hand to the plow, and looking back, is fit for the kingdom of God" (Luke 9:62). In our modern-day world, very few farmers (if any) use mules, oxen, or horses for plowing. However, can you imagine what a field of corn would be like if a farmer looked back as he plowed? It would be disastrous ... like the lives of many unbelievers, who have no sense of genuine peace and contentment. They have no basis for comparison.

Isaiah said, "Thou wilt keep him in perfect peace, whose mind is stayed on thee" (Isaiah 26:3). When our mind is "stayed on thee," we are not looking back. We have perfect peace when we abide by the truth that proceedeth from our true spiritual self ... when we "keep our mind stayed on thee."

True Christianity involves repenting and not "looking back," not clinging to the sinful ways of the past. True Christianity involves being pure in heart ... being free from evil, hate, anger, jealousy, envy, and the egotistic desire to appear special and important. There is more than enough wisdom in the teachings of Jesus for us to be saved, if only we believe and do what Jesus said.

We are beginning the twenty-first century, and religious leaders are still arguing about the biblical Scriptures. They have taken the simple and complicated it beyond understanding. Often when religious teachers have difficulty explaining the Holy Scriptures, they will exclaim, "You have to take it on faith," or "you have to believe," although it is not clear what we must take on faith or what we are to believe. What this boils down to is that they expect us to believe falsely as they themselves believe. Clearly some of their most basic, most significant beliefs are false.

Instead of teaching us the basic message that Jesus intended for us, the emphasis of religious fundamentalists is on praising Jesus, glorifying his name, and worshipping the man Jesus ... not teaching what he taught. The gospel that Jesus taught is simple. What Jesus said is understandable, practical, believable, logical,

Why Christianity Isn't Working

true, and rational ... if only we would be still and ponder what he said and understand and believe what he said.

My intention in this chapter is to make it reasonably clear that we are not being taught the message that Jesus intended for us ... at least not in a manner that we believe and comprehend. Anything that I have alluded to in this chapter will be made abundantly clear by the time you finish reading and studying the remainder of this book. The repetition you might encounter is an effort on my part to clarify and reinforce what Jesus said ... which for the most part has not been made clear for the masses of the people since the ministry of Jesus about 2,000 years ago.

John Shelby Spong, Episcopal Bishop, wrote a book titled, *Why Christianity Must Change or Die*. Christianity would flourish if Christian teachers would teach the gospel that Jesus preached, teaching it in a manner we can believe, understand and embody.

Let's face it! We do not understand the message Jesus intended for us, and we are not doing what Jesus said to do. We, our families, our society, our nation — the very world itself — are in need of a healing. The message Jesus intended for us would heal us ... if only we understand and believe — and do — what Jesus said.

In summary, Christianity is not working because the gospel that Jesus commanded his disciples to preach to every creature in the world is not being taught in the mainline churches in a manner that we believe, understand and embody.

Can you imagine? Can you comprehend what our lives, our families, our society — the very world itself — would be like if we discovered the truth that sets us free, and consequently, had peace and joy? This is the purpose for Jesus preaching the gospel. Deep inside in the soul of us, this is what every one wants.

There will never be anymore love, joy, happiness, peace, and contentment than we have the potential to enjoy this very moment ... if only we believe and embody the message Jesus intended for us. Life will never — can ever — get any better than expressing life in agreement with truth ... the same thing as being unified with God. When we are unified with God, we are saved, the subject of the next chapter.

Chapter 3
The Truth about What Will Save Us

Jesus told us about 2,000 years ago what would save us. However, what he said has been glossed over and misinterpreted. Most all religions have one goal in common, to unify with God. We are saved when we are unified with God. In another chapter I mentioned some things that might impede us from finding our way to God. In some of the Protestant churches, the confusion surrounding the concept of being saved might be one of those things that impede us from unifying with God ... that might impede us from being saved.

Some time ago, I received a letter in which the writer asked, "Is belief in Jesus Christ needed to be saved?" It was about the same time that I received this letter that I was given a pamphlet titled "What Must We Do To Be Saved?" The question was not answered in a manner that is clear and practical ... not as clear as what Jesus said. We are beginning the twenty-first century. Aren't we long overdue for knowing and understanding what will save us, according to what Jesus said?

The fact that the writer of the above question used the phrase "in Jesus" instead of "on Jesus" helped me understand a source of confusion. I have heard the Apostle Paul's statement, "Believe on the Lord Jesus Christ and thou shall be saved," several times, but always with the preposition "on," instead of "in." If we omit the prepositions "on" or "in," then we have the key to being saved: Believe Jesus — and do what he said — and we will be saved ... no confusion ... that is the key ... to believe the gospel of the kingdom of God that Jesus commanded his disciples to preach to every creature in the world.

It seems that too many people give too much significance to believing *on* Jesus. Believing on Jesus does nothing for us if we do not believe, understand, and do what he said. If we really believe what Jesus said, it seems logical that we will want to do what he

The Truth about What Will Save Us

said. After all, he said that the kingdom of God is within us. And, if we are to enjoy it, we must be saved.

If belief "on" or "in" the man Jesus were actually necessary to be saved (not the same thing as believing what Jesus said), then all before him were lost; they did not have a chance. That includes Moses, David, Job, Jeremiah, Isaiah, and many other spiritual teachers, including the Buddha.

And let us remember that Jesus said, "They that are whole have no need of the physician, but they that are sick; I came not to call the righteous, but sinners to repentance" (Mark 2:17). Jesus also said, "For the Son of man is come to seek and to save that which was lost"(Luke 19:10). These statements raise a question: Who are those who are already saved without the teachings of Jesus? This is answered clearly in Chapter 7, "Why Christians Leave Christianity."

From a simple observation of ourselves, our families, and our troubled, fractured society (with 90 percent of the families dysfunctional; about half of the marriages ending in divorce; by all the crime, violence, and suffering; with so many neurotic, anger, unhappy people; with so many people on ego trips, trying to appear special and important; where almost everyone has his or her mask; by all the pretense, unhappiness, hypocrisy, restlessness, and discontent) we realize that only a few are saved. ... that few are on the "narrow path that leads to life and few there be that find it."

It seems that what Jesus said about 2,000 years ago is true today: "Wide is the gate and broad is the way that leadeth to destruction, and many there be who follow it. Straight is the gate, and narrow is the way that leadeth unto life and few there be who find it" (Matthew 7:13-14).

By using reasoning and logic, we can discern from Jesus' teachings what we must do to be saved, which is necessary if we are to enjoy heaven. One of the most clear, direct statements by Jesus about who will enjoy heaven is in Matthew 7:21. Jesus said, "Not every one that saith unto me, Lord, Lord, shall enter into the kingdom of Heaven; but only he that doeth the will of my Father who is in heaven."

In our language, this means that only those who do the will of our true spiritual self will enjoy heaven. Think about it! There is no way to enjoy heaven except abiding by the truth that proceeds from our true self. The only way we will ever be in harmony with God — the goal of all the world's great religions — is by being in harmony with our true self. We naturally "do the will of our Father" when we are in agreement with truth. Thus, the truth that sets us free will save us from our sins and, consequently, will save us from our suffering.

Truth is the way of life—the way things are meant to be. However, fundamentalists are so captivated by the man Jesus — not by what he taught — that they are led astray from the gospel that Jesus preached. There are bumper stickers about Jesus, signs about Jesus in front of churches and along the roadways and people praising Jesus, glorifying his name, worshipping the man Jesus, singing about Jesus, and saying such things as Jesus loves you, Jesus is your friend, trust Jesus, Jesus is the way, Jesus died for our sins, Jesus is coming soon, believe on Jesus and be saved, accept Jesus as your savior ... and on and on and on. These things are not the gospel that Jesus preached.

We hear and see the name of Jesus everywhere, and the Christmas celebration of Jesus' birth is unsurpassed. It seems not to matter whether we know what Jesus said, believe what he said, or do what he said ... as long as we praise and worship Jesus and accept him as our savior.

What this boils down to is that many people are doing what we know that we are not supposed to do. Unknowingly to many people, they have made an idol of the man Jesus and they are worshipping an idol ... worshipping a false God. They are worshipping the man Jesus, rather than believing and doing what he taught.

We know from the Bible that there is only one God, and there are to be no gods before God. Jesus is not — and was not — God. Jesus said, "Why callest thou me good? There is none good but one; that is God." Jesus also said, "Thou shalt worship the Lord thy God, and him only shalt thou serve."

Jesus also said:

The Truth about What Will Save Us

- For the Son of man is come to seek and to save that which was lost (Luke 19:10).
- I came not to judge the world, but to save the world (John 12:47).
- For the Son of man is not come to destroy men's lives, but to save them (Luke 9:56).

How did Jesus attempt to save people? It wasn't by doing some of the things that fundamentalists teach. It wasn't by having them to believe *on him,* or having them to accept him as their savior, or by taking Christ into their heart, or by being "washed in the blood."

Jesus attempted to save people by preaching the gospel. There were several saviors before Jesus. Jesus was a savior in the sense that the spiritual teachers of the Old Testament were saviors. Isaiah said, "For I am the Lord thy God, the Holy One of Israel, thy Saviour. ... I, even I, am the Lord; and beside me there is no saviour" (Isaiah 43:3-11). Hosea said, "Yet I am the Lord thy God from the land of Egypt, and thou shalt know no god but me; for there is no saviour beside me" (Hosea 13:4).

Jesus preached the gospel so that those who believed would be saved. However, from the standpoint that there is something we must do to be saved, we are our own saviors. Who saved the spiritual teachers of the Old Testament? Who saved the Buddha? We are saved by communing with our own heart (our true spiritual self). Jesus' three-year ministry was devoted to helping people overcome suffering and to have peace and joy ... to enjoy the abundant life. We have peace and joy when we are saved, and we are saved by communing with our own heart.

Let's face it! Some of the things that Jesus said are not straightforward and clear. Invariably, fundamentalists interpret the things that are not clear in a manner that makes them seem to agree with false beliefs about heaven and hell ... even though the interpretations are inconsistent with the clear, essential sayings of Jesus.

Jesus' sole purpose for preaching the gospel is that we might have peace and joy. Jesus said: "These things I have spoken unto you, that in me you might have peace (John 16:33). "In me" means through his truth teachings. Jesus said clearly that those who believe the gospel would be saved. We have peace when we are saved. He also said, "These things have I spoken unto you, that my joy might remain in you, and that your joy might be full" (John 15:11). If we believe and understand the twenty selected sayings of Jesus that follow — and do what Jesus said to do — we will be saved. Thus, we do not need to know the meaning of everything that Jesus said in order to be saved. When Jesus sent his disciples to preach the gospel, he made it clear that believing the gospel will save us. Jesus said to his disciples: "Go ye into all the world and preach the gospel to every creature. ... He that *believeth* [the gospel] and is baptized *shall be saved*, but he that believeth not shall be damned" (Mark 16:16-17). Thus, Jesus attempted to save people by preaching the gospel.

The Apostle Paul said several things — that seem to have been glossed over — that let us know that there is something we must do to be saved other than just believing on Jesus and accepting him as our savior. These things are consistent with the teachings of Jesus. Actually, we know from what the Apostle Paul said that we are our own saviors. The Apostle Paul said:

- For I am not ashamed of the gospel of Christ, for it is the power of God unto salvation to every one that believeth (Romans 1:16) ... in agreement with what Jesus said about those who believe the gospel.
- Moreover, brethren, I declare unto you the gospel, which I preached unto you, which also ye have received ... by which also ye are saved ... unless ye have believed in vain (1 Corinthians 15:1-2). Thus, we are saved by the gospel if we believe and embody it.
- Meditate upon these things; give thyself wholly to them; that thy profiting may appear to all. Take heed unto thyself, and unto the doctrine; continue in them; for in doing this thou shalt both *save thyself*, and them that hear thee" (1 Timothy 4:15-16). Note that he said, "Meditate upon these things." Thus, we must do something more than just believe and accept Jesus as our savior. And note that we could *save ourselves*.
- But now much more in my absence, work out your own salvation (Philippians 2:12). This suggests that when the Apostle Paul was present with people that he helped them work out their salva-

The Truth about What Will Save Us

tion by teaching them. This also suggests that we can work out our own salvation ... that we are our own savior.

- For whosoever shall call upon the name of the Lord shall be saved (Romans 10:13). The way that this is often explained leaves the impression that we are to call upon the name of Jesus. In all simplicity, we are to call upon our true spiritual self. In this instance, the Apostle Paul used the word "Lord" in the same manner that the writers of the Old Testament used it.
- And with all deceivableness of unrighteousness in them that perish; because they received not the love of the truth, that they might be saved. And for this cause God shall send them strong delusion, that they should believe a lie; that they all might be damned who believed not the truth, but had pleasure in unrighteousness (2 Thessalonians 2:10-12).
- Be ye transformed by the renewing of your mind." Again, we must do something. We are transformed when we "clean the inside of the cup and the platter," when we obliterate the devils from our heart, when we discover the truth that sets us free.

In addition to what the Apostle Paul said, there are several clues throughout the Bible that let us know that we can work out our own salvation ... that we are our own saviors. David the Psalmist said, "As for me, I will call upon God; and the Lord shall save me (Psalms 55:16). And, "Call upon the Lord in truth. He will hear our cry and will save us" (Psalms 145:17-19). Thus, what the Apostle Paul said about "calling upon the name of the Lord" is the same thing that David the Psalmist said.

David, the Psalmist, also said, "The Lord is nigh unto all them that call upon him in truth. He will hear their cry, and will save them" (Psalms 145:17-19).

The only place we will ever discover the truth that sets us free is within ourselves. The Apostle Paul said, "So then faith *cometh* by hearing and hearing by the word of God." The "word of God" is truth. Thus, if we commune with our true spiritual self (same as calling upon the name of the Lord) and discover the truth that sets us free, we are saved.

Also, others have said things that let us know that we must do something to be saved other than just believe. Moses said, "Sanctify yourselves." James, brother of Jesus and author of "The Letter of James," said, "Purify your hearts, ye double minded." Jeremiah said, "Wash thine heart from wickedness [same thing as purifying our hearts], that thou mayest be saved." We are saved when our heart is pure.

David the Psalmist left us with one of the most simple, direct ways for doing what we must do to be saved. He said: "Be still ... commune with your own heart." We discover truth — we are saved — by being still and communing with our own heart ... same thing as calling upon the name of the Lord.

Communing with our heart is how we "clean the inside of the cup and the platter," how we cast the devils from our heart, how we purify our hearts, how we sanctify ourselves, how we become as perfect as Jesus told us to be, how we discover the truth that sets us free. In brief, communing with our own heart will save us. Thus, in the sense that we must do something to be saved, we are our own saviors.

The Apostle John said, "Howbeit when he, the Spirit of truth, is come, he will guide you into all truth" John 16:13). By communing with our own heart, the spirit of truth comes to us. It comes in an instant; however we have no way of knowing when that instant will arrive. We might meditate and commune with our heart regularly for 30 days before the spirit of truth comes. The Apostle Paul said, "Pray without ceasing" (1 Thessalonians 5:17). The point is that we must do something. James, author of the "Letter of James," said "But wilt thou know, O vain man, that faith without works is dead? ... For as the body without the spirit is dead, so faith without works is dead also" (James 2:20-26).

From this, we can surmise that if we are not among those who are alive in the spirit of truth, we are among the living dead. "Faith" is unquestioning belief. There are no "magic wands" that will save us. Professing to believe on Jesus and accepting him as our savior does not save us.

We also know from the Buddha that we are our own saviors. Buddha said, "Be ye lamps unto yourselves; seek salvation alone in truth. Those who shall not look for assistance from anyone beside themselves, it is they who shall reach the very topmost height."

The Truth about What Will Save Us

The "topmost height" is living in agreement with truth ... the same thing as being in harmony with God ... and that is heaven.

Knowing that heaven is within us and knowing that the truth that will save us dwells within our heart help us to know what we must do to be saved. We know where to look for the cause of — and the solution to — our suffering and unhappiness ... we know where to look for the truth and for the kingdom of heaven. Think about it! It's all within us.

- Jesus said, "It is done unto us as we believe." Who will change our beliefs, but we ourselves?
- Jesus said, "You shall know the truth and the truth shall make you free." Who is going to discover the truth for us, except we ourselves? No one can describe truth to us in a manner in which we can grasp and experience it.
- Jesus said, "Narrow is the way to life and few there be that find it." Truth is the way of life ... the way our life is meant to be. Who will discover the narrow way to life for us, but we ourselves? No one can — or will — do this for us.
- Jesus said, "Only those who do the will of the Father will enjoy heaven." We will not do the will our Father as long as we acquiesce to the world of the ego. No one can or will do the will of our Father for us. To enjoy heaven, we — ourselves — must do the will of our Father (our true spiritual self). We will do the will of our true spiritual self — we will serve God — when we are living in agreement with truth.
- Jesus said, "If I cast out devils, then the kingdom of God is come unto you." If we really understand the teachings of Jesus, we realize that we are the only one who can "cast the devils from our heart." We do this by communing with our own heart, which is a form of prayer (more about this in chapter 10, "Prayer that Never Fails").
- Jesus said, "Cleanse first that which is within the cup and platter, that the outside of them may be clean also" (Matthew 23:26). We accomplish this by obliterating the evil within us ... by discovering the truth that sets us free.
- Jesus said, "Except ye be converted and become as little children, ye shall not enter into the kingdom of Heaven." Who is going

to convert us, but we ourselves? How are we going to be converted, except by communing with our own heart and obliterating obscure, insidious fears and deeply held false beliefs?

- Jesus said, "Seek ye first the kingdom of God and his righteousness, and all these things shall be added unto you." Note that he told us to seek. No one — not anything — outside ourselves can seek for us. It's a do-it-yourself undertaking. We seek in the stillness of our minds, by communing with our true spiritual self.

Remember that Jesus said that those who believe the gospel would be saved. If we did any of the above, we would be saved. ... All in agreement with what Jesus said. We do not do the will of our Father — a prerequisite for enjoying heaven — if we are not in agreement with truth. And we cannot love freely and unconditionally — we cannot enjoy heaven — with fear rearing its ugly head at every turn of the road, fashioning our every thought and every action.

Also, remember that Jesus said his way is simple. His way is the way of truth. We have taken the simple and complicated it beyond anything we can comprehend ... and primarily because we have been led astray by false beliefs. In all simplicity, if we discovered the truth that sets us free, we would be saved ... we would have peace and joy.

In all simplicity, truth is the way. Truth will save us from our sins and will save us from suffering. Truth is the way of life that Jesus lived ... truth is the way that life is meant to be ... if only we would overcome the world of the ego — if only we would obliterate the devil that makes us do it — and let things be the way they are supposed to be. Thus, truth will save us, according to what Jesus said. And, truth "resteth" within our own heart.

The Apostle Paul said something that is of particular significance, but it too seems to have been glossed over. He said, "The kingdom of God is ... righteousness, and peace, and joy" (Romans 14:17). Remember that Jesus said, "The kingdom of God is within you" (Luke 17:21).

Jesus also said, "And I say unto you, ask, and it shall be given you; seek, and ye shall find; knock, and it shall be opened unto you. For every one that asketh receiveth; and he that seeketh findeth; and

The Truth about What Will Save Us

to him that knocketh it shall be opened. If a son shall ask bread of any of you that is a father, will he give him a stone? or if he ask a fish, will he for a fish give him a serpent? Or if he shall ask an egg, will he offer him a scorpion? If ye then, being evil, know how to give good gifts unto your children; how much more shall your heavenly Father give the Holy Spirit to them that ask him?" (Luke 11:9-13).

Let us pay attention to what Jesus said, "how much more shall your heavenly Father give the Holy Spirit to them that ask him?" Living in harmony with the Holy Spirit (the same thing as the spirit of truth) is the ultimate of peace and joy. When we discover the truth that sets us free, we live in harmony with truth — we are unified with God — as long as we live. Remember that Jesus said, "God is not the God of the dead, but of the living" (Matthew 22:32). Note that it is our heavenly Father who gives us the Holy Spirit; in our language, it is our true divine spiritual self. We are saved when we are living in agreement with the spirit of truth, which resteth in our heart.

Many people suffer all their life from life-draining, negative things such as hate, anger, jealousy, fear, resentment, guilt, worry, anxiety, and depression ... they suffer hell. All the while they believe that they will enjoy peace and joy — they will enjoy heaven — after they die.

Jesus' only purpose for preaching the gospel is that we might have peace and joy *now* ... not after we die. Regardless of how one might twist the Scriptures — trying to make them agree with his or her false beliefs — there is no other explanation for Jesus preaching the gospel. Jesus said, "seek ye first the kingdom of God and his righteousness," and "the kingdom of God is within you." Remember that the Apostle Paul said, "The kingdom of God is righteousness, and peace, and joy" (Romans 14:17).

Recently, I heard an evangelist say that we are not perfect and that we never will be. But, conversely, our true spiritual self is already perfect. We tend to discount or overlook — or add to or take from — biblical Scriptures that let us know we are created in the image and likeness of God, which is characterized by love, truth and perfection. We enjoy our true perfection when we discover the truth that sets us free.

Before you scoff at the thought of being perfect, we inherently desire to free ourselves from our false ego-self and to express life in harmony with our true self. Our true spiritual self is perfect, created in the image and likeness of God. Remember that Jesus said, "Be ye therefore perfect, even as your Father who is in heaven is perfect." He also said, "Cleanse first that which is within the cup and platter." Did Jesus expect us to do the things that he said to do? When we have "cleaned the inside of the cup and the platter," we are as perfect as Jesus told us to be ... a prerequisite for enjoying heaven.

When we are in harmony with our true self, we are in harmony with God and nature. When we are at one with ourselves, and consequently, unified with God, we enjoy heaven ... the abundant life consistent with what Jesus taught ... if only we would let things be the way they are meant to be ... which is in harmony with truth, God, and nature.

Jesus taught the divinity of all people, not just himself. About his works, he told his disciples that they would do greater works than he himself did. Jesus said, "Verily, verily, I say unto you, He that believeth on me, the works that I do shall he do also; and greater works than these shall he do" (John 14: 12).

For clarification, the man Jesus is not our savior; however, the gospel that Jesus preached will save us ... if we understand and believe what he said. If only we had faith in the man Jesus (not the same thing as worshipping the man Jesus) and believed what he said and accepted what he said and did what he said, we would be saved. However, saying that we accept him as our savior does not mean that we understand what he said, believe what he said, and do what he said to do ... doesn't mean that we are saved.

Going through the ritual of being saved does not mean that we have "cleaned the inside of the cup and the platter;" it doesn't mean that we know the truth that sets us free; it doesn't mean that our heart is pure, a prerequisite for enjoying heaven; it doesn't mean that we believe and comprehend the gospel of Jesus ... it doesn't mean that we are saved.

The Truth about What Will Save Us

It is our fearful, false ego-self — the Satan within us — that keeps us alienated from our true perfection ... alienated from God ... and that is hell. And the sole purpose of being saved is to avoid the suffering of hell and, consequently, to enjoy peace and joy — to enjoy heaven — while we are alive on planet Earth.

Although the Apostle Paul said some insightful things, Jesus said everything we need to know to be saved. And Paul's teachings were not as clear and concise as those of Jesus. One of the most often quoted statements about being saved is by Paul and Silas when they were in prison: "Believe on the Lord Jesus Christ, and thou shalt be saved."

The conditions under which Paul and Silas made the statement about believing on the Lord Jesus Christ is interesting. Paul and Silas had been imprisoned because they had been teaching the gospel, and this was creating disorder among the people at the market place. A great earthquake occurred while the jailer was asleep. It jarred the doors of the cells loose so that the prisoners could have escaped. The jailer's duty was keeping Paul and Silas safely. To let prisoners escape was a serious offense for jailers.

The jailer was not aware of an earthquake and thought that he had been negligent. In the words of the Scripture: "And the keeper of the prison awaking out of his sleep, and seeing the prison doors open, he drew out his sword, and would have killed himself, supposing that the prisoners had fled. But Paul cried with a loud voice, saying, 'Do thyself no harm; for we are all here.' Then the jailer called for a light, and sprang in, and came trembling, and fell down before Paul and Silas, and ask, 'What must I do to be saved?'"

It is interesting that the jailer was fearful that he might be executed for letting the prisoners escape, and Paul and Silas responded, "Believe on the Lord Jesus Christ, and thou shalt be saved, and thy house." This particular statement became one of the most often quoted passages about being saved. Insofar as being saved is concerned, this particular statement is useless and misleading. Teachers would be far more helpful if they explained something else that Paul said: "Work out your own salvation."

Paul also said, "For by grace are ye are saved through faith; and that not of yourselves; it is the gift of God: Not of works, lest any man should boast." To understand Paul's statement, we must note that he was speaking about the false ego-self, speaking of "yourselves." It's the false ego-self that strives to be known by works and likes to boast. Communing with our true spiritual self and discovering the truth that sets us free saves us.

We were given the power to choose. And with the stranglehold that Satan (our elephantine ego) has on us, we are prone (paraphrasing the Buddha) to be "led astray thinking delusion is better than truth" ... and, consequently, we are prone (paraphrasing Jesus) to "stay on the wide road to destruction."

It's easy to go through the ritual of being saved as many religious leaders advocate and still be a hypocrite. There is a level of peace and joy that a hypocrite will never understand until he or she knows from the experience. Deep inside the soul of us, we all yearn to live in agreement with truth and nature and to have genuine peace and joy. We are saved when we know the truth that sets us free of all the stuff hidden in our subconscious mind that wreaks havoc with our peace of mind and inner serenity.

We know from the teachings of Buddha that suffering will arise repeatedly until we free ourselves from the impurities in our subconscious mind.

Often times when we think of abiding by the Ten Commandments, we tend to gloss over the first and most important commandment and focus on the others. For example, we tend to focus on: "Thou shalt not kill. Neither shalt thou commit adultery. Neither shalt thou steal. Neither shalt thou bear false witness against thy neighbour. Neither shalt thou desire thy neighbour's wife, neither shalt thou covet thy neighbour's house, his field, or his manservant, or his maidservant, his ox, or his ass, or any thing that is thy neighbour's" (Deuteronomy 5:17-21).

If we exercise self discipline and consciously refrain from doing these things — having glossed over the first and the greatest of the commandments — we tend to think that we are abiding by the Ten Commandments. We might even think that we are a Christian. Refraining from doing these things — and doing good deeds — do not save us. The Apostle Paul let us know that we are not saved by works alone.

The Truth about What Will Save Us

Regardless of how diligently and conscientiously we abide by nine of the Ten Commandments — glossing over the first and the greatest — there is a level of peace, joy, and inner serenity we will not experience until we love as Jesus commanded us to love.

Jesus told us that the first and the greatest commandment is: "Thou shalt love the Lord thy God with all thy heart, and with all thy soul, and with all thy mind" (Matthew 22:37). This is essentially the same thing Moses said several hundred years before the ministry of Jesus. However, Jesus added: "This is the first and great commandment. And the second is like unto it, Thou shalt love thy neighbour as thyself. On these two commandments hang all the law and the prophets" (Matthew 22:38-39).

Sophocles, dramatist of ancient Athens, said, "One word frees us of all the weight and pain of life; that word is love."

We cannot love anyone until we abide by the first commandment; we cannot love anyone until we love ourselves. We are saved when we abide by the first and the greatest of the commandments. Quite naturally, we abide by the other commandments if we abide by the first and the greatest. If we abide by the first commandment, we are a Christian in a strict sense of the word. When we "love thy neighbor as thyself," we "do unto others as we would have others do unto us."

In addition to the Ten Commandments, Jesus also said, "This is my commandment, That you love one another, as I have loved you" (John 15:12). The Apostle Paul sums up what Jesus said about the commandments very simply and briefly: "Owe no man any thing, but to love one another; for he that loveth another hath fulfilled the law. For this, Thou shalt not commit adultery, Thou shalt not kill, Thou shalt not steal, Thou shalt not bear false witness, Thou shalt not covet; and if there be any other commandment, it is briefly comprehended in this saying, namely, Thou shalt love thy neighbour as thyself. Love worketh no ill to his neighbour; therefore love is the fulfilling of the law" (Roman 13: 8-10).

Can you imagine? Can you comprehend what our lives, our families, our society — the very world itself — would be like if only we loved as both Moses and Jesus commanded us to love? We would be as perfect as Jesus told us to be, "even as your Father who is in heaven is perfect." If we, individually and collectively as a society, were as perfect as Jesus told us to be, the very world itself would be perfect ... in harmony with God and truth.

We are saved when we love as Jesus commanded us to love. However, we cannot love freely and unconditionally — the way Jesus commanded us to love — with insidious fear rearing its head at every turn of the road. We cannot love as Jesus commanded us to love unless our heart is pure ... thus, the explanation for Jesus preaching of the gospel.

Jesus said to his disciples: "Go ye therefore and teach all nations ... teaching them to observe all things whatsoever I have commanded you" (Matthew 28:19-20). "All things whatsoever I have commanded you" include the following twenty selected sayings of Jesus.

These sayings are more than ample for us to understand the message Jesus intended for us. Focusing on these sayings of Jesus can help keep us from being overwhelmed by the entire Bible and, consequently, not grasping what Jesus said. Jesus said everything we need to know to be saved ... if only we study, assimilate, and comprehend what he said.

Most of the Bible would be redundant if we mastered the following 20 sayings of Jesus. Actually, most of Jesus' teachings would be redundant if we mastered one of the following sayings of Jesus. For example, notice the significance of what Jesus said: "If I cast out devils, then the kingdom of God is come unto you." If we cast the devils from heart, we are in harmony with truth and God ... we are saved ... the prerequisite for enjoying heaven.

Twenty selected sayings of Jesus — essentials of the gospel that Jesus preached — follow:

1) You shall love the Lord thy God with all your heart, and with all your soul, and with all your mind. This is the first and great commandment (Matthew 22:38).
2) Love thy neighbor as thyself (Matthew 22:39). [It is significant to note that Jesus said, "On these two commandments hang all the law and the prophets." Thus, most of the Bible would be redundant if we loved as Jesus commanded us to love.]

The Truth about What Will Save Us

3) This is my commandment, That you love one another, as I have loved you (John 15:12).
4) You shall know the truth and the truth shall make you free (John 8:32). If we do not discover the truth that sets us free, we are not free to love freely and unconditionally. And, consequently, we are dead in spirit.
5) Seek ye first the kingdom of God and his righteousness; and all these things shall be added unto you (Matthew 6:33). Jesus was speaking about seeking the kingdom of God *now*. And he told us that it is within us, Thus, heaven is not something that Jesus has "gone to prepare." The Apostle Paul said, "The kingdom of God is not meat and drink; but righteousness, and peace, and joy" (Romans 14:17). We enjoy peace, joy, and righteousness when we discover the kingdom of God that is within us ... now, not after we are dead and gone.
6) It is done unto you as you believe (Matthew 8:13).
7) Be ye therefore perfect, even as your Father who is in heaven is perfect (Matthew 5:48). We are as perfect as Jesus told us to be when our heart is pure. Our heart is pure when we have "cleaned the inside of the cup and the platter;" when we have obliterated the devils from our heart.
8) Not every one that saith unto me, Lord, Lord, shall enter into the kingdom of heaven; but he that doeth the will of my Father which is in heaven (Matthew 7:21). When we are abiding by the truth that proceedeth from our true spiritual self, we are doing the will of the "Father" ... God is reigning in our heart.
9) Ask, and it shall be given you; seek, and ye shall find; knock, and it shall be opened unto you (Matthew 7:7). If we ask and seek, we will discover the heaven within us. One of easiest ways of seeking is to do what David, the Psalmist said to do: "Commune with your own heart."
10) Blessed are the pure in heart; for they shall see God (Matthew 5:8).
11) Except ye be converted, and become as little children, ye shall not enter into the kingdom of heaven (Matthew 18:3). Little children are pure in heart until they are corrupted by a sinful

environment into which they are born ... a family and an environment out of harmony with truth, God, and nature.
12) Except a man be born again, he cannot see the kingdom of God (John 3:3). We know that Jesus did not mean for us to literally enter into our mother's womb and be born again. So, what did he mean? When we are converted and are as humble as little children (a requirement for enjoying heaven), when we have obliterated the devils from our heart, when we know the truth that sets us free, we have "been born again."
13) If I cast out devils, then the kingdom of God is come unto you (Matthew 12:28). Jesus was speaking about the present, not about life after death. The kingdom of God comes unto us when we obliterate the devils (obscure, insidious fears and deeply held false beliefs) from our heart.
14) I and my Father are one (John 10:30). This is the same thing as being unified with God. Jesus is an example for Christians. Jesus wanted us to be in the state of purity and perfection that he enjoyed, that "where I am there ye may be also." He wanted us to be "as perfect even as our Father who is in heaven is perfect." We cannot enjoy heaven with sin and evil in our hearts. We cannot enjoy heaven until we are as perfect as Jesus told us to be.
15) The kingdom of God is within you (Luke 17:21). Again, Jesus was speaking about the present, not about going to heaven after we die. Some Christians are letting the statement by Jesus, "I go to prepare a place for you," distort their understanding of the gospel that Jesus preached. It isn't wise to interpret a statement, which we do not understand, to mean something that is not consistent with the message that Jesus intended for us.
16) Cleanse first that which is within the cup and platter, that the outside of them may be clean also (Matthew 23:26). We are pure in heart when we have "cleaned the inside of the cup and the platter." Then we love with all our heart, soul, and mind.
17) Sanctify them through thy truth; thy word is truth (John 17:17). [To sanctify is to save. Thus, truth will save us.]
18) Whosoever eateth my flesh and drinketh my blood hath eternal life (John 6:54). Translating the idioms, this means that if we

The Truth about What Will Save Us

comprehend the true teachings of Jesus, we will be fully alive in the spirit of truth as long as we live. The Apostle John said, "... the blood of Jesus Christ his Son cleanseth us from all sin." This means that the true teachings of Jesus, if believed and comprehended, will free us from sin.

19) He that believeth [the gospel] and is baptized shall be saved, but he that believeth not shall be damned (Mark 16:16).
20) The true worshippers shall worship the Father in spirit and in truth (John 4:23). [A clear understanding of this statement (explained in Chapter 11, "The Essential Teachings of Jesus") helps unravel the mystery of Jesus' teachings.]

If we study any one of those statements by Jesus until we believe, understand, and embody it — until we are be in agreement with truth — we are saved from our sins and saved from our suffering ... we are happy, satisfied, and contented ... at peace with ourselves and at peace with God. Quite naturally, we adhere to the Ten Commandments, and we "do unto others as we would have others do unto us."

However, instead of focusing on what Jesus said, we are prone to gloss over it. We can read and speak about truth without really understanding what we are reading and talking about ... without knowing what truth is, where it is, and how we discover it. Thus, we tend to gloss over Scriptures pertaining to truth and go on with something else. What this boils down to is that we gloss over the message Jesus intended for us.

The foregoing sayings of Jesus include the essentials of the gospel that Jesus preached. We could waste time arguing about statements in the Bible that no one really understands — and we could misconstrue and misunderstand some of the things that the Apostle Paul said — and miss the message Jesus intended for us.

What difference does it make about what Isaiah meant when he said, "Behold, a virgin shall conceive and bear a son?" What difference does it make what Jesus meant about going to prepare a place for those who are saved? The important thing is to be saved, and Jesus told us that those who believe the gospel would be saved. And he told us that the kingdom of God is within us. And we know from the teachings of Jesus that we will not enjoy the kingdom of

God unless we are saved ... unless we discover the truth that sets us free. ... free from fear, free from sin, and consequently, free to love as Jesus commanded us to love.

The Apostle Paul said, "The wages of sin is death." If we do someone wrong — e.g., taking from another by cheating and stealing, stabbing another in the back — it leaves us with deep-down negative feelings. To do something ugly leaves us feeling ugly. If we do something to hurt another, we hurt ourselves. We may not be aware of what is going on within us, but doing another wrong leaves us anxious, guilty, depressed ... it saps us of life and energy ... it makes us sick. It takes the joy out of living ... we are no longer fully alive and fully living ... thus we are dead in spirit. And the negative emotions that cause the death of our spirit can lead to the physical death of our body.

According to the Commandments, we are not to lie. Lying is more than simply not telling lies. We are lying when we are wearing our mask, pretending to be something other than the way we believe and think in our heart. How many people do you know, how many Christians do you know who are not wearing a mask? Rare is the person in our society who is not wearing a mask. We will never enjoy heaven — the inherent goal of everyone — until we discover truth and are free from our masks. We will be free of our masks when we are saved, and Jesus told us clearly what would save us.

Jesus used the phrase "my Father," and he also used the phrase "your Father." The significant thing to know is that the Father is within everyone. When we are expressing life in agreement with truth, we will quite naturally do the will of our "Father," which is a prerequisite for enjoying heaven ... which is within us. The will of the Father is the will of God. Thus, when we are expressing life in harmony with truth, we are serving God ... the same thing as doing the will of the "Father." God is characterized by truth, love, peace, and perfection. Our true self is created in the image and likeness of God.

Life will not — cannot — get any better — now or ever — than it is when we are living in agreement with truth, God, and nature ... deep inside the soul of us what everyone of us desires.

The Truth about What Will Save Us

We are in agreement with truth — we are unified with God — when we believe and embody the gospel that Jesus preached.

What is the gospel that Jesus preached? It is the gospel of the kingdom of God. Luke said, "The law and the prophets were until John; since that time the kingdom of God is preached." In "The Gospel According to Mark" we find, "After John was put in prison, Jesus went into Galilee, preaching the gospel of the kingdom of God. ... And saying, The time is fulfilled, and the kingdom of God is at hand; repent ye, and believe the gospel" (Mark 1:14-15). Remember that Jesus said, "the kingdom of God is within you."

The gospel of the kingdom of God is the essence of Jesus' teachings. **The gospel is what Jesus preached and what he commanded his disciples to preach to every creature in the entire world.** The Apostle Paul, who wrote about two-thirds of the New Testament, was hopeful of getting the gospel of Jesus in all churches. If we fail to get Jesus' gospel of the kingdom of God, then we have failed to get the message that Jesus intended for us.

Strictly speaking, according to Jesus, only those who abide by the truth that proceedeth from their true spiritual self (in Jesus' language, only those who do the will of the Father) — only those who are converted and become as humble as little children — will enjoy heaven. Thus, only those who are holy — those who are sinless — will enjoy heaven. We become holy — we find salvation — by communion with God.

Note how things are simplified for us if we understand and believe what Jesus said. If we believe and comprehend the gospel, we will be saved. It's not necessary to understand the whole Bible, not necessary to understand all the information in the Old Testament and some in the New Testament, not necessary to understand all the visions of John in "The Revelation to John" to be saved ... if only we believe and comprehend the gospel that Jesus preached.

We have a tendency to complicate the simple. The Reverend Norman Vincent Peale said, "We struggle with the complexities and avoid the simplicities." In all simplicity, truth will save us.

Let us note where Jesus made it clear that truth will save us ... thus simplifying matters considerably. Jesus revealed the real secret to what will save us when he was praying for the apostles. He said, "Sanctify them through thy truth; thy word is truth" (John 17:17). "Sanctify" is defined as saved from our sins. And, we are sanctified through truth ... thus, truth will save us. When Jesus was speaking of "thy truth" and "thy word," he was speaking of the "truth" and the "word" that comes from the Father within us. "Thy" refers to the Father. And the word "Father" as used by Jesus is (in our language) our true spiritual self ... the same thing as the Holy Spirit that dwells within us. Thus, the truth that will save us comes from our innermost being, the place within us that knows the difference between what is false and what is true. The truth that will save us resides in the place within that David, the Psalmist, alluded to as the "secret place of the most high."

We're beginning the twenty-first century. Aren't we long overdue for understanding what Jesus said, rather than blindly saying, "I accept Jesus as my savior"? When Jesus spoke of "the narrow path to life and few there be who find it," he was alluding to those who are living in harmony with truth. And when Jesus spoke of the "broad path that leads to destruction and many there be who are on it," he was speaking of those who are damned ... those who do not believe the gospel, and consequently, are not saved.

To be clear about the concept of being saved, it helps to know that what we are striving for is to be saved from ourselves ... saved from our fearful, false ego-self, which is the hidden source of all our mental suffering, restlessness, and discontent. God as a deity outside ourselves does not punish us. The Satan that causes suffering is our fearful, false, elephantine ego-self. Again, it's all within us, both the source of our joy, peace, and happiness and the cause of our suffering, restlessness, and discontent.

When Jesus spoke about false prophets arising and deceiving many, he was speaking about teachers who do not teach the gospel that he commanded his disciples to teach. He was speaking about teachers who are not teaching us the truth about the truth, who are not teaching us that heaven is within us ... who are not teaching the gospel of the kingdom of God that Jesus commanded his disciples to teach to all creatures in all the world.

The Truth about What Will Save Us

Jesus told us who would not enter into the kingdom of Heaven: "That except your righteousness shall exceed the righteousness of the scribes and the Pharisees, ye shall in no case enter into the kingdom of Heaven." That includes hypocrites, people wearing their masks, pretending to be different from the way they believe and think in their heart.

On this point, the Apostle Paul was more specific. He said, "Know ye not that the unrighteous shall not inherit the kingdom of God? Be not deceived; neither fornicators, nor idolaters, not adulterers, nor effeminate, nor abusers of themselves with mankind, nor thieves, nor covetous, nor drunkards, nor revilers, nor extortioners, shall inherit the kingdom of God" (1 Corinthians 6:9-10).

The Apostle Paul described people who are not in agreement with truth and nature ... not in harmony with God ... who would not enjoy genuine peace and joy. Remember that the Apostle Paul described heaven as peace, joy, and righteousness.

In our language, if we harbor any abnormal addiction, desire, or neurotic need for power, adulation, recognition, money, sex — anything that is inharmonious with truth, God, and nature — we will not enjoy genuine peace, joy, and tranquillity of mind. Instead of peace and joy, these unhealthy desires lead from one disastrous situation to another ... all leading to alienation, loneliness, and suffering in one manner or another.

The messy morass in which we find ourselves is what we have created. We create our own hell. We do not create heaven. It is already created for us and is ours to enjoy once we know the truth that sets us free and have overcome the world of the ego.

Without fear there can be no psychological stress, anxiety, depression, worry, hatred, jealousy, possessiveness, revenge, greed, tension, apprehension, conflict, or mental turmoil. All these are products of fear and ego, the "world" that Jesus alluded to in John 16:33 when he said, "In the world ye shall have tribulations, but be of good cheer; I have overcome the world."

Jesus' disciples also had overcome the world of the ego. Jesus said, "They are not of the world, even as I am not of the world." We too can overcome the world of the ego by "cleaning the inside of the cup and the platter," by discovering the truth that sets us free, by "being converted and becoming as humble as little children" ... by abiding by the truth that dwells in our heart rather than abiding by the dictates of our false ego-self.

No one can overcome the false ego-self for us. No one can discover the truth for us ... it is a do-it-yourself task. What this boils down to is that although there are those who can teach us and guide us, in the final analysis, we are our own savior; our true spiritual self is our savior. Similarly, the Lord (the true spiritual self) was the savior of the spiritual teachers of the Old Testament. It is by communing with our true spiritual self that we discover the truth that sets us free. Teachers, ministers, therapists, and others can only serve as guides.

From the "Book of Thomas," which did not become part of the New Testament, we find where Jesus was attributed with saying, "If you bring forth what is within you, what you have will save you." (From the previously quoted book, *The Five Gospels — What Did Jesus Really Say?*).

If we study and assimilate what Jesus said, we realize that he was speaking of the truth that "proceeds from the Father," which is within us. And we realize that truth will save us ... we bring it forth by being still, calming our mind, and listening to ourselves.

In summary, truth will save us from our sins and save us from suffering. Truth is the only thing that will free us from hatred, anger, depression, anxiety, jealousy, resentment, envy, evil, guilt, the egotistic desire to appear special and important ... all that negative stuff that robs us of love, peace, and joy ... that robs us of the life of our spirit. When we have obliterated obscure, insidious fears and deeply held false beliefs, what remains must be true. Then, we must be in harmony with truth, God, and nature ... deep inside the soul of us what everyone desires.

Chapter 4
Truth Is the Way

Life will never get any better than it is when we are living in harmony with truth ... thus the wisdom of noted thinkers:
- Better than living a hundred years not seeing the highest truth is one day in the life of a man who sees the highest truth. — Buddha
- Time is precious, but truth is more precious than time. — Disraeli
- Truth is the cry of all, but the game of the few. — George Berkeley
- You shall know the truth and the truth shall make you free. — Jesus
- Our minds possess by nature an insatiable desire to know the truth. — Cicero
- Rather than love, than money, than fame, give me truth. — Thoreau

The explanation for the insatiable desire to know truth is the fact that it is the only thing that will bring us the love, joy, peace, health, happiness, and inner serenity that we all crave. The old myths "time heals all wounds" and "truth hurts" are not true. Time heals nothing. Nature heals physical wounds. Truth heals emotional wounds and emotionally induced (psychosomatic) illnesses. Truth does not hurt. On the contrary, truth is the only thing that frees us from suffering, and consequently, brings us inner peace and joy.

Why all the misunderstanding, misinformation, mystery, and confusion about truth? Truth really is no mystery. It's no guarded secret. Truth is not something that only the mystics, masters, saints and sages can comprehend. Very simply, according to Webster, "Truth is that which is true." When we free ourselves of obscure, insidious fears and false beliefs, what remains must be true ... so simple, yet so elusive. Truth is the absence of that which is false.

Discovering truth is the single most significant discovery we can possibly make ... it is the greatest lesson life has to offer. What have we gained if we "gain the whole world but lose our soul" ... if we are basically restless, discontented, dissatisfied, and unhappy? ... if we are alienated from that which is true? ... if we are alienated from our true self? ... if we are alienated from God? Truth has the power to render our families loving, happy, harmonious, functional, and stable. Truth has the power to obliterate all social problems ... crime, violence, spousal abuse, child abuse, drug abuse ... and on and on and on.

The noted psychoanalyst, Erich Fromm, said, "Man must strive to recognize the truth and can be fully human only to the extent to which he succeeds in this task."

This statement by Fromm gets to the heart of the gospel that Jesus preached. Jesus said, "People honoureth me with their lips, but their heart is far from me." Their heart is far from being in harmony with truth ... a prerequisite for being fully human. When we are in harmony with truth, we are pure in heart, a prerequisite for having peace and joy ... a prerequisite for enjoying satisfying relationships ... the solution to anger, hatred, restlessness, discontent, and unhappiness ... a prerequisite for enjoying heaven.

One of the greatest of mysteries is why truth has eluded us for so many years. We have an abundance of knowledge about all sorts of things, except one of the most simple and most important things we will ever know, which is knowing ourselves and knowing the truth that sets us free ... something that we already know ... if only we would be still and pay attention.

We've explored almost everything from the bottoms of the oceans to outer space, except the most important thing, our inner selves ... herein lies the truth that sets us free ... free from fear and free to love freely, free to be happy, satisfied, contented ... free to enjoy heaven ... here and now ... all in agreement with what Jesus said.

Aren't we long overdue for discovering truth? It's the essence of the teachings of Jesus, who taught about 2,000 years ago. It's the essence of the teachings of the Buddha, who taught about 500 years BC. Truth is the solution to all our unhappiness, all mental suffering, restlessness, and discontent.

In some instances in which Jesus used the pronouns "I" and "me" we can substitute the word "truth." Jesus was the personifi-

Truth Is the Way

cation of truth. Jesus said, "I am the way, the truth, and the life; no man cometh unto the Father, but by me" (John 14:6). In our language that is simple to understand, truth is the way and the life. Truth is the life of the spirit in us. As long as we are alive on planet earth, our spirit is alive when we are in harmony with truth. The goal of all great religions is unification with God. In our language, Jesus' statement, "no man cometh to the Father, but by me," means that no one is unified with God, but by truth.

If we were unified with God — *if* we were living in harmony with truth, God, and nature — we would be "the way, the truth, and the life." Think about what a difference it would make if we (individually and collectively as a nation) were the way, the truth, and the life. It's what Jesus wanted for the entire world.

Both the life of the Buddha and the life of Jesus were the way of truth. Both the Buddha and Jesus were the personification of truth, love and compassion. Buddha was devoted to teaching people the absolute truth. Buddha's meditations were on truth, his thoughts were on truth ... and he said, "my self has become the truth." Although using different words and phrases, both Jesus and Buddha taught truth and unconditional love.

Although truth is an essential aspect of the teachings of Jesus, I am not aware of any mainline churches that are teaching its members how to discover the truth that sets them free ... at least, not teaching in a manner that one can understand and embody. Churches will undergo a major transformation when enough religious teachers grasp the significance of Jesus' basic message of truth ... and, most importantly, learn how to teach truth in a manner that we can understand, embrace and embody.

Although, deep inside, we desire to live in agreement with truth, we do not always welcome it, as evidenced by the following comments:

- The men the American people admire most extravagantly are the most daring liars; the men they detest most violently are those who try to tell them the truth. — H. L. Mencken
- Whoever tells the truth is chased out of nine villages. — A Turkish proverb

- He who speaks the truth must have one foot in the stirrup. — Armenian proverb.
- Just as serpents close their ears, so do men close their eyes to truth. — Galileo
- Man is cold as ice to the truth, hot as fire to falsehood. — La Fontaine
- You will observe with concern how long a useful truth may be known and exist, before it is generally received and practiced on. — Benjamin Franklin
- They abhor him that speaketh uprightly (Amos 5:10).

Actually, truth is not what we resent and resist. Most of us do not know what truth is. Deep inside, truth is what we are really seeking. What we resent and resist — what we detest and hate — is someone telling us the truth. People with evil in their heart do not want anyone telling them the truth. People who are caught up in the world of the ego — pretending to be something they are not — do not like their falseness, pretense, and hypocrisy being exposed.

Our false ego-self loses all power over us in the light of truth. Truth obliterates the influence of our false, elephantine ego-self — the devil that makes us do it — rendering it powerless, useless, and unimportant ... something it will resist to the end. Thus, it hangs on tenaciously — keeping us in its thrall — until we discover the truth that sets us free. Truth frees us from the masks we wear, pretending to be something we are not. Truth frees us from unwarranted fear, sin, evil, and suffering. Truth frees us from anger, hatred, jealousy, anxiety, depression, and psychosomatic illnesses. Truth frees us from the need to appear special and important. Truth frees us from negative thoughts that rob us of peace and joy.

It is no less than tragic how we have taken the simple and complicated it to the degree that our society seems hopelessly bent on total social collapse. As it is, about 90 percent of the families are dysfunctional. About half of marriages end in divorce, and a majority of the couples who remain together is unhappy and dissatisfied. Few people are genuinely happy, satisfied, and contented. Almost everyone wears a mask, pretending to be something they are not ... pretending to be important and happy. Crime, violence, and

Truth Is the Way

suffering are rampant. Clearly, something is missing in the teachings of the churches ... clearly, something is not working.

Our mind has the potential to make us sick, depressed, anxious, restless, discontent, miserable, and unhappy. It also has the potential to make us happy, satisfied, and contented ... if only we lived in agreement with the truth that rests within our heart. It all depends on what is repressed in our subconscious mind. It all depends on "how we believe and think in our heart."

From The Bhagavad-Gita we learn, "For him who has conquered the mind, the mind is the best of friends; but for one who has failed to do so, his mind will remain the greatest enemy." We conquer our mind in the quietness of our mind, by freeing ourselves from obscure, insidious fears and deeply rooted false beliefs.

Let's note what a difference it makes when we know truth ... when we know ourselves. There is one hidden cause of all our inner turmoil and unhappiness: obscure, insidious, fears, intertwined with deeply held, false beliefs. This is characteristic of our false ego-self—the "devil that makes us do it."

Our false ego-self compels us to think, do, and say things that cause us to:

- Feel agitated, frustrated, irritated, impatient, angry, resentful, jealous, uneasy, aggressive, possessive, discontented, and restless ... any state of mind unlike love, joy, peace and inner serenity.
- Say and do those things we think will make us appear special, important, and impressive ... things to gain attention, recognition, praise and adulation ... to do those things that we can boast about and gloat over.
- Subconsciously think on those things that cause us to have tension headaches and a host of the dreaded psychosomatic illnesses ... those illnesses caused by the mind, which account for a vast majority of illnesses.
- Think on those things that make us confused, depressed, and anxious ... those things that cause us to need antidepressants, tranquilizers, and something to help us sleep.
- Subconsciously dwell on deeply held false beliefs that cause problems in loving relationships and sex.

- Be alienated from our true self, alienated from that which is true ... alienated from God, and that is hell.

In brief, our false ego-self compels us to think, do and say those things that cause us to experience states of mind unlike love, joy, happiness, peace of mind, and contentment ... and, consequently, that cause us to engage in behavior and do those things that bring all sorts of unhappiness and suffering.

From the book, *A Course In Miracles*, by the Foundation For Inner Peace, we find: "Remember that you always choose between truth and illusion; between the real Atonement that would heal and the ego's 'atonement' that would destroy."

At anytime, we are either acting or reacting — we are choosing — based on that which is either true or false. Only good comes from that which is true; only suffering comes from that which is fearful and false. We know the difference, if only we would be still and pay attention.

When we admit, acknowledge, and understand obscure fears and false beliefs, they vanish. When falsehoods vanish, what remains must be true. Then our insidious fears and deeply rooted, false beliefs lose all power over us. David the Psalmist, said: "I acknowledged my sin unto thee, and mine iniquity have I not hid. I said, I will confess my transgressions unto the Lord; and thou forgavest the iniquity of my sin" (Psalms 32:5). More about this later, but for now, note what forgave David of his sin.

When we rid ourselves of the impurities in our mind, when we "clean the inside of the cup and the platter," when we cast the devils from our mind, when we discover the truth that sets us free:
- We are free to be free ... free to enjoy life to its fullest.
- We are free to be healthy, happy, loving, loved, satisfied, and contented.
- We are free to live in agreement with truth and nature.
- When we are in harmony with our true self, we are in harmony with truth and nature ... we are in harmony with God ... we experience the "peace that passeth all understanding" ... and that is heaven.

Truth Is the Way

Our false ego-self chooses falsity over truth, death over life ... death of our spirit while our body is alive ... and actually the physical death of our body by some dread disease, rather than surrender to truth, the same thing as surrendering to God. Our false ego-self is elusive, relentless, and determined to be right and to appear special and important.

Although we can improve our overall well-being by following some of the Ten Commandments and doing what some of the great teachers such as the Buddha and Jesus told us to do, the real secret to finding peace and joy — the real secret to discovering the truth that sets us free — is to do what they themselves did ... they retreated within themselves for meditation and contemplation ... they retreated within themselves for wisdom and understanding.

In brief, to discover truth, we must learn to calm the mind (in the words of Jesus, we must learn to *shut the door*) and commune with our true spiritual self. We gain wisdom and understanding — we discover the truth that sets us free — by being still and listening to ourselves.

The Buddha achieved enlightenment by meditating beneath a tree regularly for about seven years. After becoming enlightened, the Buddha taught the Four Noble Truths and the Eight-fold Path that leads to truth and salvation, and he admonished his followers to persevere with diligence.

Saints and sages have long recognized and cherished the value of the quiet mind. The Psalmist found great solace in the quiet mind, calling it the secret place of the Most High. The quiet mind is a prerequisite for gaining wisdom and understanding. We simply cannot discover the truth that sets us free with our mind engaged in its typical chatter, rationalizing, analyzing ... all the while being swayed by our fearful, false ego-self.

Mohammed, founder of Islam, gained wisdom and understanding by retreating within a secluded cave for solitude and for meditation and contemplation.

When David, the Psalmist, was sad and depressed, he knew that the fault was in himself: "My tears have been my meat day and night ... Why art thou cast down, O my soul? And why art thou disquieted in me? ... Who can understand his errors? Cleanse thou me from secret faults." He cleansed himself of secret faults by getting wisdom and understanding within himself. He gained wisdom by understanding the cause of his suffering.

Wisdom and understanding lead to an understanding of the truth that sets us free. Sometimes it seems that people draw a blank when the idea of discovering truth is mentioned. Yet, discovering the truth that sets us free is the essence of the teachings of Jesus.

In my first book, *Listening To Ourselves — The Key To Everything That Matters,* with three techniques for calming the mind and also several exercises, I go so far as to say that you cannot follow the 30-day program — practicing the exercises seriously and conscientiously — without discovering truth ... or at least be well on your way. It's simple, yet elusive.

One of the things that renders truth so elusive to discover is that we do not know what we are searching for until we have found it ... until we know from the experience. Some people are confused about the concept of truth, thinking in terms of "your truth and my truth" ... as if different people have a different truth. The universal truth that sets us free is the same for everyone.

We will never discover truth by searching outside ourselves. It's within our own heart. Here again, we would do well to keep simple things simple. Something is either true, or it is false. It cannot be both at the same time. And in regard to the truth that sets us free, we know what is true and what is false ... if only we would be still and pay attention.

Jesus' message is simple, yet we are relentless in trying to complicate it. We can spend a lifetime trying to sort out things we cannot understand (the myths, dreams, visions, prophesy), all the while the simplicity of what Jesus said eludes us. Yet, the gospel that Jesus preached would save us ... if only we would believe and comprehend what he said.

Jesus said, "Suffer the little children to come unto me, and forbid them not, for of such is the kingdom of God. ... Verily I say unto you, whosoever shall not receive the kingdom of God as a little child, he shall not enter therein. ... They that are whole have no need of the physician, but they that are sick; I came not to call the righteous, but sinners to repentance."

Truth Is the Way

Children are not born sinners. They become sinners when outside influences — a sinful environment — program their minds to that which is contrary to truth and nature. David, the Psalmist, said something that is sometimes misinterpreted. He said, "Behold, I was shapen in iniquity; and in sin did my mother conceive me" (Psalms 51:5). We do not know the exact situation; however, his mother must have been sinful. We do know that David did not receive the love, mothering, and nurturing that children need. David suffered from depression and other afflictions. He said, "Lord, remember David, and all his afflictions" (Psalms 132:1). An unhealthy childhood environment has a bearing on most afflictions. Webster defines "affliction" as "an afflicted condition; pain; suffering; anything causing pain or distress; calamity."

The part about "shapen in iniquity" seems to get glossed over, and the part "in sin did my mother conceive me" is misinterpreted to mean that we are sinners when we are born. David (like most people) was born into a sinful environment and consequently molded and shaped psychologically by an environment that is inharmonious with truth.

The November 15, 1999, issue of *U.S. News and World Report,* has an article titled, "Behavior beats genes." The article suggests that "... environmental influences may explain more behaviors than previously thought." It also suggests that genes do not control some of the things that scientists have attributed to them.

The article goes on to say, "Scientists are hunting for genes that control everything from happiness to aggression ... scientists know that infant animals may reprogram neurons depending on how they're treated."

The article confirms what is generally known in psychological circles. Psychologically and behaviorally, we are products of our environment. Our environment molds us and shapes us psychologically into the way we are ... the way we believe and think in our heart.

Jesus' message — if believed and understood — would uproot the negative programming that keeps us treading the "broad way that leadeth to destruction, and many there be who follow it."

All that is required to get on the narrow path to life that few find is discovering the truth that sets us free. Life does not get any better than heaven, and all that is required for us to enjoy heaven is to live in agreement with truth ... the same thing as being in harmony with God and nature. And we need not make a great mystery out of understanding truth.

Very simply, Jesus said, "And ye shall know the truth, and the truth shall make you free." To a great extent we gloss over this statement with no inkling of a practical understanding. Perhaps we confuse two levels of thinking about truth. Whereas there is only one ultimate truth, there are millions of truths about facts. For example, it's true that the world is round, not flat as people once believed.

The ultimate truth — the ultimate reality — is simply that which is in agreement with God and nature. ... that which is true ... that which is real. In all simplicity, truth is what is. Harmony with truth is the way things are supposed to be as created by our Creator. When we are free from fear — when we are in harmony with truth — our life is the way it is meant to be ... peaceful and harmonious ... not characterized by stress, struggle, and strain.

Describing what it is like being in harmony with truth is elusive. No one can describe truth to us in a manner that we can comprehend. To understand the experience of being in harmony with truth, we must experience it. Similarly, we would never have known the taste of an apple without the experience of tasting one. Being in harmony with truth is the state of consciousness that Jesus enjoyed; thus, his statement, "I and my Father are one."

The only way we can comprehend the state of consciousness that is in agreement with truth is by experience. The only way we can experience the peace that is characteristic of living in agreement with truth is by freeing ourselves of subconscious fears and false beliefs; it is then that we are in agreement with truth; it is then that we experience the "peace that passeth all understanding." Thus, experienced-based learning is the only way to understand what living in agreement with truth is like.

The truth that sets us free is not some esoteric gem of wisdom that once we find it, we have the wisdom to be set free. Truth is

Truth Is the Way

undistorted perception ... undistorted by ignorance and our false ego-self. Until we are in agreement with truth — until we perceive clearly — "we see through a glass darkly." What we perceive is distorted and, consequently, we are inharmonious with truth.

One way of thinking about what truth is is to meditate to the point of transcending all fearful, negative thoughts. Then notice what you are experiencing. With no traces of negative thoughts, we must be experiencing peace. However, it is easy to let our false ego-self deceive us, having us think we are a positive thinker; all the while, negativity is ruling our life. We experience peace when we are in harmony with truth.

The most difficult aspect of the discovery of the truth is taming our mind to the point that we transcend the chatter evolving from our false ego-self. When we succeed in transcending all negative, fearful, false thinking, all is peace. There are no negative thoughts to stir up anything contrary to peace. If we have not experienced absolute peace in our meditation, then we have not succeeded in quieting the chatter that is typical of our mind.

In my use of the phrase, false ego-self, I am alluding to the place inside of us where all negative emotions and all mental suffering originate. Every emotion within us proceeds from either fear or love; there is no other basic emotion; all emotions — negative and positive — evolve from either love or fear.

There are many negative states of mind: anger, hate, jealousy, resentment, irritation, insecurity, possessiveness ... all associated with fear. And then there are fears of being rejected, of not being loved, of failure, of lack, and the fear of being abandoned ... and on and on and on. Every negative state of mind proceeds from *unwarranted* fear.

All unwarranted fear is associated with our ego. All negative states of mind — all unwarranted fear — bring suffering in one manner or another. Thus, all mental suffering evolves from our false ego-self. Speaking of the false ego-self might be easier to grasp than speaking of Satan, but they are the same thing.

The best way of understanding what our false ego-self is — of understanding what Satan is — so that we know that we know that we know is by being still, meditating, and becoming aware and understanding what it is that is causing our suffering ... our negative emotions that can literally destroy us ... that can wreak havoc with our health, happiness, and overall well-being ... that can wreck families (even nations) ... and on and on and on. Insights in the quietness of our mind provide this understanding. The key to this understanding is being still and paying attention to the insights that flourish in the quietness of our minds.

Perhaps one of the explanations of why religious teachers have not explained Satan and hell in a manner that is reasonably understandable is that we have come to believe such outrageous things about Satan and hell ... things that are incomprehensible. The descriptive language that has been used to describe Satan is so horrifying that we do not even consider that Satan is something within us.

Similarly, the descriptive language that has been used to describe hell is so indescribably unbearable (and the fact that we have been led to believe that hell is something the unsaved suffer after death), we do not consider our mental turmoil (such as hate, anger, guilt, jealousy, anxiety, depression, unwarranted fears, confusion, possessiveness, resentment, insecurity) as hell.

The fact that Satan and hell dissipate once we transcend all fearful, false ego thinking demonstrates that they are within us and that they are false and temporary. Our suffering dissipates once we know the truth that sets us free. Truth is the only thing that endures. Thus, when we discover truth, we enjoy life everlasting ... meaning to be fully alive in the spirit of truth as long as we live.

Anyway we slice it, a troubled mind is tormenting ... is hell. However, unlike the hell described by some fundamentalists, hell is an understandable, comprehensible experience. The best way to get an understanding of hell is by discovering the truth that sets us free ... by experiencing the "peace that passeth all understanding." Then we know the difference. Then we know what we have been missing.

In our troubled, fractured society, we think our negative, commonplace emotions that produce all sorts of suffering as being natural and normal; they are not. Thus, we do not realize and acknowledge that we are already in hell. The Buddha said the worst

Truth Is the Way

tormenting pain is a bad conscience. A bad conscience — a troubled mind — is hell.

Cervantes, Spanish writer, said, "Make it thy business to know thyself, which is the most difficult lesson in the world."
- Cicero, Roman writer, said, "Everyone is least known to himself, and it is very difficult for a man to know himself."
- Havelock Ellis, British psychologist and author, said, "Men who know themselves are no longer fools; they stand on the threshold of the Door of Wisdom."
- Hermann Hesse, author of *Siddhartha*, states, "The true profession of man is to find his way to himself."

According to Erich Fromm, "Know thyself" is the "mainspring of all psychology." "Know thyself" is also the mainspring of knowing the hidden secret of the ages ... of discovering the truth that sets us free. When we know ourselves, we know the truth that sets us free.

Regardless of what others believe about us, it is what we believe — it is our thoughts, not the thoughts of others — that create our reality ... "It is done unto us as we believe."

It seems rational and logical that if we eradicate obscure fears and deeply held, false beliefs from our subconscious mind, then what remains is true. We eradicate obscure fears and deeply held, false beliefs — beliefs we hold about ourselves that are contrary to our true perfection — by acknowledging them and understanding them. We gain an understanding of them by pondering them in the quietness of our minds ... by letting our mind take us to where it needs to go to discern that which is false from that which is true.

To understand the truth that sets us free, it helps to understand the fears and false beliefs that contribute to our mental aberrations; it helps to understand why we are restless and discontent; to understand why we are uneasy and *afraid to live;* to understand our motivations ... why we do what we do that we ought not to do, and why we do not do those things that we ought to do. And it helps to know that our false ego-self is very deceiving in leading us astray from anything that leads to the truth that sets us free.

To discover truth we need not learn anything new ... we need only to *unlearn* obscure fears and deeply held false beliefs. When we free ourselves from obscure, insidious fears and deeply held false beliefs — when we "clean the inside of the cup and the platter" — what remains must be true ... so simple, yet so elusive. The freedom we seek is the freedom we experience when we free ourselves from fear ... it's like "being born again." Charles F. Haanel, author of *The Master Key,* said: "When you come to know that every form of disease, sickness, lack and limitation are simply the results of wrong thinking, you will have come to know 'the Truth that will make you free.' "

Once we get the knack for calming our mind and listening to ourselves, we reach the point alluded to by Emerson when he said, "There is a guidance for each of us, and by lowly listening we shall hear the right word. Certainly, there is a right for you that needs no choice on your part. Place yourself in the middle of the stream of power and wisdom that flows into your life. Then, without effort, you are impelled to truth and to perfect contentment."

Perfect contentment is peace and joy, the purpose for Jesus preaching the gospel. We have peace and joy when we discover the truth that sets us free.

The foregoing statements by Emerson are consistent with what Jesus, the Apostle Paul, the spiritual teachers of the Old Testament, and other religious teachers taught. Note that "Lowly listening" leads to truth and perfect contentment. "Lowly listening" must be the same thing as "communing with our own heart," as alluded to by David the Psalmist. "Perfect contentment" must be the same thing as "the peace of God, which passeth all understanding," as alluded to by the Apostle Paul.

Emerson also said, "Nothing can bring you peace but yourself." Thus, we must be our own saviors. Nothing outside ourselves makes us angry, hateful, guilty, emotionally insecure, resentful, frustrated, dissatisfied, and unhappy. And nothing outside ourselves makes us happy, joyful, peaceful, satisfied, and contented.

Our false ego-self (Satan within us) would have us cling to false, age-old, religious beliefs rather than admit that we are the cause of our suffering ... rather than have us confess that we are a hypocrite. Our false ego-self would have us believe that Jesus died on the cross to save us from our sins so that we will be peaceful

Truth Is the Way

and happy after we are dead and gone, rather than have us explore our inner selves and surrender to the truth that sets us free.

We cannot lowly listen — we cannot commune with our own heart — without calming our mind ... without "shutting the door" (using the words of Jesus) ... without "being still" (using the words of David the Psalmist). We cannot get an inner knowing and understanding — we cannot gain wisdom and understanding — with our mind running rampant with its everyday chatter, dominated by our false ego-self that is defensive and always denying, resisting, analyzing, and rationalizing ... a tactic of our false-ego self, which circumvents truth, wisdom, and understanding.

In his book, *As A Man Thinketh*, James Allen said, "Only by much searching and mining are gold and diamonds obtained, and man can find every truth connected with his being, if he will dig deep into the mine of his soul ... and utilizing his every experience, even to the most trivial, everyday occurrence, as a means of obtaining that knowledge of himself which is Understanding, Wisdom, Power."

A prerequisite for discovering truth is a quiet, meditative state of mind ... somewhat a dreamy state, somewhat akin to daydreaming ... somewhat a diffused sense of awareness. Thus, if you do not already know how to calm your mind and meditate — to stop the chatter of the false ego-self — then this is a first priority. Pascal said, "All the troubles of man come from his not knowing how to sit still."

Our false ego-self will resist and attempt to lead us astray at every step of the way. It will have us conceal, rather than reveal. It will have us trying to appear special and important, trying to impress others and gain recognition, praise, and attention. It will have us lashing out at others and committing evil acts ... anything and everything, except to accept truth.

The false ego-self will, in its deceitful way, attempt to protect us from hurt, but in so doing — in everything it does — it brings only more hurt and suffering. Our false ego-self will not willingly accept truth ... which ends suffering. The ultimate wisdom is knowing the truth that sets us free ... is knowing ourselves ... the greatest lesson life has to offer.

Fundamentalists caution us against taking verses of Scripture out of context of the entire passage; however, they do this quite regularly. The statement, "We cannot lean on our own understanding," is an example. Fundamentalists use this statement to refute a logical, rational, plausible explanation that is contrary to their own false religious beliefs. Fundamentalists take this statement out of the context of the passage in which it is written and give it the opposite meaning of what the author of the passage intended. The only way we can understand the truth that sets us free is by our own understanding.

In essence, what fundamentalists say is that we cannot use our power of reasoning and common sense to understand the Scriptures. The complete passage is in "The Proverbs": "Trust in the Lord with all thine heart and lean not unto thine own understanding. In all thy ways acknowledge him, and he shall direct thy paths" (Proverbs 3:5-6).

Translated into the language of our time, this means that we are to trust our true spiritual self with all our heart ... and not be guided by the chatter from our false ego-self. "In all thy ways acknowledge him, and he shall direct thy paths" means the same thing as doing what Jesus did; he did the will of his Father, a prerequisite for enjoying heaven. Thus, we must follow the guidance of the truth that proceeds from our true spiritual self if we are to enjoy the peace and joy of heaven.

Remember that the authors of the Old Testament used the word "Lord" in the same manner that Jesus used the word "Father." And whatever we call it, it is our true spiritual self. Thus, we are to trust our true spiritual self with all our heart and lean not on the understanding of our false ego-self. Incidentally, "trusting in the Lord with all our heart" is the *secret* to being happy. This is made abundantly clear in Chapter 9, "Wisdom and Understanding."

The author of the subject passage was stressing the point that we must listen to our "heart," not our "head." We must listen to our true spiritual self ... that quiet place within that knows what is true ... that place within us where we gain wisdom and understanding. Thus, we must use our own understanding if we are to understand

Truth Is the Way

the message Jesus intended for us ... if we are to discover the truth that sets us free.

The author of the subject passage did not say that we are not to use knowledge, common sense, and the power of reasoning; "lean not" is not the same as "do not." And the fact is that we must do both—use our logical, rational thinking, conscious mind and do what David, the Psalmist said to do: "Commune with your own heart." Not to use our God-given gifts is a denial of God.

Listening to ourselves is the key to knowing ourselves. When we know ourselves, we know truth ... and vice versa. Knowing ourselves is the key to love, joy, happiness, peace of mind, and contentment ... deep inside, what every one of us wants.

This must be the hidden secret of the ages: Discovering ourselves is the secret to discovering truth, which is the secret to discovering the kingdom of Heaven. And it's all within us. When obscure fears and false beliefs are obliterated, truth and love fill the void. We cannot love freely and unconditionally with obscure, insidious fears and deeply held false beliefs rearing their ugly heads at every turn of the road. Fear and love do not occupy the same space at the same time ... it is either one or the other.

Although we are not aware of it, fear underlies a vast majority of the things we do and say. Until we achieve a breakthrough to awareness — until we discern that which is true from that which is false — we have no inkling about how much we do and say is dictated by fear.

A common myth is that truth hurts. The ego causes hurt—not truth. All mental and emotional suffering (guilt, anger, hatred, anxiety, depression) evolve from fear ... not from truth. Truth is the only thing that will bring us genuine love, joy, happiness, peace of mind, and inner serenity ... deep inside, what every one wants.

You might bear in mind that there is nothing anyone detests more — nothing anyone hates more — than having someone tell them the truth; yet there is nothing we want more than the truth ... nothing we want more than to live and love in harmony with truth ... the same thing as being in harmony with God and nature.

People who think they have been hurt by truth stand to learn the most important lesson life has to offer, if only they will ponder the hurt in the stillness of their mind until they understand the falseness (the ego's influence) underlying the hurt ... a lesson that comparatively few people learn in a lifetime. Once we learn this lesson — which is very simple, yet very elusive — then it is clear to us why Jesus said, "Narrow is the way to life and few there be who find it."

About 50 years BC, Lucretius said, "So it is more useful to watch a man in times of peril and in adversity to discern what kind of man he is, for then at last words of truth are drawn from the depths of his heart, and the mask is torn off and reality remains."

Discovering truth is comparatively simple; it requires comparatively little time in comparison with all the stress, struggle, and strain involved in following the dictates of our false ego-self. When we know truth, we know our real self. Quimby, a mental healer during the 1800s, said: "When we find our real self, everything afterwards is easy." Quimby believed that illness is caused by false beliefs and that people can be healed by suggestion ... can be healed by a mind open to the wisdom of God.

Our false ego-self has us thinking that we can fill the emptiness within — that we can end our sense of isolation and separation — by doing and saying those things that seem to make us appear impressive and important. However, there are not enough hours in a day, enough days in a week, enough weeks in a year — there is not enough of nothing — to fill the void. A million times nothing is nothing. It is little wonder that stress, fatigue, and tension headaches are common complaints.

Emanuel Swedenborg, Swedish scientist, philosopher, and theologian, said, "To be able to discern that what is true is true, and what is false is false, this is the mark of character and intelligence."

We are able to make the distinction between what is true and what is false in the stillness of our minds by paying attention. Remember the Proverb, "As he thinketh in his heart, so is he." The only way of knowing what we believe in our heart is by being still and paying attention. From Taoism we learn, "To the mind that is still, the whole Universe surrenders."

Alexander Lowen, author of *Narcissism — Denial of the True Self,* states, "Therapy is a process of getting in touch with the self.

Truth Is the Way

Traditionally, the approach to the self has been through analysis. Every therapy must include a thorough analysis of the patient's history to discover the experiences that have shaped the patient's personality and determined his or her behavior. Unfortunately, that history is not readily available. The suppression and denial of feelings result in a repression of significant memories. The facades we erect hide our true selves from us as well as from the world."

The "history" that is not readily available — that is the cause of all mental suffering and unhappiness — becomes available to us in the stillness of our minds. The insights that let us discern what is true from what is false come to us in the stillness of our minds.

Discovering truth does not require more reading, studying, seeking and searching, interpreting this, interpreting that, and deciphering what others have said, and it does not require listening to more lectures and more sermons. Instead, it involves being still and listening ourselves; it involves an understanding of the "history" that is not readily available to us ... old memories from the past that deprive us of peace, joy, and happiness.

Perhaps you might be thinking, "But I do not want to be reminded of my childhood experiences." Subconsciously we are reminded of them most of the time ... even when we are asleep and dreaming. Obscure, fear-based memories from the past influence our every thought and every action. They lose power over us once we acknowledge and understand them ... which we can do in the stillness of our minds.

Remember that Jesus' mission is that we might have peace. We cannot have genuine peace with old memories from the past — hidden from our conscious awareness — influencing our every thought and every action. We enjoy genuine peace only when we discover the truth that sets us free ... free from the old memories that determine the way we believe and think in our heart.

Everything we need for understanding ourselves — for discovering truth — is within us. We gain knowledge from books and teachers; however, we gain wisdom and understanding from within ourselves. Others can talk about truth, but they cannot impart truth to us. It's already within us. The gift of God has already been given (the gift of truth, life, spirit, heaven), awaiting our understanding and acceptance ... awaiting our transcending the world of the ego and surrendering to truth.

We could listen to teachers and sermons all our lives and we could study the Bible from cover to cover as long as we live and never discover what we are searching for. We will never discover the truth that sets us free in the Bible. Teachers and the Bible are guides. The truth that sets us free dwells within us. ... the only place we will ever find it. Thus, to discover truth, the only place to seek is within ourselves. The only way to seek is by being still and communing with our true spiritual self.

A simple exercise, which you can do in the quietness of your mind, can shed more light on psychology and religion than all the reading and studying you can ever do ... than all the lectures and sermons you could hear in a lifetime. It's how you can discover the truth that will set you free ... it's how you can learn the greatest lesson life has to offer.

Here's the exercise: In the quietness of your mind, bring a recurring situation that regularly triggers your anger or anxiety (any recurring negative emotion) to your conscious awareness. In your mind's eye — in your inner vision — "see" yourself in a typical recurring situation that disturbs you. Then in the quietness of your mind, let your mind take you to where it needs to go for you recognize what it is that disturbs you. Just be in the scene, be with the experience, and note and pay attention to the insights as they come to you.

With a little experience you will develop the knack — the intuition — for noticing insights. Like the white puffy clouds on a sunny day, they are there, but we do not particularly notice them unless we pause and pay attention. Herein lies the secret to discovering the truth ... being still and paying attention. A calm mind is a prerequisite.

Anything that robs us of joy, peace of mind, and inner serenity must be false. And it must be something that we have learned since birth. We simply were not born with false beliefs embedded in our subconscious mind ... with fearful, false beliefs that cause our restlessness, discontent, and suffering. In the quietness of our mind, we have the wisdom to know what is fearful and false.

Truth Is the Way

I would be remiss if I did not caution you. This process could get you in touch with some old childhood hurts that could cause anguish ... the "gnashing of teeth." You will suffer as long as you harbor old childhood hurts. However, confronting these old hurts directly might just temporarily intensify the suffering.

Thus, if you have a serious psychological problem (if you are seeing a therapist, or are in need of a therapist, if you are psychotic, if you have a tendency to break with reality), then do not try this process without the help of a qualified professional therapist.

Instead of anything dreadful, most people should be able to get insights and reach an understanding of the cause of mental conflicts ... and simply get an "aha" feeling. Once you get the understanding to give you that "aha" feeling, you will realize that you have something that is invaluable ... you are on the threshold of learning life's greatest lesson ... a lesson most people do not learn in a lifetime.

In an inner exploration, it helps to know that we are not looking for a specific true statement that will set us free. Similarly, we are not looking for a specific false belief that is the cause of our suffering. It helps with the inner exploration to notice what we sense and what we feel and then notice the insights of those things that have a bearing on our negative feelings and sensations ... those things that cause us to perceive things in a negative manner.

When we are experiencing any negative emotion, we are harboring unwarranted fears and false beliefs. In the stillness of our minds, by observing the negative experiences and the insights bearing on them, we recognize the fears and false beliefs that are contrary to truth, and consequently, we know what is true.

Oliver Wendell Holmes, American writer and physician, said, "A moment's insight is sometimes worth a life's experience." We gain insights by observing negative experiences in the quietness of our minds until we understand the underlying cause of them. Insights flourish in the quietness of our mind ... never from the chatter coming from our false ego-self. These insights lead to the discovery of the truth that sets us free.

Once we begin a process of being still and communing with our heart, the insights we receive are cumulative. We have no way of knowing when we will discover the truth that sets us free or when we will unify with our true spiritual self—when we will unify with God. However, if we will be patient ("wait upon the Lord," our true spiritual self) and persevere, we will be transformed ... we will discover the truth that sets us free.

- But of that day and that hour knoweth no man, no, not the angels which are in heaven, neither the Son, but the Father. Take ye heed, watch and pray; for ye know not when the time is (Mark 13:32-33).
- Howbeit when he, the Spirit of truth, is come, he will guide you into all truth (John 16:13). Bear in mind that "he, the Spirit of truth," that will guide us into all truth is our true spiritual self.

Peace and harmony permeate everything in nature. Peace and harmony are in us and all around us. A scuba diving experience (being on the bottom of the ocean about 80 feet deep) helped me to appreciate and understand this. Other than the presence of scuba divers, nothing was occurring 80 feet deep, on the bottom of the ocean, except what is in agreement with nature. There was not anything causing the exquisite peace and harmony. It's just the way things are when we let things be the way they are supposed to be. The fish swam about ever so gently. The marine flora on the bottom of the ocean swayed gently. A couple of barracudas seemed to be suspended, motionless in the water. Their movement was effortless.

The peace, harmony, and quietness were inspiring ... a spiritual experience. Reflecting on the experience, I realize I did not have to go to the bottom of the ocean to know that peace and harmony permeate everything in nature. In thinking back on the experience, which separated me from the typical everyday world of activity and commotion, I realize that wherever we look in nature (nature that has not been disturbed by humans and if it is not mating time), fish, birds, and animals are peaceful and contented.

To realize this is true, observe the cattle grazing in the pasture fields, or lying under the shade trees; notice undisturbed pets. Notice and observe that peace and harmony permeate everything in nature. From noticing and observing nature, we realize that fish, animals, and birds — left undisturbed — enjoy a peace and harmony that is their natural state of being.

Truth Is the Way

Our natural state of being is peaceful and harmonious; however, we have chosen stress, struggle, and strain ... pretense over truth and nature. We are so far alienated from truth and nature that we have no inkling of what it is like ... we have no basis for comparison. The Apostle Paul made it clear that God is characterized by peace. And we know from the Old Testament that we are created in the image and likeness of God.

We enjoy peace, harmony, joy — we enjoy heaven — when we discover the truth that sets us free ... when we understand and embody the message that Jesus intended for us. Truth is the way of life ... the way life is meant to be ... if only we would overcome our fearful, false ego-self and let things be the way they are meant to be, which is in agreement with truth, God, and nature.

Truth will save us—our families, our society ... the very world itself. Truth is the solution to all mental suffering and all unhappiness ... the solution to all psychosomatic illnesses, the solution to crime, violence, dysfunctional families, the breakup of families ... and on and on and on.

In the book, *The Religions of Man*, by Huston Smith, the author states, "Of all the philosophers of the West, Spinoza stands closest to Buddha on this question of the mind's potential. ... 'To understand something is to be delivered of it' — these words come close to summarizing Spinoza's entire ethic." The statement, "To understand something is to be delivered of it," means the same thing as knowing the truth that sets us free.

In summary, truth is the way. The truth that sets us free is the secret to finding genuine peace, joy, happiness, and contentment. We discover the truth that sets us free by being still, paying attention, and listening to our true spiritual self. We discover the truth that sets us free by doing what David the Psalmist said to do about 3,000 years ago: "Commune with your own heart." Discovering the truth that sets us free is the greatest lesson life has to offer.

Chapter 5
Understanding What Jesus Said

Jesus' ministry was almost 2,000 years ago, and recently I saw an article alluding to the archaic language of the Bible and posing a question about the possibilities if no one really understood what Jesus said. A fact is that many Christians do not understand the gospel that Jesus preached.

The difficulty in understanding Jesus' teachings is much more than the archaic language in the Bible and the idiom of that time and place in history. Much of the difficulty in understanding what Jesus said is the manner in which he said it. Jesus' own disciples had difficulty understanding what he said. Understanding the idioms that Jesus used is a prerequisite for understanding what he said.

One of the difficulties in understanding what Jesus said is that ancient, false beliefs are so firmly embedded into the minds of many people that they are not open-minded to what Jesus said; they do not have "ears to hear" what he said. How could people possibly believe what Jesus taught when they harbor false, age-old beliefs about such things as God, heaven, hell, devil, and Satan ... beliefs that are not in agreement with what Jesus taught?

Both the Buddha and Jesus understood how people are prone to cling to false, age-old beliefs. In the book, *What The Buddha Taught*, the author, Walpola Rahula, states: "The Buddha's teaching does not support this ignorance, weakness, fear, and desire, but aims at making man enlightened by removing and destroying them, striking at their very root. According to Buddhism, our ideas of God and Soul are false and empty. ... These ideas are so deep-rooted in man, and so near and dear to him, that he does not wish to hear, nor does he want to understand, any teaching against them."

- Men willingly believe what they wish. — Julius Caesar
- With how much ease believe we what we wish! — John Dryden

One of the greatest difficulties in understanding the Holy Scriptures is understanding the idioms. Translators of the Scrip-

Understanding What Jesus Said

tures translated the language, but they did not explain the meaning of the idioms. A fundamentalist is one who believes in a literal interpretation of the Bible. We cannot understand the message that Jesus intended for us and literally interpret the idioms that Jesus used. Some idioms are reasonably clear; e.g., when Jesus said "Cleanse first that which is within the cup and platter that the outside of them may be clean also," it is clear that he was speaking of purifying our heart, not literally cleaning the cup and the platter.

How interesting that many people realize some passages of the Holy Scriptures are not to be taken literally; for example, "Whoso eateth my flesh and drinketh my blood hath eternal life." We know that Jesus did not mean to eat the flesh or drink the blood from his body. Yet, fundamentalists take other passages they do not understand and interpret them literally. They twist some passages of the Holy Scriptures and add to them to make them seem to agree with what they believe.

To understand the idioms that Jesus used, it helps to note what he said when he did not use idioms. For example, Jesus said that those who believe the gospel would be saved. This is not an idiom. This statement has essentially the same meaning as "Whosoever eateth my flesh and drinketh my blood hath eternal life." Translated into our language, this means that those who believe, understand, and embody the gospel that Jesus preached will be fully alive in spirit of truth as long as they live ... they will have peace and joy.

To understand Jesus' meaning of the phrases "kingdom of God" and "kingdom of Heaven," it helps to keep in mind his mission: that we might have peace. Too, it helps to remember how the Apostle Paul described heaven. The Apostle Paul said, "For the kingdom of God is ... righteousness, and peace, and joy" (Romans 14:17). Heaven is the state of mind of the "peace that passeth all understanding."

When all aspects of our mind are in agreement with truth — when our ego self and our spiritual self are one — that is heaven ... and life will never get any better than heaven.

Jesus said, "I am the resurrection and the life; he that believeth in me, though he were dead, yet shall he live. And whosoever liveth and believeth in me shall never die."

From this passage we realize that Jesus was not speaking of dead people as we typically think of dead people. "He that believeth" could not possibly be dead as we typically think of being dead. The word "dead" as used in many places in the Bible means dead in spirit, not dead as we typically think of the word "dead." Thus, Jesus was talking about those who were dead in spirit. Clearly, when Jesus said "shall never die," he was not speaking in terms of never dying as we typically think of dying. And it does not mean what some fundamentalists think it means, that people will live for eternity after they die.

The Apostle Paul said, "Therefore if any man be in Christ, he is a new creature; old things are passed away; behold, all things are become new. And all things are of God, who hath reconciled us to himself by Jesus Christ" (2 Corinthians 5:17-18).

We are "a new creature" (like "being born again"), and we are unified with God when we believe and comprehend the gospel that Jesus preached. We are unified with God (the goal of all great religions) when we "clean the inside of the cup and the platter;" when we obliterate the devils from our heart; when we are as perfect as Jesus told us to be ("even as your Father who is in heaven is perfect"); when we are converted and are as humble as little children; when we know the truth that sets us free; when we love as Jesus commanded us to love. In brief, we are "a new creature" when we believe, understand, and embody the teachings of Jesus.

Thus, to understand the teachings of Jesus, we must take into account the idioms, metaphors, and the descriptive language that Jesus used. And it is important to use some common sense to understand the sayings of Jesus. When Jesus said, "Let the dead bury their own dead," he was speaking of people who do not believe the gospel and who are dead in spirit. Dead people — as we think of dead people — do not bury other dead people. When the Apostle Peter spoke of preaching the gospel to the dead, he was speaking of people dead in spirit.

One of the most often quoted passages of Scripture that fundamentalists use to justify their belief in a literal hell is the passage about the rich man and Lazarus. To understand that passage, it is important that we know that Jesus is not saying that the rich man and Lazarus died as we typically think of people dying. Jesus said, "And it came to pass that the beggar died and was carried by the angels into Abraham's bosom; the rich man also died and was buried; and in hell he lift up his eyes, being in torments, and seeth Abraham afar off, and Lazarus in his bosom. And he cried and said, 'Father Abraham, have mercy on me and send Lazarus, that he may dip the tip of his finger in water and cool my tongue; for I am tormented in this flame' " (Luke 16:24).

"Flame" is an idiom, meaning a troubled, tormented mind ... troubled by such things as fear, anxiety, guilt, shame, anger. Also, note the phrase, "carried by angels." Often when the word "angel" appears in the Bible it refers to a vision; a vision is not reality.

Logic and common sense tell us that if the rich man were dead (as we typically think of being dead), he did not see Lazarus in Abraham's bosom, and no one literally saw or heard the rich man crying out for help. Dead bodies do not see or hear anything, as people who interpret the Bible literally seem to think the rich man did. Religious fundamentalists twist this Scripture — adding to it and taking from it — to make it seem that Jesus said something about hell that he did not say.

Nothing in that passage — nothing in the teachings of Jesus — suggests that heaven and hell are places where people go after death. The message in this passage is not to explain heaven and hell. Had Jesus believed that heaven and hell are places where people go after death, surely he would have made that reasonably clear sometime during his ministry. Obviously, Jesus did not believe that. Otherwise, he would not have said plainly and clearly "For behold, the kingdom of God is within you" (Luke 17:21).

The primary thing that Jesus emphasized in the passage about the rich man and Lazarus gets to the heart of his teachings. Jesus makes it clear that what matters most in life is the condition of our heart. It's not our outer appearance ... it's not our riches and material things that matter most in life.

Regardless of how rich a person might be, his or her money and material things cannot buy peace of mind, inner serenity, joy, happiness, and contentment ... all of which are free and accrue to us naturally when we are in agreement with truth, God, and nature.

No amount of money will free us from repressed anger, guilt, shame, anxiety, depression, inner turmoil, a lack of self-esteem, emotional insecurity. No amount of money will free us from the obscure, insidious fears and false beliefs (the devils in our mind) that rob us of love, joy, peace, and happiness.

Remember, the Apostle Paul said, "Heaven is peace, joy, and righteousness." Money cannot buy peace, joy, and righteousness ... money cannot buy heaven. The richest of the rich suffer the torments of hell — a mind in mental turmoil — if they are led astray from truth ... if they are alienated from God.

A pure heart is a prerequisite for enjoying the "peace that passeth all understanding." A pure heart is a prerequisite for enjoying heaven. Jesus said, "Blessed are the pure in heart; for they shall see God." The passage about the rich man and Lazarus, a beggar, suggests that Lazarus was pure in heart.

It helps to understand the passage of Scripture about the rich man and Lazarus to keep in mind that Jesus' purpose for preaching the gospel is that we might have peace and joy. Often when we think of prosperity, we think in terms of money and material wealth. The Apostle John said "Beloved, I wish above all things that thou mayest prosper and be in health, even as thy soul prospereth" (3 John 1:2). "Even as thy soul prospereth" is not related to riches. The soul thrives on the spirit of truth, which brings peace and joy. Note that the Apostle John wished this above all things ... the kind of life that Jesus wanted for us.

Let's face it! Parts of the Holy Scriptures are not clear; we simply do not know and understand what some of the Holy Scriptures mean. How can fundamentalists be so certain that Lazarus was dead when Jesus' own disciples had questions regarding his condition?

Note the following scripture in which Jesus said that Lazarus was asleep, and then he said that Lazarus was dead ... and the disciples wondered (John 11:11-14): "Now a certain man was sick, named Lazarus ... Jesus said, 'Our friend Lazarus sleepeth; but I go, that I may awake him out of sleep.' Then the disciples said,

Understanding What Jesus Said

'Lord, if he sleeps, he shall do well.' ... Howbeit Jesus spake of his death, but they thought that he had spoken of taking of rest in sleep. Then said Jesus unto them plainly, 'Lazarus is dead.'"

It is obvious and clear that many Christians do not accept and believe what Jesus said about heaven being within us. Otherwise, why would they twist and stretch what Jesus said about the rich man and Lazarus — adding to it and taking from it — to make it seem that Jesus was speaking about a literal hell and heaven after death.

For fundamentalists to suggest that the subject passage of Scripture alludes to a literal hell is an example of what Jesus alluded to when he said, "You blind leaders, who strain at a gnat and swallow a camel." What fundamentalists try to do is make the subject passage of Scripture agree with their false beliefs about heaven and hell.

Another passage of Scripture to which fundamentalists resort to prove that heaven is a place where the saved go after they die is Chapter 21 in "The Revelation to John." Resorting to this passage to prove their point, fundamentalists do not realize that they do not really believe, understand, and accept what Jesus said. And, they do not understand the nature of visions. Again, visions are not reality. Remember that Jesus said, "The kingdom of God is within you."

John's description of the heavenly Jerusalem is another way of describing heaven. Isaiah used different descriptive words. He said: "Seek ye the Lord while he may be found; call ye upon him while he is near. Let the wicked forsake his way and the unrighteous man his thoughts; and let him return unto the Lord. ... For ye shall go forward with joy and be led forth with peace; the mountains and the hills shall break forth before you into singing, and all the trees of the field shall clap their hands" (Isaiah 55:6-12). We know that the mountains and the hills will not literally sing and the trees will not clap their hands. This was Isaiah's way of describing the peace and joy that we will experience when we find our true spiritual self and know the truth that sets us free.

John's description of the heavenly Jerusalem is consistent with what Isaiah said and also what the Apostle Paul said: "Heaven is peace, joy, and righteousness."

And note that the Apostle John said, "And I John saw these things, and heard them. And when I had heard and seen, I fell down to worship before the feet of the angel which showed me these things" (Revelation 22:8). Thus, the things that John "saw" and "heard" were visions ... were in his inner image. The Apostle John was in prison during the time that he had the visions described in "The Revelation to John." He was imprisoned because he was preaching the gospel.

And what the Apostle John said in verse 27 of Chapter 21 is in agreement with what Jesus said. The Apostle John said, "And there shall in no wise enter into it [the heavenly Jerusalem] any thing that defileth, neither whatsoever worketh abomination, or maketh a lie; but they which are written in the Lamb's book of life" (Revelation 21:27).

We know from the teachings of Jesus that only those who do the will of the Father — only those who are converted and are as pure in heart of little children — will enjoy heaven. Thus, in John's vision, those who are saved are "they, which are written in the Lamb's book of life" ... a vision.

Another passage of Scripture to which fundamentalists refer to support their belief in a literal hell after death begins with: "When the Son of man shall come in his glory, and all the holy angels with him, then shall he sit upon the throne of his glory. And before him shall be gathered all nations and he shall separate them one from another, as a shepherd divideth his sheep from the goats" (Matthew 25:31-32). And in verse 41, we find: "Then shall he say also unto them on the left hand, Depart from me, ye cursed, into everlasting fire, prepared for the devil and his angels."

If we study and assimilate the message Jesus intended for us, we realize that this passage of Scripture is not consistent with the other teachings of Jesus. And, according to the book, *The Five Gospels — What Did Jesus Really Say?* by Robert W. Funk, Roy W. Hoover, and The Jesus Seminar, these are inauthentic Jesus words.

If we study and assimilate what both Jesus and the writers of the Old Testament said, we realize that hell is a troubled, tormented

Understanding What Jesus Said

state of mind ... something we experience while we are alive, not after we die.

In intense personal growth workshops, it is commonplace to observe wailing and gnashing of teeth. And the people wailing and gnashing are like people we encounter every day. However, in everyday life, we do not realize how much pain many people are bearing. In everyday life, we do not see an adult (either man or woman) curled up in the arms of a woman who is playing the part of a mother, holding a baby bottle and letting the adult nurse from the bottle, letting the adult get some sense of the mothering and nurturing that he or she did not get as a baby.

From an observation of some of these people when they get into their pain — kicking, screaming, vomiting — in the throes of anger, hate, hurt, resentment, revenge, jealousy — it is obvious that they "lifted up their eyes in hell." ... there was "gnashing of teeth."

When we harbor anger and guilt, we have a troubled mind ... we experience hell. We never really enjoy genuine inner peace and serenity when we are troubled with anger and guilt.

If we study — and assimilate — what Jesus said, we realize that when we are expressing life in the light of truth, we experience peace and joy. When we are living in darkness (out of harmony with truth), we experience suffering ... "weeping and gnashing of teeth."

Fundamentalists describe hell as being the most intense suffering one can possibly imagine — a hell of fire and brimstone — for eternity after one dies. If fundamentalists teach this kind of stuff as a means of scaring worshippers into salvation, it simply does not work. A far more rewarding approach — one that will not fail — is to teach the gospel that Jesus preached ... teaching it in a manner that we believe and understand. After all, everyone insatiably desires to live in harmony with truth and to have peace and joy.

Perhaps fundamentalists are the only people who teach that heaven and hell occur after death. Jesus, Buddha, the writers of the Old Testament and other great teachers did not teach this.

If we really understand Jesus' teachings, we realize that God has never — and will never — cast anyone into hell. We do it to ourselves. We cast ourselves into hell with our insidious fears and deeply rooted false beliefs ... and while we are alive on planet Earth, not after we are dead and gone ... all in agreement with what Jesus taught ... "It is done unto us as we believe."

To benefit from the teachings of Jesus, we must be guided by the truth that lies within our heart. Where are we to find peace and joy except within ourselves? Where are we to find heaven except within ourselves? Remember what Jesus said, "Neither shall they say, Lo here! or, lo there! For, behold, the kingdom of God is within you" (Luke 17: 21).

Jesus' message is quite simple. He said, "Ye shall know the truth and the truth shall make you free." Truth will save us. Yet, instead of focusing on something this important, we are swayed to focus on things we do not understand ... misled by stuff that distracts us from Jesus' basic message of love and truth, that distracts us from the gospel that Jesus preached.

In addition to literally interpreting the idioms that Jesus used, fundamentalists literally interpret visions and stuff we really do not understand. Let's face it! We simply do not know what much of the Scriptures regarding the ascension and the transfiguration means. Even some of the people, who were present and understood the language and idioms, did not know what to believe.

The following are some examples of things that the people of that time had difficulty understanding and believing.

- It was Mary Magdalene, and Joanna, and Mary the mother of James, and other women that were with them, which told these things unto the apostles. And their words seemed to them as idle tales, and they believed them not (Luke 24:10-11).

- Yea, and certain women also of our company made us astonished, which were early at the sepulchre; and when they found not his body, they came, saying, that they had also seen a vision of angels, which said that he was alive (Luke 24:22-23). [Note that they were talking about a vision, not reality.]

- And, behold, there was a great earthquake; for the angel of the Lord descended from heaven, and came and rolled back the stone from the door, and sat upon it. His countenance was like lightning, and his raiment white as snow. ... And the angel answered and said unto the women, Fear not ye; for I know that ye seek Jesus, which

Understanding What Jesus Said 111

was crucified. He is not here; for he is risen (Matthew 28:2-6). Again, Angels are seen in visions.
- And when they saw him, they worshipped him; but some doubted (Matthew 28:17).
- And after six days Jesus taketh with him Peter, and James, and John, and leadeth them up into a high mountain apart, and he was transfigured before them. And his raiment became shining, exceeding white as snow; so as no fuller on earth can white them. And there appeared unto them Elias with Moses; and they were talking with Jesus. ... And there was a cloud that overshadowed them; and a voice came out of the cloud, saying, This is my beloved Son; hear him (Matthew 17:1-5).
- And as they came down from the mountain, Jesus charged them, saying, "Tell the vision to no man, until the Son of man be risen again from the dead" (Matthew 17:9).
- And they kept that saying with themselves, questioning one with another what the rising from the dead should mean (Mark 9:10).

Note that the apostles — who were with Jesus at the time — were not clear about what Jesus meant. Thus, even the people at that time had doubts about what was being said and what people saw. A fact is that we simply do not know what transpired. Yet, fundamentalists are adamant about their beliefs about what transpired. They seem to believe that Jesus rose from the grave and ascended up into the clouds into heaven. Let us not forget that Jesus said, "The kingdom of God is within you."

Whatever transpired in the high mountain, Jesus called it a vision. Again, visions are not reality. We know that Jesus' followers did not literally see Jesus talking with Moses and Elias. Moses had been dead for several hundred years. And logically and rationally, we know that they did not actually hear a voice come out of a cloud. Clearly, what they heard and saw was imaginary ... a vision, not reality.

Thomas, one of Jesus' most devoted apostles, was called a doubter because he doubted what other apostles were saying about the ascension. Yet today, we have religious teachers who literally interpret the Scripture — visions and all — about the ascension, believing that Jesus ascended up into the clouds and that he will return from the clouds.

Regardless of what all that stuff about the ascension means, it does not change what we must do to discover the truth that sets us free ... what we must do to be saved. Literally interpreting the Scripture about the ascension hinders one from understanding the message Jesus intended for us.

There is nothing in all that stuff about the ascension and the transfiguration that suggests that heaven is within us, which is what Jesus taught. False beliefs about that stuff cause confusion about what and where heaven is. These false beliefs detract from a simple, clear statement by Jesus: "The kingdom of God is within you" (Luke 17:21).

From my experiences in meditation, mind regression, reincarnation, training and experiences in hypnotism, and dream interpretation, it seems clear to me that much of what was going on was in the mind ... not reality. It is uncanny what we can imagine in the quietness of our mind.

I am reminded of a group exercise involving reincarnation, people being regressed to "previous life times." The responses of participants were quite interesting. The images and visions in our mind are limited only by our imagination.

We need not get bogged down and misdirected, twisting the Scripture about visions and things that we cannot understand, trying to make it confirm something we wish to believe. The Heaven we seek is within us, not someplace up in the heavens, not someplace up in the sky. English lyric poet, Percy Bysshe Shelley, said, "Where is the love, beauty, and truth we seek, but in our mind?"

An abundance of evidence in the Holy Scriptures lets us know that heaven is within us (peace, joy, and righteousness). Most significantly, let us not forget that Jesus said it very clearly: "The kingdom of God is within you" (Luke 17:21).

Paul alluded to the mystery of the gospel when he said: "And for me, that utterance may be given unto me that I may open my mouth boldly to make known the mystery of the gospel. ... That I may speak boldly, as I ought to speak."

Understanding What Jesus Said

From the book, *The Secret Teachings Of Jesus – Four Gnostic Gospels*, translated by Marvin W. Meyer, we find that Jesus said: "I disclose my mysteries to those who are worthy of my mysteries. Do not let your left hand know what your right hand is doing. ... Whoever finds self is worth more than the world. ... For whoever does not know self does not know anything, but whoever knows self already has acquired knowledge about the depth of the universe."

The secret to a joyous, peaceful, happy contented life was summed up in two words by the Seven Sages of Greece about 500 years BC: "Know thyself." When we know ourselves, we know the truth that sets us free. When we know the truth that sets us free, we know ourselves. It's one and the same. ... thus, the same message that Jesus "was sent" to preach ... and without the mystery.

At one point Jesus gave thanks, "I thank thee, O Father, Lord of Heaven and earth, that thou has hid these things from the wise and prudent" (Matthew 11:25).

For whatever the reasons, Jesus did not intend for his parables to be understandable to all people. Jesus' disciples ask him, "Why speakest thou unto them in parables?" He replied, "Because it is given unto you to know the mysteries of the kingdom of Heaven, but to them it is not given."

Jesus said, "Therefore speak I to them in parables; because they seeing see not; and hearing they hear not, neither do they understand. And in them is fulfilled the prophecy of Esaias, which saith, By hearing ye shall hear, and shall not understand; and seeing ye shall see, and shall not perceive; For this people's heart is waxed gross, and their ears are dull of hearing, and their eyes they have closed; lest at any time they should see with their eyes and hear with their ears, and should understand with their heart, and should be converted, and I should heal them" (Matthew 13:13-15).

Isaiah said something similar to what Jesus said. If we study, assimilate, and understand what Isaiah said, we realize that he was speaking of the present time, not prophesying about something to happen several hundred years later; he was not prophesying the birth of Jesus.

In "The Book of Isaiah," we find: "I heard the voice of the Lord, saying, Whom shall I send, and who will go for us? Then said I, Here am I; send me. And he said, Go, and tell this people, Hear ye indeed, but understand not; and see ye indeed, but perceive not. Make the heart of this people fat, and make their ears heavy, and shut their eyes; so that they see with their eyes, and hear with their ears, and understand with their heart, and convert, and be healed" (Isaiah 6: 8-10).

Note that Isaiah said, "so that they would understand with their heart." This is the same thing as "communing with your own heart," as advocated by David, the Psalmist. Communing with our own heart is the way we are converted and healed.

In "The Gospel According to Matthew" we find, "In those days came John the Baptist, preaching in the wilderness of Judaea, And saying, Repent ye; for the kingdom of heaven is at hand. For this is he that was spoken of by the prophet Esaias, saying, The voice of one crying in the wilderness, Prepare ye the way of the Lord, make his paths straight" (Matthew 3:1-3).

In "The Book of Isaiah," we find: "Comfort ye, comfort ye my people, saith your God. ... The voice of him that crieth in the wilderness, Prepare ye the way of the Lord, make straight in the desert a highway for our God. Every valley shall be exalted, and every mountain and hill shall be made low; and the crooked shall be made straight, and the rough places plain; And the glory of the Lord shall be revealed, and all flesh shall see it together; for the mouth of the Lord hath spoken it" (Isaiah 40:1-5).

Note that Isaiah said, "the mouth of the Lord hath spoken it." The "mouth of the Lord" is (in our language) our true spiritual self. Isaiah got wisdom and understanding from the Lord within him, the same way that Moses got wisdom and understanding ... the same way that Jesus got wisdom and understanding from the Father.

Too, note that Isaiah was speaking about the present ("the mouth of the Lord hath spoken"), not prophesying something to happen several hundred years later. In this instance, Isaiah was speaking about the present in the same sense that he was speaking about the present when he said: "Seek ye the Lord while he may be found; call ye upon him while he is near. Let the wicked forsake his

Understanding What Jesus Said

way and the unrighteous man his thoughts; and let him return unto the Lord. ... For ye shall go forward with joy and be led forth with peace; the mountains and the hills shall break forth before you into singing, and all the trees of the field shall clap their hands" (Isaiah 55:6-12).

Notice that once we find the Lord — once the glory of the Lord is revealed — that we have peace and joy. Remember that the Apostle Paul said, "Heaven is peace and joy." Thus, what Isaiah said is in agreement with what the Apostle John said, "The kingdom of heaven is at hand" ... meaning in the present moment ... when we find the Lord. In our language finding the Lord is the same thing a finding our true spiritual self. Once we are unified with our true spiritual self, this is the same thing as being unified with God ... the same thing as Jesus being one with the Father.

Isaiah's descriptive language of what we experience once we find the Lord blends in with what Jesus said: "Seek ye first the kingdom of God, and his righteousness; and all these things shall be added unto you" ... things like peace and joy ... "the hills shall break forth before you into singing, and all the trees of the field shall clap their hands" ... that must be the joy and peace of heaven.

It's easier to understand the mystery of Jesus' teachings when we realize that Jesus was a human being and had an earthly father. However, he learned things of a spiritual nature from his spiritual Father ... "because I go unto the Father." One of the things that made Jesus special (one of the most influential teachers of all time) is that he discovered truth, he overcame the world of the ego ... he harmonized with God. And, importantly, he lived what he taught. He was humble and compassionate; he abided by the will of his Father.

Jesus said to his disciples privately, "Blessed are the eyes which see the things that ye see; for I tell you, many prophets and kings have desired to see those things ye see, and have not seen them, and to hear those things ye hear, and have not heard them."

Some of the things Jesus said could be simpler to grasp if we simply said them in the language of our time. About his commandment, "This is my commandment that you love one another as I have loved you," the same message can be conveyed simply, "we must have a loving heart" ... what the Buddha taught about 500 years BC.

It helps to unravel the mystery of Jesus' teachings if we realize that in some instances (not always) where Jesus used the pronouns "me" and "I," we can substitute the word "truth." ... and we are not taking away or adding to what he said ... only understanding what he said. Interpreting what Jesus said is quite different from taking from and adding to what he said to make it seem that he did not say what he said.

In the following, note how we can get a clear understanding of what Jesus said, if we think in terms of "truth" — if we think in terms of the message Jesus intended for us — rather than focusing on the man Jesus. Jesus said, "I am the way, the truth, and the life; no man cometh unto the Father, but by me" (John 14:6). This is simpler to grasp if we substitute the word "truth" for the pronouns "I" and "me." Thus, truth is the way and the life of the spirit; no one unifies with God, but by truth.

Jesus knew that his parables, proverbs, metaphors, and his manner of teaching were not clear to many people, including not only the Jews but also his own disciples. In "The Gospel According to John," Jesus, speaking to the Jews, said, "Yet a little while am I with you, and then I go unto him that sent me. Ye shall seek me, and shall not find me; and where I am, thither ye cannot come." "Then said the Jews among themselves, Whither will he go, that we shall not find him? will he go unto the dispersed among the Gentiles, and teach the Gentiles?" (John 7:33-35). We know from other things that Jesus said that "him that sent me" is the Father (his spiritual self).

In John 16:16-29, we find where Jesus was speaking to his disciples: "A little while, and ye shall not see me; and again, a little while, and ye shall see me, because I go to the Father. Then said some of his disciples among themselves, What is this that he saith unto us, A little while, and ye shall not see me; and again, a little while, and ye shall see me; and, Because I go to the Father? They said therefore, What is this that he saith, A little while? we cannot tell what he saith."

Understanding What Jesus Said

Jesus said: "These things have I spoken unto you in proverbs; but the time cometh, when I shall no more speak unto you in proverbs, but I shall show you plainly of the Father. ... I came forth from the Father, and am come into the world; again, I leave the world, and go to the Father " (John 16:25-28).

When Jesus said, "am come into the world; again, I leave the world," he was not speaking of the world as we typically think of the world. He was speaking of the world of the ego. Jesus also said, "Ye have heard how I said unto you, I go away, and come again unto you. If ye loved me, ye would rejoice, because I said, I go unto the Father; for my Father is greater than I" (John 14:28).

Not understanding the language that Jesus used, some fundamentalists think that Jesus will return to earth. Jesus went unto the Father and "came again" several times during his brief ministry. He retreated to the Father within. He retreated to the place alluded to by David the Psalmist as "the secret place of the most High."

Note also that Jesus said, "I shall show you plainly the Father." No one has ever seen God, and no one can see the "Father." So, what did Jesus mean by the verb "show?" He must have meant that he would explain what the "Father" is. However, if he ever explained this, he did not make his explanation clear. We know from the many ways in which Jesus spoke of the "Father" that the "Father" is the same thing as the "Lord" alluded to by the spiritual teachers of the Old Testament. And, in our language, the "Father" is the true divine, spiritual self.

Perhaps one of the greatest mysteries of Jesus' teachings pertains to who, what, and where the Father is. The disciples wanted to know, but they could not get a clear answer. Jesus said so much about the Father that it is an exercise in futility to read and study what Jesus said without knowing what and where the Father is.

Jesus said, "All things are delivered to me of my Father, and no man knoweth who the Son is but the Father, and who the Father is, but the son. ... I am in the Father and the Father in me. He also said, "All things the Father hath are mine. ... Whatsoever ye ask of the Father in my name he will give it to you. ... A little while and ye shall not see me and again, a little while and ye shall see me, because I go to the Father."

The disciples, who knew the language that Jesus used, reacted: "What is this that he saith unto us. ... Because I go to the Father. ... We cannot tell what he saith. ... Lord, we know not whither thou goest. ... Lord, show us the Father. ... Where is thy Father? ... Lo, speakest thou plainly and speakest no proverb."

About the most that the disciples got in way of an answer was, "Ye neither know me nor my Father. If ye had known me, ye should have known my Father also."

Knowing what and where the Father is and also knowing where the truth that sets us free resides help us to understand the mystery of Jesus' teachings. It helps to know that the Father is in everyone and that the truth proceeds from the Father. This is clear from Jesus' teachings ... if only we will ponder and assimilate his teachings, rather than gloss over them, thinking he is saying something that he did not say.

Following his baptism, Jesus began speaking in terms of the Father. In "The Gospel According to Matthew" there are about twenty statements by Jesus in which he spoke in terms of *your* Father, *thy* Father, and *our* Father. The following examples are more than enough to let us know that Jesus was speaking of something that is within us. And bear in mind that Jesus told us that heaven is within us (Luke 17:21). Jesus said:

- Be ye therefore perfect, even as *your* Father which is in heaven is perfect (Matthew 5:48).
- Take heed that ye do not your alms before men, to be seen of them; otherwise ye have no reward of *your* Father which is in heaven (Matthew 6:1).
- But thou, when thou prayest, enter into your closet, and when thou hast shut thy door, pray to *your* Father which is in secret; and *your* Father which seeth in secret shall reward you openly (Matthew 6:6).
- *Your* Father knoweth what things ye have need of, before ye ask him (Matthew 6:8).
- After this manner therefore pray ye: *Our* Father which art in heaven, Hallowed be thy name (Matthew 6:9). [Remember that Jesus said heaven is within us.]

Understanding What Jesus Said

- For it is not ye that speak, but the Spirit of *your* Father which speaketh in you (Matthew 10:20).

In addition to the foregoing, note the significance of the following, realizing that the *Father* is our true divine spiritual self. Jesus said:

- For if ye forgive men their trespasses, *your* heavenly Father will also forgive you (Matthew 6:14). From this we realize that it is our true spiritual self that does the forgiving.
- But if ye forgive not men their trespasses, neither will *your* Father forgive your trespasses (Matthew 6:15).
- Not every one that saith unto me, Lord, Lord, shall enter into the kingdom of heaven; but he that doeth the will of my Father which is in heaven (Matthew 7:21). This means that only those who do the will of their true spiritual self will enjoy heaven.
- And every one that hath forsaken houses, or brethren, or sisters, or father, or mother, or wife, or children, or lands, for my name's sake, shall receive an hundredfold, and shall inherit everlasting life (Matthew 19:29). ... For whosoever shall do the will of my Father which is in heaven, the same is my brother, and sister, and mother" (Matthew 12:50). When we, individually and collectively as a group, are unified with our true spiritual self (what Jesus meant when he said, "I and my Father are one"), we are unified as a group ... we are as one body. ... the same in the spirit of truth— free from sin and evil.
- "And call no man your father upon the earth; for one is your Father, which is in heaven" (Matthew 23:9).

Thus, there are several passages of Scriptures that let us know that the *Father*, as alluded to by Jesus, is the same thing as our true spiritual self. Perhaps one of the examples in which Jesus makes this clear is when he was telling his disciples what to expect when they were preparing to teach the gospel, bearing in mind that the disciples were ordinary human beings. Jesus told them, "take no thought how or what ye shall speak, for it shall be given you in that same hour what ye shall speak. For it is not ye that speak, but the Spirit of your Father who speaketh in you" (Matthew 10:19).

We also know from the prayer Jesus prayed that the Father is within us. He began the prayer with, "Our Father who art in heaven." Note that he said "*our* Father," and he had already told us that heaven is within us. And he said, "Pray to your Father who is in secret." Clearly, the "Father" is in us.

The following statement by Jesus, "For *your Father* knoweth what things ye have need of before you ask him," sheds light on what and where the Father is. Who or what is it that knows our needs other than some aspect of ourselves? It is not some mystical being up in the clouds someplace.

Jesus said, "The words that I speak unto you I speak not of myself; but the Father that dwelleth in me, he doeth the works." Perhaps this gets glossed over because we think of Jesus as being a divine person without an earthly father and because we do not realize that the Father is within us. It helps us to understand the teachings of Jesus to know that the Father is within us. Whatever we wish to call it, "our Father" is an aspect of our mind ... that part of the psyche that is not in the immediate field of awareness. Thus, *our* "Father" is within us. And we, too, can communicate with our true spiritual self by doing what Jesus did. We can "shut the door" and listen to our inner most self for wisdom and understanding ... for discovering the truth that sets us free.

This is not to say that there is not a Force — that there is not a God — outside us. Quite to the contrary, God is all there is ... in all and through all. Our ultimate goal in life is to harmonize with God, which we can do by discovering the truth that sets us free ... which we can do by communing with our own heart. Jesus' life was centered on doing the will of his Father. And he said that only those who do the will of the Father would enter heaven. He attributed his works and his understanding to his Father. He said, "I do nothing of myself, but as my Father hath taught me, I speak these things. ... And he that sent me is with me; the Father hath not left me alone; for I do always those things that please him."

If we ponder this statement for a moment — in light of other things that Jesus said — we realize that "he that sent me" is the Father within. Remember that Jesus told his disciples, "It is not ye that speak, but the Spirit of your Father which speaketh in you (Matthew 10:20). And we know Jesus said, "I must be about my Father's business." Jesus attributed most everything he believed, most everything he taught, and most everything he did to the Father within ... "because I go to the Father."

Jesus said, "For I have not spoken of myself; but the Father who sent me, he gave me a commandment, what I should say and what I should speak. ... whatsoever I speak therefore, even as the Father said unto me, so I speak."

If we assimilate some of the teachings of the spiritual teachers of the Old Testament, asking a few simple questions and noticing how they refer to the *Lord,* we realize that Jesus used the word *Father* in the same manner that the spiritual teachers of the Old Testament used the word *Lord.* As examples, think about the following questions: Who or what was Moses with for forty days and forty nights when he wrote the Ten Commandments, except something within himself? An angel of the Lord appeared unto Moses. Angels appear in the inner vision. What Moses saw and heard was within him. In our language, Moses was communing with his true spiritual self.

Isaiah said, "Seek ye the Lord while he may be found; call ye upon him while he is near." Who or what were the people to seek, except something within themselves, something that was near?

David, the Psalmist, said: "Bless the Lord, O my soul, and *all that is within me.* ... The Lord is my strength and song, and is become my salvation. ... forget not all his benefits ... who forgiveth all thine iniquities ... who healeth all thy diseases ... who redeemeth thy life from destruction. ... In my distress I cried unto the Lord, and he heard me. ... O Lord my God, I cried unto thee, and thou hast healed me. ... Lord, remember David, and all his afflictions. ... Many are the afflictions of the righteous; but the Lord delivereth him out of them all."

Who or what did David credit for all the good that came unto him, except the Lord within himself ("all that is within me")? There are two parts to the answer to this question. The first part is that David communed with his own heart, the Lord within him (in our language, his true spiritual self). This is how he gained the wisdom for knowing the truth that set him free from his afflictions.

However, in the final analysis, the one and only universal God does the healing. Before God heals us, there is something we must do, and we do it as advocated by David, the Psalmist: "Commune with your own heart." ... the "heart" being the *Lord* within (in our language, the true spiritual self). Communing with our own heart is the same thing as communing with God.

If we really believe the gospel, then we know there is something we must do to be saved. God does for us according to our deeply held beliefs and desires, according to the way we believe and think in our heart: "As a man thinketh in his heart, so is he." And, "It is done unto us as we believe."

From *The Koran*, the sacred book of the Muslims, we learn, "God changes not what is in a people, until they change what is in themselves." Who is going to change what is in us but we ourselves? Who is going to change our beliefs but we ourselves?

When we "clean the inside of the cup and the platter," when we obliterate the devils from our mind, when we are converted and become as humble as little children, when we discover the truth that sets us free, we are in harmony with God—we have a pure heart, we are saved; we are healed; we have peace and joy. ... we enjoy heaven.

One of the most significant things about understanding that Jesus used the word *Father* in the same manner that the spiritual teachers of the Old Testament used the word *Lord* is that we realize that whatever we call it (true self, sacred self, spiritual self, higher self, "secret place of the most high," etc.), it is something within us. Borrowing from something that the Apostle Paul said about the natural man and "he who is spiritual," I have chosen to use the phrase *spiritual self*. The Apostle Paul said, "It is sown a natural body; it is raised a spiritual body. There is a natural body, and there is a spiritual body" (1 Corinthians 15:44).

Understanding that our true spiritual self is the same thing as the *Father* as alluded to by Jesus and the *Lord* as alluded to by the spiritual teachers of the Old Testament helps us understand the gospel that Jesus preached. This understanding can help us break the cycle of doing what Jesus said that religious teachers did about 2,000 years ago. They taught their own tradition, rejecting the commandments of God.

Understanding What Jesus Said 123

In "The Gospel According to Mark" we find: "Then the Pharisees and scribes asked him [Jesus], Why walk not thy disciples according to the tradition of the elders ... He answered and said unto them, Well hath Esaias prophesied of you hypocrites, as it is written, This people honoureth me with their lips, but their heart is far from me. Howbeit in vain do they worship me, teaching for doctrines the commandments of men. For laying aside the commandment of God, ye hold the tradition of men, as the washing of pots and cups; and many other such like things ye do. And he said unto them, Full well ye reject the commandment of God, that ye may keep your own tradition" (Mark 7:5-9).

Isaiah said, "... this people draw near me with their mouth, and with their lips do honour me, but have removed their heart far from me, and their fear toward me is taught by the precept of men" (Isaiah 29:13).

We are beginning the twenty-first century and still today many Christians are doing what Jesus said that people were doing about 2,000 years ago. Think about it! Many people are clinging to false doctrine, rather than believing and following the gospel that Jesus preached.

Some things that Jesus *did not* say are implicit in what he said. For example, Jesus said, "These things I have spoken unto you, that in me ye might have peace. In the world ye shall have tribulation, but be of good cheer; I have overcome the world" (John 16:33).

Note that Jesus told people things to help them have peace. Implicit in the statement, "but be of good cheer; I have overcome the world," is that through his teachings ("that in me") we too would overcome the world and have peace (speaking of overcoming the world of the ego).

Many Christians suffer varied tribulations; however, they discount these as something to be expected and endured in this lifetime. They believe they will have peace and joy after they die and go to heaven. They quote the part of the above statement by Jesus about having tribulations with no true understanding of the latter part of the statement. Actually, many so-called Christians, with their false beliefs about such things as Jesus being God in human flesh, gloss over what Jesus said about overcoming the world.

Overcoming the world of the ego indicates that Jesus was human, and we can do what he did; we can overcome the world of the ego.

Webster defines "tribulation" as, "Great misery or distress ... something that causes suffering or distress." "Tribulations" include such things as anxiety, guilt, jealousy, anger, depression, hatred, and stress-induced illnesses. Fear is a hidden culprit underlying tribulations. Thus, using Jesus as our example, when we overcome the world of the ego — when we are unified with our true spiritual self (the same thing as being unified with God) — we will be free from tribulations. We overcome our tribulations — we have peace and joy — the moment we discover the truth that sets us free.

David the Psalmist was delivered from all his afflictions (another word for tribulations) by communing with his own heart ... the same thing as communing with God. We can do the same thing that David did. We can commune with our own heart and consequently discover the truth that sets us free from all our tribulations ... free from the insidious fears and deeply held false beliefs that cause all our mental suffering.

There are those who say "Jesus was God in human flesh." In the sense that Jesus was God in human flesh, we are all God in human flesh. Jesus taught that we are all children of God. We are all divine, created in the image and likeness of God.

If we study and assimilate what Jesus said, rather than gloss over it, we realize that Jesus said several things that let us know that he was human. Note the following: Jesus asked his disciples, "Whom do men say that I the Son of man am?" They gave varying answers, but not the correct answer. Thus, Jesus answered his question: "He that soweth the good seed is the Son of man" ... in other words, he was human. Although it seems to have been glossed over and misunderstood, in the above comments, Jesus alluded to himself twice as the "Son of man." This needs no special interpretation. Jesus alluded to himself as being the Son of man in the same sense that some of the spiritual teachers of the Old Testament alluded to being the Son of man. Ezekiel began several passages with, "And the word of the Lord came unto me, saying, Son of man."

Understanding What Jesus Said 125

Jesus said, "Because of your unbelief; for verily I say unto you, if ye have faith as a grain of mustard seed, ye shall say unto this mountain, remove hence to yonder place; and it shall remove; and nothing shall be impossible unto you." This was Jesus' answer to the disciples when they ask him why they themselves were unable to heal a lunatic. From Jesus' response, we realize that the disciples had the same ability that Jesus had ... if only they believe. It was not that Jesus could heal lunatics because he was God in human flesh.

Jesus said, "Verily, verily, I say unto you, he that believeth me, the works that I do shall he do also; and greater works than these shall he do, because I go unto my Father." This explains the source of Jesus' success in the miracles he performed: the Father within. And, to think! It's all within us. Note that Jesus told his disciples, "Greater things than these ye will do." This means that we have the potential to do "greater things than these."

Note also the significance of the clause: "because I go unto my Father." This takes on added significance when we realize that the Father is within us. Just imagine the possibilities if we cultivate our oneness with the Father ... oneness with our true spiritual self.

In addition, note what Jesus said concerning those who believe the gospel and are saved: "And these signs shall follow them that believe. In my name shall they cast out devils. ... they shall lay hands on the sick, and they shall recover" (Mark 16:15-18).

Note that the disciples could do what Jesus did, cast out devils and heal the sick. ... all in the name of truth ... all by believing and doing what Jesus did and what he taught. Think about it! We have the potential for doing what they did ... if only we believe and comprehend the true teachings of Jesus.

Let us remember that the disciples were human like we are. Thus, from the foregoing statements, we realize that we have the potential for doing the things that Jesus did ... if only we believe and comprehend what he said ... if we learn to trust, cherish, and embrace our true spiritual self and abide by it.

We find in the Book of Numbers that Moses said, "Hereby ye shall know that the Lord hath sent me to do all these works, for I have not done them of mine own mind" (Numbers 16:28). This is similar to what Jesus said about doing the will of his Father who sent him.

The above statements by Jesus seem very compelling that he was a human being, and especially in view of the fact that there is nothing in the teachings of Jesus or in the teachings of the spiritual teachers of the Old Testament about Jesus being God in human flesh. There is nothing to suggest that Jesus was not an ordinary person in the sense of being human. However, in the sense of being truthful — in the sense of being unified with God — he was extraordinary; he was the personification of truth.

Understanding Jesus' mission helps us understand what he said. If we understand Jesus' mission, we are not prone to add to and take from what he said, trying to make it seem to agree with false beliefs. His mission was not to save us so that we might go to heaven after we die, as many Christians believe. If we study and assimilate what Jesus said, we realize that his purpose for preaching the gospel was quite simple: that we might have peace.

Generally speaking, if we read isolated statements by Jesus — glossing over what he said — we do not get the full significance of what Jesus said. For example, Jesus said, "These things I have spoken unto you, that you might have peace" (John 16:33).

It is particularly easy to gloss over what Jesus said in this statement when we believe that heaven is a place of peace and joy where Christians go after they die. It is much easier to grasp what Jesus said when we know that peace and joy characterize heaven and that heaven is within us. If we assimilate what Jesus said, his teachings become clear. His mission that we might have peace becomes clear in the following few paragraphs.

In the following, notice what Jesus said, keeping in mind that he was speaking about the present, not about life after death. Moreover, Jesus did not teach anything about heaven being a place where the saved go after they die. In addition, let us remember the Apostle Paul's description of heaven: "peace, joy, and righteousness." The Apostle Paul also called the gospel of Jesus the gospel of Peace: "How beautiful are the feet of them that preach the gospel of Peace and bring glad tidings of good things!" ... speaking about the present.

Understanding What Jesus Said

With the foregoing in mind, note what Jesus said pertaining to peace and joy:
- These things I have spoken unto you, that in me you might have peace (John 16:33).
- These things have I spoken unto you, that my joy might remain in you, and that your joy might be full (John 15:11).
- Take my yoke upon you, and learn of me; for I am meek and lowly in heart; and ye shall find rest unto your souls. For my yoke is easy, and my burden is light (Matthew 11:29).
- Peace I leave with you, my peace I give unto you; not as the world giveth, give I unto you. Let not your heart be troubled, neither let it be afraid (John 14:27).
- I am come that they might have life, and that they might have it more abundantly (John 10:10).
- Seek ye first the kingdom of God, and his righteousness; and all these things shall be added unto you (Matthew 6:23).
- The kingdom of God is within you (Luke 17:21).
- Come unto me, all ye that labour and are heavy laden, and I will give you rest (Matthew 11:28).
- Blessed are the peacemakers; for they shall be called the children of God (Matthew 5:9).
- Have salt in yourselves, and have peace one with another (Mark 9:50).
- Ask, and ye shall receive, that your joy may be full (John 16:24).
- If I cast out devils by the Spirit of God, then the kingdom of God is come unto you (Matthew 12:28).

The foregoing statements are by Jesus. Following are selected statements related to peace and joy by other spiritual leaders of biblical times. And, bear in mind that both Jesus and the spiritual leaders of the Old Testament were speaking about the present.
- I will hear what God the Lord will speak; for he will speak peace unto his people (Psalms 85:8).
- Light is sown for the righteous, and joy for the upright in heart (Psalms 97:11).
- Then thou shall have great joy in the Almighty, and shall lift up thy face unto God (Job 22:26).

- This day is holy unto our Lord; neither be ye sorry; for the joy of the Lord is your strength (Nehemiah 8:10).
- I will greatly rejoice in the Lord, my soul shall be joyful in my God; for he hath clothed me with the garments of salvation (Isaiah 61:10).
- Thou hast turned for me my mourning into dancing; thou hast ... girded me with gladness (Psalms 30:11). ["Gladness" is joy and happiness.]
- Peace, peace to him that is far off, and to him that is near, saith the Lord; and I will heal him. But the wicked are like the troubled sea, when it cannot rest, whose waters cast up mire and dirt. There is no peace, saith my God, to the wicked" (Isaiah 57:19-21).
- Now the Lord of peace himself give you peace always by all means (2 Thessalonians 3:16).
- And let the peace of God rule in your hearts, to the which also ye are called in one body; and be ye thankful (Colossians 3:15).
- And the peace of God, which passeth all understanding, shall keep your hearts and minds (Philippians 4:7).
- The wisdom that is from above is first pure, then peaceable. ... And the fruit of righteousness is sown in peace of them that make peace (James 3:17).
- For I know the thoughts that I think toward you, saith the Lord, thoughts of peace, and not of evil (Jeremiah 29:11).
- And these things write we unto you, that your joy may be full (1 John 1:4).
- The Lord will give strength unto his people; the Lord will bless his people with peace (Psalms 29:11).
- Depart from evil, and do good; seek peace, and pursue it (Psalms 34:14).
- Great peace have they which love thy law; and nothing shall offend them (Psalms 119:165). To "love thy law" is to "do the will of the Father," a requirement for enjoying heaven. "Thy law" is the same thing as the truth that proceeds from our true spiritual self.
- Thou wilt shew me the path of life; in thy presence is fullness of joy (Psalms 16:11). Let us not gloss over what the Psalmist said. Who or what is it that will show us the "path of life" except our true spiritual self? And when we find "the path of life," we experi-

Understanding What Jesus Said

ence the fullness of joy. Note the word "is" in the phrase, "in thy presence *is* fullness of joy." ... meaning in the present moment.
- Restore unto me the joy of thy salvation; and uphold me with thy free spirit (Psalms 51:12). We have a free spirit when we know the truth that sets us free.
- Deceit is in the heart of them that imagine evil; but to the counsellers of peace is joy (Proverb 12:20).
- Thus saith the Lord, Stand ye in the ways, and see, and ask for the old paths, where is the good way, and walk therein, and ye shall find rest for your souls (Jeremiah 6:16). Remember that Jesus said, "learn of me and ye shall find rest unto your souls."
- When a man's ways please the Lord, he maketh even his enemies to be at peace with him (Proverb 16:7).
- I will *rejoice* in the Lord, I will *joy* in the God of my salvation. The Lord God is my strength (Habakkuk 3: 18-19).
- The meek shall inherit the earth and shall delight themselves in the abundance of peace (Psalms 37:11).
- Thou wilt keep him in perfect peace whose mind is stayed on *thee*. (Isaiah 26:3). "Thee" as alluded to here is our true spiritual self. When "our mind is stayed on thee," we follow the guidance of our true spiritual self. In Jesus' language, we "do the will of our Father," a prerequisite for enjoying heaven.
- And the work of righteousness shall be peace; and the effect of righteousness quietness and assurance forever (Isaiah 32:17).
- And all thy children shall be taught of the Lord; and great shall be the peace of thy children (Isaiah 54:13).

All of the above is about peace and joy — the abundant life — and there is nothing in the teachings of Jesus or the spiritual teachers of the Old Testament about being saved so that we will enjoy peace and joy — so that we will enjoy heaven — after we die.

Note the significance of the last statement above. It is easy to gloss over this statement, yet it is packed with wisdom. If we teach our children about the Lord, they will have great peace. What greater gift could we give our children than to love them and teach them about the Lord?

Abiding by the truth that proceeds from our true self (the Lord within us) brings peace and joy, which everyone insatiably desires. No one will ever be totally satisfied and contented until they have peace and joy. Abiding by the false ego-self brings suffering. Think about it! If we love our children and teach them about the Lord, they will have peace and joy. In turn, they will pass onto their children peace and joy. In due time planet earth would be a utopia ... like, "a new heaven and a new earth."

From the above list, we realize that the purpose of the teachings of both Jesus and the spiritual teachers of the Old Testament is that we might have peace and joy. And there is nothing in the Bible to support the fundamentalist belief that Jesus was sent to save us so that we would enjoy heaven after we die. If we attempt to assimilate passages of Scriptures about heaven and hell after death (similar to what I did above with passages of Scriptures pertaining to peace and joy), there is nothing to assimilate. Although the words "heaven" and "hell" appear many times in the Bible, they are not mentioned one time in a manner that indicates that they are places where people go after they die.

And, it's a mistake to select two or three passages of Scripture that we do not understand and interpret them to mean something that leads us astray from the message Jesus intended for us. And, it's a mistake to resort to the visions of John in "The Revelation to John" and interpret the visions in a manner that supports a false belief about heaven and hell. For example, there are fundamentalists who believe that John's vision of the heavenly Jerusalem alludes to an eternal home in heaven, a place where the saved go after they die. This belief is not consistent with the gospel that Jesus preached.

The "path of life" alluded to by David, the Psalmist, is the same "narrow way" alluded to by Jesus when he said, "Narrow is the way that leadeth unto life and few there be who find it." We have peace when we find the narrow way to life and do the will of our true spiritual self ... the same as Jesus doing the will of the Father. And according to Jesus, only those who do the will of the Father will enjoy heaven ... will enjoy "the peace that passeth all understanding."

Understanding What Jesus Said

Note the significance of the statement by Jesus above: "If I cast out devils, then the kingdom of God is come unto you." Jesus was speaking about the present. The kingdom of God is within us, and we enjoy it when we are pure in heart. We are pure in heart — we are saved — when we cast the devils from our heart. When our heart is pure, we are unified with God (same thing as Jesus and his Father being one). Thus, the moment we cast the devils from our mind, we enjoy peace and joy; we enjoy heaven ... now, not after we are dead and gone. Truth obliterates devils.

Being clear about the significance of that one saying of Jesus, we realize that we do not have to understand the whole Bible — we do not have to understand everything that Jesus said — in order to understand the message that Jesus intended for us ... in order to discover the truth and be free ... in order to discover heaven here and now. If we master this one saying of Jesus, we realize that we need not get bogged down in a lot of myths, dreams, visions, and prophesy, trying to understand what it is that we really want to know ... which is the truth that sets us free.

Jesus said, "Take my yoke upon you, and learn of me ... and ye shall find rest unto your souls." Simply said in our language, if we understand the teachings of Jesus, we would find "rest unto our souls." Remember, Jesus also said, "And those who believe the gospel [those who "learn of me"] will be saved." When we are saved, we find "rest unto our souls." From the above, we realize that the purpose of the teachings of both Jesus and the spiritual teachers of the Old Testament is that we might have peace.

We enjoy peace and joy when we are abiding by the truth that proceeds from our true spiritual self, as opposed to following the dictates of our false ego-self, which is the source of suffering and evil ... which is the source of destructive acts and behavior. Our false ego-self always wants to appear special and important — thriving on attention and recognition — and is the source of our suffering, restlessness, anxiety, and discontent ... the source of a troubled mind, which is hell.

In addition to the foregoing, the word "peace" is used extensively in the teachings of the Apostle Paul, who alluded to God as the God of peace. Paul said, "Be of one mind; live in peace, and the

God of love and peace shall be with you. ... And let the peace of God rule in your hearts ... And the peace of God, which passeth all understanding, shall keep your hearts and minds."

Let us not gloss over what the Apostle Paul said. The phrase, "be of one mind" means being free of the fearful, false beliefs of the false ego-self, and consequently, being one with our true spiritual self ... the same thing as Jesus and his Father being one. If we let our true spiritual self rule in our heart — the same thing as God ruling in our heart — we will live in peace.

The Apostle Paul also said, "For God is not the author of confusion, but of peace, as in all churches of the saints" (1 Corinthians 14:33), and "Let us therefore follow after the things which make for peace, and things wherewith one may edify another (Romans 14:19).

"Edify" is defined by Webster: "to instruct in such a way as to improve, enlighten, or uplift morally or spiritually." Truth teachings — the gospel that Jesus preached — uplift us spiritually and bring us peace ... if we understand, believe and embody what Jesus said.

The Apostle Paul, speaking of unbelievers (Jews and Gentiles), said: "As it is written, There is none righteous, no, not one. There is none that understandeth, there is none that seeketh after God. ... Destruction and misery are in their ways. And the way of *peace* have they not known" (Romans 3:10-17).

What the Apostle Paul said is applicable to many people who profess to be Christians. Jesus said, "Narrow is the way that leadeth unto life and few there be who find it" (Matthew 7:14). Those who believe and comprehend the gospel are saved; they find the "narrow way to life" ... they find peace and joy.

Although the word "heaven" appears many times in the Old Testament, it is not mentioned one time in a manner that suggests it is a place where the saved go after they die. The following is a sample of the ways the word "heaven" is used in the Old Testament: "In the beginning God created the heaven and the earth; look now toward heaven and tell the stars; the rain from heaven was restrained; the fowls of the heaven and the flesh of thy saints unto the beasts of the earth; heaven was black with clouds; the flame of the city ascended up to heaven; that is in heaven above or that is in the earth beneath; the dew of heaven and the fatness of the earth."

The point is that there are no references to the word "heaven" in either the Old Testament or the New Testament to suggest that heaven is a place where the saved go after they die. Perhaps such a concept of heaven is something someone has made up. Knowing that heaven is within us, and that it is characterized by peace and joy, facilitates discovering it. However, we will not grasp what genuine peace and joy are until we experience them ... until we discover the truth that sets us free.

Living in harmony with truth is comparatively easy. When we are in harmony with truth, we do not get burdened with demands and expectations. We do not take off on tangents doing those things that the false ego-self compels us to do. We have no concern about appearing special and important ... we have no need to keep up with the Joneses. Life is much simpler and much more satisfying when we are simply in harmony with truth and nature.

In a nutshell, Jesus' message is about changing the way we believe and think in our heart, so that we might have peace and joy ... so that we might have life and have it more abundantly. We experience the abundant life that Jesus had in mind for us when we "clean the inside of the cup and the platter," when we "cast the devils out of our subconscious mind" ... when we discover the truth that sets us free.

Jesus said to his disciples, "Go ye therefore, and teach all nations ... Teaching them to observe all things whatsoever I have commanded you; and, lo, I am with you always, even unto the end of the world."

Note the part, "I am with you always, even unto the end of the world." Jesus' teachings are simpler to grasp and apply when they are explained in our language. Once we understand and embody the teachings of Jesus they remain with us as long as we live. The truth that sets us free — programmed into us by God — is already within us.

We have the choice of surrendering to — and abiding by — truth ... the only thing that will bring us genuine joy and peace; or, choosing to follow the dictates of our false ego-self, which always brings alienation, mental suffering, restlessness, and discontent. Following the dictates of the bloated, elephantine ego and doing those things that are showy, conceited and the things that seem to make us appear special and important — doing things that are "savored by man [the false ego-self]" — cause a confused, troubled, tormented mind, which is hell. Following the inner guidance of our true spiritual self and being humble, genuine, real, and in harmony with truth, God, and nature bring inner peace and joy, which is heaven.

Jesus taught the gospel for the same reason that the Buddha taught what became known as Buddhism, that we might have peace ... that we might overcome mental suffering. The ultimate goal of religion, psychiatry, the teachings of Jesus, the writers of the Old Testament, Buddha, and other great teachers is the same—that we might have peace. We have peace when we are in harmony with truth, God, and nature.

We can accomplish the goal of psychiatry, religion, and the teachings of Jesus by learning to do what Jesus told us to do: shut the door, know the truth, clean the inside of the cup and the platter, cast out devils, be as perfect even as our true self is perfect, be as honest, free, humble, and spontaneous as little children.

We can also accomplish the goal of psychiatry, religion, and Jesus by doing what the Buddha taught: "Be ye lamps unto yourselves; seek salvation alone in truth."

We can accomplish the goal that Jesus had for us by doing what David, the Psalmist, said to do: "Commune with your own heart" ... the same thing that Jesus did when he "went unto the Father."

The Apostle Paul said, "Be ye transformed by the renewing of your mind." The greatest transformation we might experience and the most profound renewal of our mind are brought about when we discover the truth that frees us from the devils in our minds. It is then that we experience the "peace that passeth all understanding." It is then that we are in harmony with truth, God, and nature.

There is no simpler way of renewing our mind and, consequently, being transformed than to free ourselves of obscure, insidious, unwarranted fears and deeply rooted, false beliefs. And when

Understanding What Jesus Said

we do this one comparatively simple thing, we are in agreement with truth ... we are free to love freely ... we are pure in heart ... our heart is right with God ... we are happy, satisfied, and contented ... it is like "being born again."

In many ways Jesus helped clarify some of the Old Testament teachings. He made it clear that God is love and that heaven is within us. However, in some ways — in his manner of teaching — he made some things that he said difficult to grasp, especially when he used the pronouns of "I" and "me." The following passages by Jesus are examples. What the prophet, Micah, author of The Book of Micah, said, helps clarify what Jesus said.

Jesus said, "Think not that I am come to send peace on earth; I came not to send peace, but a sword. For I am come to set a man at variance against his father, and the daughter against her mother, and the daughter in law against her mother in law. And a man's foes shall be they of his own household. He that loveth father or mother more than me is not worthy of me; and he that loveth son or daughter more than me is not worthy of me ... He that findeth his life shall lose it; and he that loseth his life for my sake shall find it" (Matthew 10:34-39).

In "The Gospel According to Luke," Jesus said, "I am come to send fire on the earth ... Suppose ye that I am come to give peace on earth? I tell you, Nay; but rather division; For from henceforth there shall be five in one house divided, three against two, and two against three. The father shall be divided against the son, and the son against the father; the mother against the daughter, and the daughter against the mother; the mother in law against her daughter in law, and the daughter in law against her mother in law" (Luke 12:49-53). And, "If any man come to me, and hate not his father, and mother, and wife, and children, and brethren, and sisters, yea, and his own life also, he cannot be my disciple" (Luke 14:26).

Incidentally, the mere fact that Jesus alluded to some people who thought that his purpose was to bring peace is indicative that there were those who believed that Jesus' purpose for preaching the gospel is that we might have peace ... which was his sole purpose.

So, what did Jesus mean by the foregoing passages? In his manner of teaching, what Jesus said is a powerful way to make a point. In other passages, Jesus said so much about love that we know he did not literally expect us to hate anyone, including our father, mother, wife, children, brothers, and sisters. Jesus taught unconditional love. Jesus said, "This is my commandment, that you love one another, as I have loved you. ... Love your enemies, bless them that curse you, do good to them that hate you, and pray for them which despitefully use you, and persecute you."

The phrase (in the above passage), *and his own life also,* helps explain what Jesus said. We realize that Jesus was speaking of hate in the same manner that David, the Psalmist, said, "I hate every false way." Jesus was speaking of hating the false ways of the ego ... even the false ways of those we cherish the most. Those who give up the way of the ego for the way of truth find the narrow path to life that few find ... they find peace and joy ... the abundant life.

Jesus knew how difficult it is for people to let go of their deeply held false beliefs and replace them with his truth teachings. Jesus knew how our false ego-self (Satan within us) hangs on tenaciously, resenting and resisting truth. Erroneous beliefs are so thoroughly embedded in us that we can read something that is true — but that differs from our false beliefs — and immediately our mind jumps to some explanation that seems to disprove the true statement we have just read. Thomas Carlyle, Scottish essayist and historian, said, "No iron chain, or outward force of any kind, could ever compel the soul of man to believe or to disbelieve." Jesus understood this long before Carlyle said it.

So, what is the "sword"? What is it that brings division? That sets people at variance with others? It's the truth teachings of Jesus; it's the gospel that Jesus preached.

Jesus knew that believing what he taught was contrary to what others believed and that this could cause alienation from others. Yet, there is nothing more important than abiding by the guidance of our true spiritual self (the same thing as doing the will of the Father), which we will do if we believe and comprehend the gospel that Jesus preached. Jesus knew that the gospel — that the way of truth — will bring us peace and joy. According to Jesus, only those who abide by the guidance of their true spiritual self — only those who are unified with God — will enjoy heaven.

Understanding What Jesus Said

What Jesus said about 2,000 years ago is true today. You can quickly alienate Christians from you if you explain the gospel of Jesus, which is not consistent with the beliefs of fundamentalists. What Jesus said is essentially the same thing that the prophet Micah said. In The Book of Micah, we find, "Trust ye not in a friend, put ye not confidence in a guide; keep the doors of thy mouth from her that lieth in thy bosom. For the son dishonoureth the father, the daughter riseth up against her mother, the daughter in law against her mother in law; a man's enemies are the men of his own house. Therefore I will look unto the Lord; I will wait for the God of my salvation; my God will hear me. Rejoice not against me, O mine enemy; when I fall, I shall arise; when I sit in darkness, the Lord shall be a light unto me" (Micah 7: 5-8).

In Micah's words, "a man's enemies are the men of his own house." In Jesus' words, "a man's foes shall be they of his own household." Regardless of what others believe, there is nothing more important than following the guidance of our true spiritual self. The guidance of our true, divine, spiritual self — the same thing as guidance from God — is always right. And according to Jesus, following this guidance is a prerequisite for enjoying heaven.

Micah followed the guidance of the Lord ... same thing as Jesus following the guidance of his Father. And that is what Jesus expected his disciples to do, follow the guidance of their true spiritual self. And if we believe and follow the teachings of Jesus, we will follow the guidance of our true spiritual self ... the only thing that will bring us genuine peace, joy, and happiness.

Incidentally what Jesus expected from his disciples is what all religious teachers should do. Religious teachers should abide by the truth that dwells within their own heart regardless of what others may believe, think, and say, including those of his or her own family. Religious teachers should have enough faith in Jesus to believe — and teach — what he said ... even at the risk of alienating others, including members of their own family. After all, everyone desires to enjoy the life they would enjoy if they understood and embodied the message Jesus intended for us.

Following the teachings of others — abiding by most of the Ten Commandments — can help us in various ways. But, this does not save us; this is not the same thing as being free to be free ... not the same thing as living our life freely, following the guidance of the truth that proceeds from our true spiritual self.

We actually do not know what all Jesus said that did not get recorded. During his three-year ministry, he must have said much more than what is in the New Testament. If we omit the duplication of what Jesus said that got recorded in the New Testament, we could say everything that Jesus said in one lecture.

However, according to John the Baptist, Jesus said and did much more than that which got recorded. John said, "And there are also many other things which Jesus did, and if they should be written every one, I suppose that even the world itself could not contain the books that should be written."

Although some of the teachings of Jesus are somewhat mysterious and elusive to grasp — and, consequently, not matter-of-fact, straightforward, and clear — he said more than enough that is comparatively easy to grasp and understand for us to learn the most important lesson life has to offer ... if only we will study and assimilate what he said. Our understanding is enhanced by focusing on Jesus' purpose for teaching and the things he said that are reasonably clear and consistent with his purpose. For our interpretation of anything Jesus said to be practical, meaningful, and most of all, accurate, it must be consistent and in agreement with those things Jesus said that are consistent with the essential teachings of the gospel. A primary deterrent to our understanding is false beliefs that are contrary to what Jesus said.

What is the significance of all that stuff about Jesus dying for our sins, Jesus is the answer, Jesus is your friend, trust Jesus, the virgin birth, the blood, the cross, Jesus ascending up into the clouds, and on and on and on, if we do not discover the truth that sets us free? What's the significance of all that stuff if we do not learn to love unconditionally ... if we do not "clean the inside of the cup and the platter," if we do not obliterate the devils from our mind? What is the significance of all that stuff if we do not comprehend the message that Jesus intended for us? if we do not have peace and joy? if we are not happy, satisfied, and contented? In brief, what is the significance of all that stuff if we are not saved, a

Understanding What Jesus Said

prerequisite for enjoying heaven? And remember that we are saved when we believe and comprehend the gospel that Jesus preached.

This reminds me of something that Emmet Fox said in his book, *Power Through Constructive Thinking*: "There is no difficulty that enough love will not conquer; no disease that enough love will not heal. ... If only you could love enough you would be the happiest and most powerful being in the world." Is not this in agreement with the message that Jesus intended for us?

If we fail to discover the truth that sets us free — free from fear and free to love freely and unconditionally — we have missed Jesus' basic message ... we have missed what matters most. We have missed the love, joy, happiness, and peace of mind that is inherent in being unified with God.

Two things that were of tremendous help to me in understanding the teachings of Jesus were a cursory study of the teachings of the Buddha (whose basic message is the same as that of Jesus) and the practice of Transcendental Meditation® (TM), as taught by the Maharishi Mahesh Yogi. By learning the art of meditation, I learned to calm my mind and to block out the chatter that evolves from my false ego-self. I learned to listen to myself and to discern that which is true from that which is false. I learned this while I was writing my first book ... thus, the title of that book, *Listening To Ourselves: The Key To Everything That Matters*.

One of the best ways to understand what Jesus said is to learn to "shut the door" ... to do what Jesus himself did when he went to the Father within ... the same thing as calming our mind and listening to ourselves ... listening to our inner voice. We gain wisdom and understanding from the quiet place within that the Psalmist termed the "secret place of the most high." We gain wisdom and understanding by doing what the Psalmist said to do: "Commune with your own heart" ... the same thing as listening to ourselves.

We must learn to "shut the door" if we are to accomplish what the writer of the Book of Proverbs admonished: "In all thy getting, get wisdom and understanding." The only place to get the wisdom and understanding to know the truth that sets us free is within us. And the only way of accessing this wisdom and understanding is by "shutting the door"... by being still and calming our mind.

If you become still and ponder the teachings of Jesus, you will understand why the 20 selected sayings of Jesus listed in Chapter 3, "The Truth about What Will Save Us," do not include one of the most often quoted Scriptures in the Bible, John 3:16-17: "For God so loved the world that he gave his only begotten Son, that whosoever believeth in him should not perish but have everlasting life. For God sent not his Son into the world to condemn the world, but that the world *through him* might be saved."

The part, "gave his only begotten son," is not something that Jesus would have said. This is not consistent with Jesus' teachings and other biblical teachings. We know from Jesus that he was sent by his Father (God), same thing as the spiritual teachers of the Old Testament being sent by the Lord (God). And, those who "believeth in him" are those who believe the gospel that Jesus preached. And, "through him might be saved" means that sinners could be saved thorough the truth teachings of Jesus ... if only they believe, understand, and embody what Jesus said. Further, the Apostle Paul said, "For as many are led by the Spirit of God, they are the sons of God" (Romans 8:14). Thus, Jesus is not the only son of God.

Actually, often quoted passages of Scriptures, attributed to Jesus, according to red-letter editions of the New Testament, are inauthentic Jesus words, according to the book, *The Five Gospels: What Did Jesus Really Say?* by Robert W. Funk, Roy W. Hoover, and The Jesus Seminar. This includes the passage in John 3:16.

The subject book contains the "Gospel of Thomas," which did not get published in the King James Version of the Bible. Although Thomas was called a doubter because he doubted what other apostles said about the ascension, he was a very devoted apostle. When Jesus said to his disciples, "Let us go into Judaea again," his disciples cautioned him that the Jews might stone him. Thomas said, "Let us also go, that we may die with him."

Regardless of how one might interpret the passage in John 3:16, Jesus told us more than once who sent him. Jesus said, "I seek not mine own will, but the will of the Father who hath sent me" (John 5:30). Jesus also said, "The word which ye hear is not mine, but the Father's which sent me" (John 14:24). And, Jesus said, "Yet a little while am I with you, and then I go unto him that sent

Understanding What Jesus Said

me" (John 7:33). He also said, "He that sent me is with me." "With me" must mean "within me." Remember that Jesus said to his disciples, "For it is not ye that speak, but the Spirit of your Father who speaketh in you" (Matthew 10:20).

God does not make mistakes and God does not fail. If Jesus were God in human flesh — with the infinite wisdom of God — it does not seem logical that he would have failed to get people to believe (to have "ears to hear") the gospel that he preached. Jesus failed to get many people to transcend the deceiving ways of the false ego-self and to hear and believe the gospel that he preached. From observing the conditions of the world in which we live, clearly, many people do not believe and comprehend the gospel of Jesus, and consequently, do not do what Jesus said to do. And, "he that believeth not shall be damned." Jesus knew that many people would not believe the gospel ... that they would be damned.

If heaven and hell exist after death (as fundamentalists seem to believe), it behooves Christian teachers to clarify the teachings of Jesus so that people will believe and be saved. Believing the things that are emphasized in the teachings of Christianity will not save us. And there are no provisions for being saved after we die. Understanding and believing the gospel that Jesus preached — and doing what Jesus said to do — would save us. And, think what a difference it would make with our families, our society, our nation, and us if we were saved *now*. It's incomprehensible!

When we consider how the Bible was put together, it's quite possible that a mistake was made attributing the words in John 3:16 to Jesus. The Apostle John said essentially the same thing in his first Epistle to the Christian community. And he goes on to clarify who sent Jesus, using words consistent with what Jesus used. The Apostle John said: "Ye are of God, little children, and have overcome them [false prophets, false spirits]; because greater is he that is in you, than he that is in the world. They [false prophets, false spirits] are of the world; therefore speak they of the world, and the world heareth them. We are of God; he that knoweth God heareth us; he that is not of God heareth not us. Hereby know we the spirit of truth, and the spirit of error. Beloved, let us love one another; for love is of God; and every one that loveth is born of God, and knoweth God. He that loveth not knoweth not God; for God is love. *In this was manifested the love of God toward us, because that God sent his only begotten Son into the world, that we might live through him.* ... If we love one another, God dwelleth in us, and his love is perfected in us. Hereby know we that we dwell in him, and he in us ... And we have seen and do testify that *the Father sent the Son* to be the Saviour of the world" (1 John 4: 4-14). [Note: The words in italics are attributed to Jesus in John 3:16.]

The phrase, "the Father sent the Son" in the last statement of the above is consistent with what Jesus said: "Father who hath sent me" ... the Father being the true spiritual self. And note the statements in the above, "greater is he that is in you, than he that is in the world ... God dwelleth in us, and his love is perfected in us." "He," as used in the statement, "Greater is he that is in you," alludes to the true spiritual self ... the God that dwelleth in us. This is consistent with something that Jesus said: "I go unto the Father; for my Father is greater than I" (John 14:28). And to "live through him" means to believe and follow the teachings of Jesus. Note also the phrase, "than he that is in the world." The word "world" as used here alludes to the world of the ego. Note also that we (everyone) are the children of God (sons and daughters of God) and everyone that loveth is born of God.

In the sense that Jesus was sent by the "Father," the spiritual teachers of the Old Testament were sent by the Lord ... and for the same purpose. The following are a couple of examples. Isaiah said: "The spirit of the Lord God is upon me, because the Lord hath anointed me to preach good tidings unto the meek. He hath *sent me* to bind up the brokenhearted, to proclaim liberty to the captives and the opening of the prison to them that are bound ... to comfort all that mourn" (Isaiah 61:1-2).

Moses said, "Hereby ye shall know that the *Lord hath sent me* to do all these works, for I have not done them of mine own mind" (Numbers 16:28). This is similar to what Jesus said about doing the will of his Father who sent him. And, Jesus said, "I do nothing of myself; but as my Father hath taught me, I speak these things.

In "The Book of Jeremiah," we find: "Then spake Jeremiah unto all the princes and to all the people, saying, 'The Lord sent me

Understanding What Jesus Said 143

to prophesy against this house and against this city all the words that ye have heard. ... the Lord hath sent me unto you to speak all these words in your ears'" (Jeremiah 26:12-15).

There are those who say that the entire Bible is the inspired word of God and that in order to understand it, we have to be inspired. This begs the question: Where are we to get the inspiration? Besides, where are those who are inspired enough to understand the Bible? Why is there so much misunderstanding? If there are those who understand what Jesus said, why do they not teach it in a manner that others can understand? There are more than 250 denominations, a result of disagreements about the Holy Scriptures.

How could anyone honestly say that the whole Bible is the inspired Word of God when there is much of it they do not understand? When they keep studying, studying, and studying, trying to understand it? How could anyone honestly say that the whole Bible is the inspired Word of God when they really do not understand what Jesus said? And still there are Christians who believe that heaven is a place where Christians go after death. This belief does not come from the Bible. Jesus and the saints of the Old Testament did not teach this.

To believe that we have to understand the whole Bible is contrary to what Jesus taught. He taught that his way is simple ... simply being humble and living in agreement with truth and love. Most of the Bible would be redundant if only we knew the truth that sets us free ... if only we loved as Jesus commanded us to love.

Michel de Montaigne, Essayist, said, "Nothing is so firmly believed as that which we least know." Many religious fundamentalists are close-minded to almost any religious viewpoints that are not from the Bible. They do not think they need anything else ... if only they study enough to understand the inspired word of God that is found in the Bible.

They really do not understand what the inspired Word of God is. *If* we are really in agreement with truth, we are in harmony with God. *If* we are in harmony with God, then every word we utter is the inspired Word of God. How or why would it be otherwise? The inspired Word of God is the truth. The truth, according to Jesus, proceeds from our true spiritual self (what Jesus called the Father).

By using some logic and common sense, we know that every word in the Bible is not the inspired Word of God. We know for example that the God of the Old Testament has been characterized as being angry and vengeful. God is not angry and vengeful and never has been. We know from Jesus' teachings that God is love.

Those people who believe that the Bible is the inspired Word of God and that there is not a word in the Bible that is not divinely inspired by God would do well to read two books by Steve Allen: *Steve Allen on the* Bible, *Religion, & Morality* and *More Steve Allen on the* Bible, *Religion, & Morality.*

In his book, *More Steve Allen on the* Bible, *Religion, & Morality,* the author states: "There is not the slightest question but that the God of the Old Testament is a jealous, vengeful God, inflicting not only on the sinful 'pagans' but even on his CHOSEN PEOPLE fire, lightning, hideous plagues and diseases, brimstone, and other curses. The reader is advised not to waste time consulting scholarly works in the hope of finding a resolution of the contradiction. No such resolution is possible unless reason itself be cast aside."

Ernest Holmes, Founder of Religious Science, said, "The only sin is ignorance. ... All human misery is a result of ignorance; and nothing but knowledge can free us from this ignorance and its effect."

An all-knowing, loving, perfect God created a paradise for us here on Earth. To experience peace and joy we must live in agreement with truth and nature ... the same thing as being in harmony with God ... the same thing as enjoying heaven. And we do not need to know and understand every statement in the Bible to do this. An all-knowing, loving, perfect God did not create us and planet Earth to be so complicated that we have to know the entire Bible in order to live in agreement with truth and nature. Rather than being complicated, living in agreement with truth and nature is so simple, that it is elusive.

We may note that what Isaiah described several hundred years ago coincides with the purpose for Jesus' teachings. Isaiah said, "Seek ye the Lord ... and ye shall go forward with peace and joy." Jesus said, "These things I have spoken unto you that you might have peace." What Isaiah said also coincides with the Apostle

Understanding What Jesus Said

Paul's description of heaven: "For the kingdom of God is not meat and drink, but righteousness, peace, and joy."

What Isaiah said is the object of all our seeking and searching: "Seek ye the Lord." In our language, he was speaking of seeking our true spiritual self. All the books in the world, all the sermons we could ever hear, will not reveal what we are searching for, which is our true self. To discover our true self, we must seek within ourselves. We need not go looking for another book, teacher, guru — not for anything or anyone outside ourselves — but only for our true self. Confucius, Chinese philosopher, said, "What the great man seeks is in himself. What the small man seeks is in others."

Who or what is the Lord (that is near) that Isaiah told us to seek except our true spiritual self? If we study and assimilate what Isaiah and other writers of the Old Testament said, we realize that the "Lord" (as alluded to by the prophet Isaiah) is the same thing as our true, spiritual, sacred self. And when we find our true self and are abiding by that which is true, we "shall go forward with joy and be led forth with peace."

In addition to Isaiah, other spiritual leaders told people to seek the Lord. Note the following:

- And ye shall seek me, and find me, when ye shall search for me with all your heart. And I will be found of you, saith the Lord (Jeremiah 29:13-14).
- But if from thence thou shalt seek the Lord thy God, thou shalt find him, if thou seek him with all thy heart and with all thy soul (Deuteronomy 4:29).
- The Lord searcheth all hearts, and understandeth all the imaginations of the thoughts; if thou seek him, he will be found of thee; but if thou forsake him, he will cast thee off for ever (1 Chronicles 28:9).
- And they that know thy name will put their trust in thee; for thou, Lord, hast not forsaken them that seek thee (Psalms 9:10). [Note: Those who put their trust in thee (the true spiritual self) are happy. This is made clear in Chapter 9, "Wisdom and Understanding."]

The Apostle Paul said, "But the fruit of the Spirit is love, joy, peace" (Galatians 5:22). This coincides with — and helps explain

— something that Jesus said, "... the Spirit of Truth, which proceedeth from the Father" (John 15:26). Thus, the fruit of the Spirit of Truth is peace and joy ... which proceeds from within.

Following are selected gems of wisdom from various spiritual teachers, some who taught before Jesus' ministry and some who taught since his ministry. Regarding some of the most significant things that many spiritual teachers said, they said the same thing ... only the language is different.

- From *The Koran*, the sacred book of the Muslims, we learn, "God changes not what is in a people, until they change what is in themselves." Jesus said, "It is done unto us as we believe." God does for us according to our deeply held beliefs ... whether true or false, good or evil.
- The Seven Sages of Greece said, "Know thyself" ... the equivalent of knowing the truth that sets us free.
- Emerson said, "Nothing can bring you peace but yourself." We have peace when we "clean the inside of the cup and the platter." Who is going to do this for us, except we ourselves?
- The Apostle Paul said, "In my absence, *work out your own salvation.*" When we work out our own salvation, we are saved.
- The Buddha said, "Better than living a hundred years not seeing the highest truth is one day in the life of a man who sees the highest truth."
- Cicero said, "Our minds possess by nature an insatiable desire to know the truth." Jesus said, "You shall know the truth and the truth shall make you free." There is nothing we desire more than to live in harmony with truth and to be free.
- Dr. Ernest Holmes, founder of Religious Science, said, "The inherent nature of man is forever seeking to express itself in terms of freedom. ... a freedom which the soul craves."

In summary, knowing that Jesus preached the gospel that we might have peace and joy, knowing that heaven is within us, and knowing that the truth that sets us free is within us help us understand the message Jesus intended for us. When we understand and embody Jesus' message of love and truth, we enjoy peace and joy ... we enjoy the "peace that passeth all understanding" ... that is heaven ... here and now.

Chapter 6
The Hidden Cause of Suffering

If we are clear about the cause of a problem, often we can focus attention on the cause and find the solution. Otherwise, we can spend considerable time, effort, and energy going around and around in circles, trying to alleviate symptoms without correcting the cause.

If you read this chapter slowly and thoughtfully, you will know beyond a shadow of doubt that obscure, insidious fears and deeply held, false beliefs (the "devil that makes us do it") that elude our conscious awareness are the underlying causes of anxiety, depression, hate, anger, problems in relationships and sex, lack of self-esteem, divorce, dysfunction in families, crime, violence, rape, child abuse, spousal abuse, drug abuse ... any state of being unlike love, joy, happiness, and peace of mind. There is no other cause!

For eons people have associated suffering with Satan. But what is Satan, explained in modern-day language? Satan — the hidden cause of suffering — in today's language, is unwarranted, obscure, insidious fear, combined with deeply rooted, false beliefs that we hold about ourselves. Or, we might think of Satan as being our fearful, false ego-self. Or from the teachings of the Buddha, we might conclude that Satan is the impurities in our mind.

If we accept the premise that Satan is the cause of suffering, then Satan is none other than our false ego-self. All mental suffering (anger, hatred, jealousy, insecurity, fear, envy, evil, anxiety, depression, emotional instability) — all the negative stuff imbedded in our subconscious mind that robs us of love, peace, joy, and happiness — evolves from our false ego-self ... never from our true spiritual self. Thus, the only Satan that troubles us is the one buried in our subconscious mind.

Job, "the greatest of all the men of the East" in biblical times, suffered severely for many years before he discovered the cause of his suffering, which was within him. Job said, "For the thing that I greatly feared is come upon me, and that which I was afraid of is come unto me" (Job 1:3 and 3:25). He gained the wisdom and understanding to help him overcome his suffering within himself ... by understanding the cause of his suffering.

David, the Psalmist, also suffered considerably until he discovered within himself the cause of — and the solution to — his suffering. Bear in mind that this was more than 2,000 years ago before people had the benefit of the contributions to psychology by Freud and others, and consequently, the intellectual knowledge we have today about the source of our suffering and unhappiness. Both David and Job did what few people today will do. The vast majority of people will not be still, pay attention, recognize, and admit that the fault is within them.

Regardless of how much we blame others for our hate, anger, suffering, unhappiness, frustration, discontent (any emotion and behavior that is not in agreement with truth), the cause is within us. The cause of all mental suffering, all unhappiness, and all psychosomatic illnesses is hidden from us in our subconscious mind.

All mental suffering, restlessness, discontent, and dissatisfaction are resolved in our mind by understanding. Thus, both the cause and the solution are in our mind. The hidden cause is insidious fears and deeply rooted, false beliefs, and the solution is knowing the truth that sets us free.

Being clear about this — and not making an exception for our unhappiness — can help us avoid what we are prone to do, which is blaming something or someone other than ourselves for our suffering and discontent. Also, when we are unhappy, restless, frustrated and discontented, we are prone to take off on a tangent, trying first one thing and then another, trying to find something or someone outside ourselves to bring us happiness and peace of mind. People are prone to seek and search for something or someone outside themselves that will bring them love, luck, fortune, happiness, and peace of mind. This is the explanation for the booming business of psychics, astrologers and psychiatrists.

The only change that will bring us joy, happiness, and peace of mind is the change we make within ourselves. Thus, we need not focus on changing others or changing society but on changing the way we believe and think in our heart.

The Hidden Cause of Suffering 149

Some people try to overcome fear by doing the thing they fear. This technique is helpful in some situations (flying, speaking before groups), but this is not the ultimate answer for being free of fear. Doing the thing you fear to overcome the fear does not work in regard to the things that matter most. We simply cannot love freely with a mind confused with fear and false beliefs. We simply cannot communicate openly, freely, and honestly — the type of communication necessary for loving, lasting relationships — with a mind plagued with fear and false beliefs. There is no way to do the thing you fear to overcome the fear that is the hidden cause of psychosomatic illnesses.

Fears vanish when we recognize and understand them. We understand them by paying attention to insights about them. When fears are obliterated, we quite naturally move in the direction of health, happiness, joy, and peace of mind.

Jesus said, "Hearken unto me every one of you, and understand: There is nothing from without a man, that entering into him can defile him; but the things that come out of him, those are they that defile the man. ... If any man have ears to hear, let him hear" (Mark 4:23). Thus, what corrupts us is within us.

To "defile" is to corrupt the purity or perfection of; to make filthy, to make dirty, to render impure. God created us pure and perfect. Our purity and perfection are corrupted by the evil in our heart. It's the evil within us that renders impure that which by God's creation is pure.

What Jesus said about 2,000 years ago has been confirmed by Freud and others. The cause of all negative, destructive behavior, all mental suffering, all psychological problems is buried in the subconscious mind. What it boils down to is, "As a man thinketh in his heart, so is he ... It is done unto us as we believe ... The truth will set us free." It's all within us ... the source of our love, joy, and happiness and the source of our suffering and unhappiness. Jesus said, "According to your faith be it unto you" (Matthew 9:29). "Faith" is unquestioned belief.

Jesus also said, "Are you so without understanding also? Do you not perceive that whatsoever thing from without entereth into the man, it cannot defile him, because it entereth not into his heart?

... For from within, out of the heart of men, proceed evil thoughts, adulteries, fornication, murders, thefts, covetousness, wickedness, deceit, lasciviousness, an evil eye, blasphemy, pride, foolishness. All these evil things come from within, and defile the man."

Signs and symptoms of "all these evil things" are everywhere. Fear and ignorance are the cause of evil. Truth obliterates fear and ignorance, and consequently, evil.

Violence, which is evil, is rampant in our society. Violence is triggered by anger. Fear and ignorance trigger anger. Anger is so prevalent that we tend to think that it is natural and normal; it is not. People do not make us angry. When we have repressed anger, we're already angry ... we just do not express it all the time. Triggering our anger is not the same thing as causing our anger. The same hidden cause of anger is the same hidden cause of all that disturbs our peace of mind and happiness. The hidden cause is fear.

What we usually do is to blame something or someone outside ourselves for our hate, anger, jealousy, possessiveness, envy, hostility — all that stuff that causes pain and suffering — when all the while the cause is buried in our subconscious mind.

It's not what others believe and say about us that hurts us; it's what we believe about ourselves. For eons people have believed in such things as evil spirits and a Satan out there someplace (something outside ourselves) that defile us and that cause suffering ... and will cause suffering after we die. Jesus did not teach this. Instead, he taught about the evil in our heart being the cause of "all these evil things."

We were not born with evil in our heart. Evil is a product of fear. The evil in our heart is something we have acquired, something that we have fabricated in our subconscious mind. And for the most part we begin fabricating this during early childhood, because of faulty parenting ... because of parents who were not in agreement with truth.

Can you imagine? Can you comprehend what our families and our society would be like if parents lived in agreement with truth and, consequently, children were reared in an atmosphere of truth, love, happiness, and harmony? Think about it ... families and society that are characterized by love, happiness, harmony, and

The Hidden Cause of Suffering

peace ... a society in which we quite naturally do unto others as we would have others do unto us ... a society in which we love one another as Jesus told us to love.

What Jesus said about what corrupts us is consistent with what Buddha said about 500 years BC. During the course of his teaching, Buddha had a lot to say about suffering. The Buddha spoke of the impurities in our mind. David, the Psalmist, spoke of cleansing himself of secret faults. Other words having the same or similar meaning include devils, demons, unclean spirits ... all fabricated out of obscure, insidious, unwarranted fears and deeply rooted, false beliefs ... and all having a bearing on the way we think and believe in our heart. All unwarranted subconscious fears and deeply held, false beliefs are negative and destructive; they cause suffering in one manner or another.

We could study all the teachings of the great religious teachers, we could study the Bible from cover to cover, we could study the writings of Freud, and on and on and on, and what it all boils down to is what Jesus told us about 2,000 years ago, "All these evil things come from within, and defile the man."

Fear is the hidden culprit underlying "all these evil things." It's the cause of all mental suffering, from the mild impatience one experiences when the elevator is too slow to the most serious of psychological disorders. Subconscious, unwarranted fear is related to anxiety, anger, hate, depression, jealousy, envy, pride, selfishness, shyness, the ego's desire for attention and recognition, and the need to appear special and important—all that robs us of love, joy, happiness, peace, and inner serenity. Fear catapults us into a state of inner turmoil ... into hell.

In biblical times, there were comparatively few words and phrases describing psychological problems and mental suffering. The words that just about cover it all are devils, demons, Satan, lunatics, and unclean spirits.

Today we have many words pertaining to mental suffering and unhappiness. And we have words that cover a host of mental problems. For example, the word "neurotic" includes disturbed, disoriented, troubled, unstable, irrational, deranged, erratic, and aberrant. "Aberration" is defined as "partial mental derangement."

In addition to the cover-all words, we have many words for specific conditions; e.g., schizophrenia, psychosis, kleptomania, multiple personalities, phobias, addictions, and on and on and on. We do not have to be any great psychiatrist, psychologist, or religious teacher to know that these conditions are not natural and normal. A common-sense question about any of these abnormal conditions is—is it natural and normal? And the answer is a simple "no." A common-sense definition of natural and normal is that which is in agreement with truth and nature.

There are many mental problems of which many people have never heard. Munchausen by proxy (MBP) is becoming more commonly known than heretofore. I mention this terrible mental abnormality because it demonstrates the manner in which deeply held, false beliefs and obscure, insidious fears can manifest in a myriad of ways and how one's secret faults can be hidden by a carefully designed facade.

The person afflicted with MBP (usually a mother) feigns affection, tenderness, love, and caring. And often the troubled mother spends many hours and nights at hospitals with her children, hovering over them and seemingly very concerned about the child's health and well being. All the while, it's all a sham. The illness has been induced intentionally by the mother.

Many of those who have the illness have perfected such a loving, caring, protective facade that they can fool many people. Many doctors and nurses have innocently been drawn into a form of child abuse. In one case that recently made news, a child underwent many surgeries, some of which involved the removal of parts of the digestive system. It's tragic the suffering that a child endures when under the care of a mother plagued with Munchausen by proxy ... and under the guise of being a very loving, caring, and protective mother.

Although the cause of Munchausen by proxy is not clear, it is safe to say that those who are troubled with it did not receive adequate love as a child; they crave love, acceptance, and approval. Basically they are lonely and empty inside.

All that is bad flows from our fearful, false ego-self. All that is good flows from our true perfect self ... the part of us that is

The Hidden Cause of Suffering

perfect, created in the image and likeness of God. The author of Ecclesiastes said, "Lo, this only have I found, that God hath made man upright; but they have sought out many inventions."

We would be happy, satisfied, and contented if only we would understand and believe the message that Jesus intended for us ... if only we would "clean the inside of the cup and the platter" ... if only we would obliterate the devils in our mind (the hidden cause of our suffering) and overcome our false ego-self and let things be the way they are supposed to be, which is in agreement with truth and nature.

Thus, whether from religion, psychology, or whatever source, it seems clear that all our mental turmoil, emotional suffering, and unhappiness is caused by something within us. From a religious viewpoint, we can think of that something within us that causes our suffering as being Satan. And, consequently, in studying the Bible, it helps to understand that Satan is obscure, insidious fears and deeply rooted, false beliefs that are hidden from our conscious awareness.

Fear keeps us alienated from our true, spiritual, perfect self ... the self of us that is created in the image and likeness of God. Unwarranted fear keeps us alienated from God, and a separation from God is hell. Fear keeps many people trapped in their *miserable* comfort zone.

Fear leads us into all sorts of erratic behavior and actions that bring suffering in some form. It leads some people into pursuing wealth, fame, and power, which has an impact of keeping people alienated from their true self ... alienated from God. Fear causes some people to feel emotionally insecure, anxious, depressed, envious, jealous, possessive, and angry ... a troubled state of mind, which is hell. Fear is the underlying motivation that leads some people into promiscuous sex, perverted sex, kinky sex ... sex that is not natural and normal.

Fear is the underlying, hidden cause of all suffering evolving from the dreaded psychosomatic illnesses ... illnesses that are caused by the mind and that account for about 90 percent of the visits to doctors.

Fear is the underlying influence that is the cause of addictions, which take many forms: gambling, drugs, smoking, alcohol, sexual, excessive eating, and on and on and on.

Thus, fear is the hidden cause of all mental suffering, all restlessness, discontent, dissatisfaction, and unhappiness. Fear is the cause of any state of mind unlike love, joy, happiness, peace of mind, and inner serenity ... anything unlike heaven. Fear keeps us alienated from truth ... alienated from God ... and that is hell.

Before scoffing at this idea, thinking that you have no fear, think again. A deceiving trait of the ego is denial ... to deny that we are wrong ... to deny that the fault is in us ... to deny that we are afraid. Our false ego-self has us thinking that it is more honorable and acceptable to express our anger than it is to let people know that we are afraid.

Mahatma Gandhi said, "The only devils in the world are those running around in our own hearts. That is where the battle must be fought." The "only devils in the world" are our obscure, insidious fears and deeply held false beliefs.

These obscure fears and false beliefs stir up anger, hate, revenge, resentment, jealousy, possessiveness, greed, selfishness ... anything contrary to truth ... anything contrary to that which is loving, joyous, and satisfying.

If we, individually and as a society, were in agreement with truth — in agreement with our true nature — we would be very similar in our behavior. Our behavior would be predictable. We would be loving, happy, honest, truthful, peaceful, and helpful ... without masks, hiding the way we believe and think in our heart.

In spirit and in truth, nature created us quite similar; however, the traits we have acquired (both the good and the evil) render us quite dissimilar. Insidious, unwarranted fears and deeply rooted false beliefs manifest in a myriad of unpredictable and negative, destructive ways. With so much anger, hate, jealousy, and neurotic behavior in our society — with almost everyone masking the way they believe in their heart — behavior is unpredictable. Let's face it! We never know what to expect, except perhaps to expect the unexpected.

The Hidden Cause of Suffering

There is a high degree of probability that those we meet are suspicious, pretentious, and distrustful—wearing their mask, pretending to be other than the way they really believe and think in their heart. And let us be honest and face the facts. There is a high degree of probability that we are wearing a mask, pretending to be different from the way we believe and think in our heart.

Typically, we go through life unaware of the masks we wear ... unaware of how pretentious and dishonest we really are ... unaware of what it is like to simply express life in agreement with truth and nature ... unaware of the genuine peace and joy we are missing ... we have no basis for comparison.

We have no inkling of the type of life — the type of society — we would enjoy if only we understood the teachings of Jesus. We have no inkling of what life and society would be like, knowing that those we encounter in everyday life are loving, helpful, supportive, peaceful, and contented ... the kind of life — the kind of world — Jesus wanted for us ... the kind of life in which truth is the way.

Think of what a difference it would have made if religious teachers had been teaching (for about 2,000 years) the message Jesus intended for us. Think of what our society would be like if we truly did what Jesus said to do: "As ye would that men should do to you, do ye also to them likewise." Think of the significance of this one statement by Jesus.

Think of what a difference it would make if we treated others the way they would like to be treated and if we knew that others would treat us the way we would like to be treated. Think of the love, joy, and peace that would prevail. Think of how different our judicial system would be ... how many laws that would never have been enacted ... how many lawsuits that would never have been filed ... how many prisons that would never have been built ... how many psychosomatic illnesses that would not exist ... think of the families that would be loving, happy, harmonious, functional, stable ... and on and on and on ... if only we understood, believed and embodied the gospel that Jesus preached.

Think about it! All the following conditions are because people are out of harmony with truth, and this is only a partial list: psychosomatic illnesses, anxiety, depression, problems in relationships, problems in sex (and there are a myriad of abnormal sexual deviations), a myriad of emotional and mental problems, jealousy, emotional insecurity, anger, hate, child abuse, child molestation, spousal abuse, murder, rape, crime, violence, dysfunctional families, an alarming divorce rate, an alarming rate of suicides, cults, Satan worshippers, shootings in the schools, the homeless, the hopeless, crookedness in politics and government, selfishness, greed, militia groups ... and on and on and on ... and all because we are out of harmony with truth ... out of harmony with God.

To correct the cause of our suffering, it helps to know what and where the cause is and how it originated. The last thing any one of us wants is to have someone tell us that the fault is within us. Very simply, the cause of our suffering and discontent is within us, and the solution to our suffering and discontent is within us.

In all simplicity, the cause of our suffering and unhappiness is obscure, insidious fears and deeply held, false beliefs that were ingrained during infancy and childhood because of a lack of adequate love. False beliefs that become ingrained in the subconscious mind are kept intact and reinforced by fear and repetition. A child who does not get adequate love becomes fearful and angry ... infantile ways of trying to get love and to get his or her physical and emotional needs met.

Many angry, jealous, insecure, disturbed adults have not outgrown their infant ways of trying to get love; only the details are different. Much of what many unhappy people are doing that is negative, obnoxious, offensive, destructive, and that causes suffering is a cry for love.

Once you master the art of calming your mind and listening to yourself, you will become aware of the falseness of your deeply held false beliefs. Then you will understand clearly (more clearly than you can ever learn from all the reading and studying you can ever do or listening to all the lectures and sermons you can possibly ever hear) that "it is done unto you as you believe."

According to Webster, a belief is, "anything believed or accepted as true." Thus, those things that we believe or accept as true are our beliefs ... whether they are true or false. And you can be assured that they are false if you find yourself experiencing anxiety,

The Hidden Cause of Suffering

depression, hate, anger, jealousy, self-pity, irritation, frustration, restlessness, discontentment, emotional insecurity, a lack of self-esteem—any state of mind unlike love, joy, happiness, inner serenity, and peace of mind.

What are the false beliefs that cause us suffering? First let's take a look at what they are not. The false beliefs that cause us suffering are not the beliefs we have been taught verbally by others. False beliefs about such things as God, heaven, hell, Satan, and false beliefs about Jesus' teachings are not the hidden cause of our suffering. All false beliefs are a detriment in some form or another. Although false religious beliefs are not the cause of our suffering, they impede us from discovering the truth that sets us free from the false beliefs that are the hidden cause of our suffering ... the false beliefs that rob us of joy, peace of mind and contentment.

For the most part, the false beliefs that cause us suffering and unhappiness are those subconscious beliefs we hold about ourselves that are contrary to our true perfect self ... beliefs about ourselves that are not in agreement with truth and nature.

The false beliefs that wreak havoc with our overall well-being bear on such things as we are not worthy, we are not adequate, we are not okay, we are not acceptable, we do not measure up, we are not lovable, we are bad, we are no good, we are not good enough ... beliefs that render us feeling unworthy ... beliefs that rob us of self-esteem. False beliefs that bring us suffering are tainted with beliefs that we are flawed, inferior, that we are not okay the way we are ... that we are not perfect the way God created us. Ultimately, when we are out of harmony with truth, we believe that we are imperfect ... we feel like a reject. God did not create anything that is imperfect ... anything that is out of harmony with truth and nature. God did not create us with unwarranted fears, false beliefs, evil, anger, and hatred in our heart.

These types of false beliefs will have us thinking that we are failures, that we will fail, that we cannot do this, or we cannot do that, and on and on and on.

False beliefs that we hold about ourselves — beliefs that are contrary to truth — are the root cause of mental suffering and unhappiness. They rob us of the freedom to enjoy life to its fullest

... from enjoying the abundant life that Jesus wanted us to enjoy ... from enjoying heaven here and now. Remember that Jesus said, "It is done unto us as we believe."

All the evil things that come from within us that defiles us — that renders us impure and that corrupts us and causes us suffering — evolve from obscure, insidious fears and deeply rooted, false beliefs that we hold about ourselves.

If we suffer from low self-esteem, if we are emotionally insecure and are seeking approval from others, we can become troubled simply by the expression on another's face. Sensing what we sense that others might be sensing about us can enrage us. We can become embarrassed, angry, and defensive because we are sensitive and subconsciously believe that we are inferior ... because we are out of harmony with truth ... because we do not genuinely know, love, and accept ourselves. Our anger and defensiveness are false ways of demonstrating that we are *somebody* ... trying to convince others of something we do not honestly feel about ourselves.

And we can create an impenetrable facade and become defensive — we can cast ourselves into hell — simply because of our obscure, false beliefs about ourselves and the fact that we do not know, love, and accept ourselves. All the while our true self is perfect ... if only we would obliterate our false beliefs and live in agreement with our true, perfect self ... deep inside the soul of us what every one of us desires to do.

A trick that our false ego-self plays on us is that it has us creating facades to protect us from hurt. In effect, these facades keep us alienated from ourselves and alienated from others, and they block us from loving and being loved ... what we all want. Actually, in its deceitful way of protecting us from hurt, our false ego-self creates hell for us ... mental turmoil ... the gnashing of teeth. If we lash out in anger at others, it's our false ego's way of trying to demonstrate that we are right, although deep inside, we believe something about ourselves that is false.

We cannot enjoy closeness with others while keeping our facades intact. Instead of closeness, we suffer from loneliness, isolation, and separation from ourselves ... and separation from God, which is hell.

The Hidden Cause of Suffering

God did not create anything that is not perfect and that does not have a purpose ... this includes everyone ... regardless of race, creed, or color. God is love and God is perfect. Our true spiritual self is perfect, created in the image and likeness of God. Why would a perfect, all-knowing God create anything that is not perfect? It's only our ignorance and our false ego-self that make it seem that there is something inherently bad about human nature.

It is not what others do, say, and think that makes us angry and unhappy. Others do not cause our anger and mental suffering. It is what we subconsciously think and believe about ourselves. What we sense and what we perceive that causes mental confusion and turmoil is something that is contrary to truth. Thus, anytime we are in a negative state of mind — a state of mind that is contrary to peace, joy, and happiness — subconsciously, we are entertaining fearful, false thoughts.

What makes us upset and angry — in a state of mental turmoil, confusion, and indecision — is when something or someone reminds us subconsciously of the false beliefs we hold about ourselves, and this reminder triggers our feelings of being inferior ... of being flawed. Our typical reaction is to go on the defensive. Defensiveness is a false way of attempting to prove that we are right and that we are okay ... although deep inside, we are troubled.

When we become hateful, resentful, and angry, consciously we do not realize what has happened. Our reaction is a false way of our ego to protect us from hurt. However, pitifully and painfully, invariably our reaction causes more hurt. When we become defensive, angry, and upset ... we experience "gnashing of teeth" ... we experience suffering ... we experience hell.

Actually, when someone says something that makes us angry — something that causes us mental suffering — they remind us subconsciously of who we are. They remind us subconsciously of old memories from the past. If we become angry, we are a person with repressed anger ... "As a man thinketh in his heart, so is he."

We become defensive, because we do not like who we are. We do not like the way we believe and think in our heart ... we do not like living a lie. David, the Psalmist, said, "I hate every false way." Everyone hates every false way ... the false ways of the ego.

If we are living in agreement with truth, in agreement with our spiritual self — if we love and accept ourselves (a prerequisite for loving others) — then what others do or say does not throw us into a tailspin of defensiveness, anger, revenge and jealousy ... nothing negative, detrimental, and destructive. We simply remain at peace with the universe and ourselves. We do not hate others for what they say or do. Our hatred is within us, and it is caused by something within us; it is caused by our obscure fears and false beliefs.

The Apostle John said, "There is no fear in love; but perfect love castest out fear; because fear hath torment. He that feareth is not made perfect in love" (1 John 4:18). Note that "fear hath torment." A fearful, tormented mind is hell.

We free ourselves from Satan by discovering the truth that sets us free ... by casting the devils from our heart. When we discover the truth that sets us free, we can say with honesty, humility and understanding, "Get thee behind me, Satan; thou art an offense unto me; for thou savourest not the things that be of God, but those that be of men [the false ego-self]" (Matthew 16:23).

James said, "Resist the devil, and he will flee from you" (James 4:7). Where is the Satan (the devil) that gets behind us and that flees from us, except within us? When we cast the devils from our heart — when we "clean the inside of the cup and the platter" — Satan is "behind us;" then we are peaceful, joyous, happy and contented ... the purpose for Jesus preaching the gospel.

In summary, fear underlies all our mental suffering and unhappiness. Fearful, false, negative thoughts create our suffering. Our negative thoughts are formulated by our perception. Our perception is determined by what is programmed into our subconscious mind ... the way "we believe and think in our heart."

Thus, it's all within us ... our suffering and the cause of our suffering. Fortunately for us, the solution is within us. Would not it be tragic if we had to rely on others to make us happy and to free us from our suffering? Being clear about this simplifies everything. It helps us to know where we must focus our attention to discover the truth that sets us free ... free from obscure, insidious fear — free from Satan — and free to be peaceful, joyous, happy, satisfied and contented.

Chapter 7
Why Christians Leave Christianity

Christianity is the dominant religion in America; however, some Christians leave Christianity for alternative religions, for cults, for new thought groups, and some join various study groups. Some Christians leave mainline Christian churches for churches that are Christian, yet the teachings are quite different from mainline Christian churches; for example: Religious Science, Unity, Mormonism and Christian Science. Some Christians are attracted to the teachings of the Buddha. Why is this so? What did Buddha teach?

It's ironic that Christians leave Christianity for Buddhism in an effort to get the basic message that Jesus intended for us. The Buddha — like the saints of the Old Testament — taught the essentials of the gospel that Jesus preached. Although using different words and phrases — and a different manner of teaching — the Buddha taught people what will save them from their suffering ... taught them how to have peace and joy.

The following comment appears on the back cover of *Buddhism In America,* by Emma McCloy Layman: "... it was not until the sixties that Buddhism began to attract substantial numbers of adherents from the non-Oriental population of America. Since about 1965 its growth has been rapid, and in the middle seventies it shows no signs of abating."

In the book, the author states: "Actually, most Americans who leave Judaism or Christianity to become Buddhists do so not because of their preference for the beliefs of Buddhism over those of Judaism or Christianity, but either because the Judaeo-Christian establishment in its institutionalized form has failed to meet their personal needs and what they perceive to be the needs of society, or because the practices in the church seem cold, sterile, and lacking in dynamism. ... Many young people who turn from Christianity to embrace Buddhism do so because, in their idealism, they see the Christian Church as having failed to cure the ills of society. They perceive church members as hypocrites who mouth acceptance of the Ten Commandments and then break them with regularity."

Not only are there striking similarities in the teachings of Jesus and the Buddha, but also there is some similarity in the history of their lives. For clarification, "Buddha" is not the name of a person. The word Buddha, meaning "enlightened one," was an epithet applied to Siddhartha Gautama, the founder of the religion that came to be known as Buddhism. Similarly, "Christ" became associated with Jesus of Nazareth.

Siddhartha Gautama was born into a wealthy family, and his birth attracted special attention. There was a celebration surrounding his birth. A wise old sage cried when he visited the family a few days after the birth of Siddhartha. He recognized him as being special and someone who would be a great teacher and spread his teachings in all the world, trying to eradicate suffering. The wise old sage was sad because he would not be present to witness the great works of such a great teacher.

This wise old sage was correct in his prophecy. When Siddhartha Gautama reached enlightenment at about age 35, he realized he had discovered something that would free people from suffering, and he spent the remainder of his life (about 45 years) teaching people the Four Noble Truths and the Eight-fold Path to enlightenment ... a path to a liberation from suffering ... a path to truth, love, and freedom.

Buddha taught his followers to refrain from killing, stealing, committing adultery, being deceitful, cursing, lying, boasting, coveting, insulting, flattering, and becoming angry or vengeful ... quite similar to the Ten Commandments taught by Moses and that are taught in Christianity.

In the book, *What The Buddha Taught,* by Walpola Rahula, we find that Buddha said: "Let not one deceive another nor despise any person whatever in any place. In anger or ill will let not one wish any harm to another. ... Let one's thoughts of boundless love pervade the whole world — above, below, and across — without any obstruction, without any hatred, without any enmity. ... Just as a mother would protect her only child even at the risk of her own life, even so let one cultivate a boundless heart towards all beings

... Not to do any evil, to cultivate good, to purify one's mind, this is the Teaching of the Buddhas."

The "Teaching of the Buddhas" is in agreement with the teaching of Jesus. Note the comment above about "boundless love." This alludes to loving like Jesus commanded us to love, "with all our heart, soul, and mind." And note the part "to purify one's mind" ... the same thing as "cleaning the inside of the cup and the platter." When we purify our mind, we are transformed; we are saved ... like "being born again."

The Buddha said, "Therefore, seek the life that is of the mind. Where self is, truth cannot be; yet when truth comes, self will disappear. Therefore, let your mind rest in truth.... In the truth you shall live forever. Self is death and truth is life. The cleaving to self is a perpetual dying, while moving in the truth is partaking of Nirvana which is life everlasting.... The truth remains hidden from him who is in the bondage of hate and desire. Nirvana remains incomprehensible to the vulgar whose minds are beclouded with worldly interests.... Let us guard our thought that we do no evil, for as we sow so shall we reap.... The man who walks in the noble path lives in the world, and yet his heart is not defiled by worldly desires.... The craving of selfishness is destroyed, and the truth is attained. This is true deliverance; this is salvation; this is heaven and the bliss of a life immortal." (*Sayings of Buddha*," by The Peter Pauper Press).

Note the similarity with what Jesus taught. "Seeking the life that is of the mind" is the same thing as seeking the guidance of the Father, the guidance of the true spiritual self. And, note the clause, "where the self is, truth cannot be." We are either abiding by that which is true or that which is false; it's one or the other. And note that "the man who walks in the noble path lives in the world, and yet his heart is not defiled by worldly desires." Jesus and his disciples had overcome the sinful world of the ego. Speaking of his disciples, Jesus said, "They are not of the world, even as I am not of the world."

Also note the use of the phrases by the Buddha, "In the truth you shall live forever" and "Nirvana which is life everlasting." Both Jesus and the Buddha spoke in terms of eternal life and life everlasting, meaning to be fully alive in spirit of truth while we are alive on Planet Earth, rather than being spiritually dead ... rather than suffering. Similarly, when the spiritual teachers of the Old Testament spoke in terms such as, "that they mayest live," they were speaking about being alive in the spirit of truth.

A book published in 1997, titled *Jesus And Buddha — The Parallel Sayings,* edited by Marcus Borg with Introduction by Jack Kornfield, addresses the similarities between the teachings of Jesus and the Buddha. The author states, "Whether speaking of love, material wealth, temptation or salvation, they were two masters with one message. ... They taught that what is inside a person matters, not his or her outward appearance."

Jack Kornfield states in the introduction: "If we could read, listen to, take to heart and enact even one verse from these teachings, it would have the power to illuminate our hearts, free us from confusion and transform our lives."

Can you imagine? Can you comprehend? What our lives, our families, and our society would be like if we could read, understand, take to heart and enact the gospel that Jesus preached!

And notice what both the Buddha and Jesus taught: "What is inside a person matters, not his or her outward appearance." This is supported by Jesus' statement, "Clean first that which is within the cup and platter, that the outside of them may be clean also," and the passage about the rich man and Lazarus.

The Apostle Paul said, "Be ye transformed by the renewing of your mind." There is no better way to renew our minds, no better way to purify our mind, no better way of "cleaning the inside of the cup and the platter," no better way of ridding ourselves of the impurities in our mind (the same thing as casting out devils), than to discover the truth that sets us free.

In its simplest form, Buddha's parable about the piece of cloth is that if we soak a piece of soiled and dirty cloth in a dye (of pink, yellow, red, or blue color), it will have a dirty color. If we soak a piece of clean cloth in a dye (of pink, yellow, red, or blue color), it will have a clean color.

Similarly, if our mind is contaminated with impurities, then we can expect a troubled future; we can expect suffering, loneliness, anger, hate, jealousy, rage, isolation, alienation, and an emptiness that nothing outside ourselves can fill. In brief, we can expect hell, which is a confused, troubled state of mind.

If our mind is pure — free of impurities — then we can expect a happy future, free from mental turmoil and suffering. We can expect love, joy, happiness, peace of mind, and inner serenity. We know from the teachings of Jesus that a pure heart is a prerequisite for enjoying heaven.

Where is our hate, anger, jealousy, resentment, guilt, the ego desire to appear important — all that negative stuff that robs us of peace and joy — except within our mind? Where is the truth that sets us free from all that negative stuff that robs us of peace and joy, except within our mind? If we obliterate the impurities in our mind — if we "clean the inside of the cup and the platter" — we have a pure heart ... all in agreement with what the Buddha and Jesus taught.

When we obliterate the impurities from our mind, we experience the present moment, not tormented by anxiety about tomorrow, or unwarranted fears, guilt, and deeply held false beliefs from the past. Instead, we experience peace and joy. We experience mental confusion, turmoil, and suffering when we are harboring impurities in our subconscious mind; impurities are contrary to truth.

Buddha's first step of the Eightfold Path is right understanding, a prerequisite for mastering the remaining seven steps, which lead to enlightenment ... the same state of mind characteristic of heaven ... a state of mind in agreement with truth.

Buddha's primary aim was to help people overcome suffering. Supposedly, if one studies the Four Noble Truths and follows the Eight-fold path diligently, then he or she will reach a state of enlightenment called Nirvana, which is defined as a condition of great peace or bliss. This is the way the Apostle Paul described heaven, "peace, joy, and righteousness."

If one reaches the state of enlightenment called Nirvana — the condition of great peace and bliss — then he or she knows the truth that sets him or her free. In other words, if we discover the truth that sets us free, we have reached the state of enlightenment ... the state of Nirvana, which is a state of mind of peace and bliss. Both

Jesus and Buddha taught that we might have peace in the present moment ... not after we die.

Suffering is so prevalent that we seem to think that it is inherent in human life ... somewhat similar to the erroneous beliefs of some people that human nature is inherently sinful. Perhaps suffering only seems inherent in human life because there is so much of it. Suffering is not programmed into us by God. Suffering arises from fear and ignorance, something we learn that is not in agreement with our true nature.

An all-knowing, perfect God did not create human nature that is sinful and inherently plagued with suffering. We have the power of choice. Out of ignorance (being in the thrall of the false ego-self), we have chosen suffering ... led astray, trying to find fulfillment by doing and saying things that seem to make us appear special and important.

Jesus' ministry was about 500 years after the teachings of the Buddha. Jesus preached the gospel of the kingdom of God. He said, "It is done unto us as we believe." He also said, "Repent, for the kingdom of Heaven is at hand" ... meaning peace and joy ... here and now. If there is a shortcoming in the teachings of Jesus, it is not what he said but what he did not say ... or at least make clear for the masses. He did not tell us — or at least make clear — how to discover the truth that sets us free, how to clean the inside of the cup and the platter, and how to be as perfect as he told us to be.

This is at least a part of the explanation of why some Christians leave Christianity. They want to learn how to do some of the things that orthodox Christian teachers are not teaching. Our most basic goal is to discover the truth that sets us free from our suffering, and consequently, sets us free to be in harmony with truth, God, and nature.

Thought precedes feelings and actions. We think, we feel, and we act. Thoughts are formulated by our perceptions. Our perceptions are formulated by what is programmed into our subconscious mind ... by the way we believe and think in our heart. When we obliterate the aberrations in our mind (the hidden cause of suffering), then the way we think in our heart is in agreement with truth.

There is a deep-down longing of the people in our hustle-bustle, troubled society (a society wreaked with crime, violence, stress, anxiety, suffering, restlessness, and discontent) to return to a life that is in agreement with truth and nature.

Often we attempt to fill the void in our lives by seeking all sorts of attractions ... all sorts of things to see and to do. Attractions become distractions. Temporarily, attractions distract us from our loneliness and isolation; however, they also distract us from discovering what we are seeking, which is our true self. We end up running from ourselves ... and regardless of how fast or how long we run, we do not run away from the longing to return to our true self ... we do not escape the longing to harmonize with God.

If only we understood and embodied the basic teachings of either Jesus or the Buddha, we would experience what every one in his or her own way is seeking, which is to live in agreement with truth and nature ... which is to discover our true self ... which is to discover the "peace that passeth all understanding" ... which is the same thing as being in harmony with God and nature.

In essence, the basic message of both Jesus and Buddha is truth, love, and peace, which is the solution to all mental and emotional suffering. Truth will bring us love, joy, happiness, peace of mind, and inner serenity ... the things that matter most in life, and they are free.

In his book, *"The Varieties of Religious Experience,"* William James, speaking about Buddhism and Christianity, said: "They are essentially religions of deliverance: the man must die to an unreal life before he can be born into the real life. ... There are two lives, the natural and the spiritual, and we must lose the one before we can participate in the other."

This must mean the same thing that Jesus said, "Except a man be born again, he cannot see the kingdom of God" (John 3:3).

It's incomprehensible to think of how much time, energy, effort, and money are directed toward our outer appearance, including the plastic smiles (the masks we wear to hide the inner pain), pretending to be righteous and happy ... regardless of how frustrated and wretched we feel inside. Think of all the time, money, and effort that go toward impressing others, trying to appear special and important, trying to "keep up with the Jones" ... and all because we are out of harmony with truth, God and nature! Think of all the things we own or do that we can gloat over: things that are bigger, better, faster; things that are more refined, more exquisite, more outrageous than those of others ... and on and on and on. All the while, what matters most in life is the way we believe and think in our heart ... what matters most is being in harmony with truth, God and nature.

It's incomprehensible how much time, energy, and effort that people devote to seeking and searching, trying to find something to add meaning to their lives ... trying to find something that will bring them love, joy, happiness, peace of mind, and inner serenity ... trying to find something that will make them satisfied and contented ... thus, a part of the explanation of Christians leaving Christianity for Buddhism.

Jesus told us everything we need to know to be happy, satisfied, and contented ... if only we believed and comprehended what he said. A pure heart is a prerequisite for enjoying heaven. Purifying our heart is the essence of the teachings of both Jesus and the Buddha.

Fundamentalist ministers often use the word "eternity" in their sermons. And it is used in the context of "Where will you spend eternity after you die, in heaven or in hell?" Some ministers can be very compelling and dramatic in their preaching. It is nothing less than amazing how dramatic and compelling some ministers can be. Just imagine the impact on us, our families, our society — the very world itself — if ministers could be as enthusiastic and convincing about the gospel that Jesus preached as they are about their own beliefs ... some that are false and misleading. Jesus did not use the word "eternity" in his teaching. The word "eternity" is not in the New Testament. It appears only one time in the Old Testament (in "The Book of Isaiah") ... and not used in the manner that fundamentalists use it.

Note what Jesus said to a lawyer who asked him a question: "And, behold, a certain lawyer stood up and tempted him, saying, 'Master, what shall I do to inherit *eternal life?*'" Jesus said unto him, 'What is written in the law? How readest thou?' And the lawyer answering said, 'Thou shalt love the Lord thy God with all thy heart, and with all thy soul, and with all thy strength, and with all thy mind; and thy neighbour as thyself.' And Jesus said unto him, 'Thou hast answered right; this do, and *thou shalt live.*'" The lawyer was already alive; thus, in the language of that time, Jesus was equating *eternal life* to being fully alive and fully living ... while alive on Planet Earth ... having nothing to do with what happens after we die.

Let's also note another example where Jesus is not speaking of death as we typically think of death. "Verily, verily, I say unto you, He that heareth my word and believeth on him that sent me, hath everlasting life and shall not come into condemnation, but is passed from death unto life. Verily, verily, I say unto you, the hour is coming, and *now is*, when the dead shall hear the voice of the Son of God; and they that hear shall live" (John 5:24-25). Here again, Jesus is speaking about the dead in spirit becoming *awakened* (to use an expression from the teachings of the Buddha). And "now is" means the present. Thus, the phrase, "hath everlasting life," means to be fully alive in the spirit of truth as long as one lives.

Jesus was not talking about dead people — as we think of dead people — coming alive. He was talking about people being dead in spirit and becoming alive in the spirit of truth, which is accomplished by discovering the truth that sets us free and, consequently, by harmonizing with God. We might also note that Jesus said that the hour "now is," not after we are dead and gone.

For clarification, "him that sent me" is the Father within (in our language, the "Father" is our true spiritual self). When we hear the word of truth that comes from our true spiritual self and abide by it, we are alive in the spirit of truth.

What this boils down to is that you will not find anywhere in the teachings of either Jesus or the Buddha where they spoke in terms of an eternity — or everlasting life — in heaven or hell after death, as some fundamentalists believe. Nevertheless, these age-old beliefs about heaven and hell are so firmly embedded in the minds of many people — somewhat like being brainwashed — that they are not open-minded to hearing what Jesus said, which is in agreement with what Buddha said about 500 years BC.

It seems that Christianity as we know it today focuses too much attention on things out there, up there, and life after death ... and stuff cloaked in a mystery that no one can understand. From the above statements by Jesus, clearly he was speaking of the present moment. Obviously, those who "heareth my word" are already alive as we typically think of being alive. Thus, those who "hear the word of truth shall live." His phrase "shall live" must have a special meaning, like being fully alive in the spirit of truth rather than dead in spirit ... rather than being troubled, stressed, depressed, anxious, fatigued, jealous, angry, hateful, resentful ... all that negative stuff that saps us of the life of our spirit.

The spiritual teachers of the Old Testament also spoke of hell as being in the present. Let's note a few examples: In "The book of Deuteronomy," we find: "For a fire is kindled in mine anger, and shall burn unto the lowest hell" (Deuteronomy 32:22). In the book of *Jonah*, we find: "Then Jonah prayed unto the Lord his God out of the fish's belly. And said, I cried by reason of mine affliction unto the Lord, and he heard me; out of the belly of hell cried I, and thou heardest my voice" (Jonah 2:2). And from "The Psalms" we find: "The sorrows of death compassed me, and the pains of hell gat hold upon me; I found trouble and sorrow. ... Whither shall I go from thy spirit? Or whither shall I flee from thy presence? If I ascend up into heaven, thou art there; if I make my bed in hell, behold thou art there" (Psalms 18:4). Surely the Psalmist was speaking about the present, not about life after death.

Some fundamentalists judged the Buddha as being atheist, primarily because he did not teach about heaven and hell after death; neither did Jesus. There is nothing in the Scriptures about a heaven or a hell after death like fundamentalists describe. Twisting the Scriptures — adding to and taking from them — does not make it so.

When fundamentalists resort to the "Revelation to John" in order to support their beliefs in a literal heaven and hell after death, we might know that he or she does not really understand and accept what Jesus said, and he or she does not really understand the nature of visions. Many people who read and study "The Revelation to John" do not take into account the fact that the passages in "red" letters are not the words of Jesus. These are things that the Apostle John "saw" and "heard" in his visions.

And when fundamentalists read descriptive language about the suffering of hell — weeping and gnashing of teeth — they seem to jump to the conclusion that it is about hell after death. Yet, weeping and gnashing of teeth are common in our society ... *now.*

The point is that Jesus, the Buddha, and the spiritual teachers of the Old Testament taught about overcoming suffering and finding peace and joy *now* ... not after the death of the body. This must be at least a part of the explanation of why some Christians leave Christianity for Buddhism, or for some other alternative teaching, trying to find something that will help them to find peace, joy, inner serenity, and happiness *now.*

If we make a cursory observation of the membership of the church and what the church is accomplishing, we might conclude that the church is failing to accomplish its mission ... if its mission is teaching people the gospel that Jesus preached and teaching people how to be saved from their sins and saved from their suffering ... if the mission includes helping people to accomplish what Jesus said, "Ye shall know the truth and the truth shall make you free."

It seems that the success of a church is measured to a great extent by its membership, whether or not it is helping people to comprehend the gospel that Jesus preached and whether or not it is helping people find their way to God.

It is a well-known fact that church membership and attendance are enhanced immensely by increasing social activities. Some churches are resorting to a casual church atmosphere to help stem the tide of declining attendance. This casual atmosphere includes a varied assortment of extracurricular activities, including pop music.

A great attraction for many of the churches is the music. Music has a tremendous impact on us, regardless of what kind of music it is—gospel, rock, classical, country, jazz, pop, whatever. And even if we do not agree with some of the words in some of the old gospel hymns, the music can still be uplifting.

Also, what attracts many people to the churches and keeps them there is that churches provide the best environment of any organizations in our nation for people to enjoy socialization and camaraderie with others ... what some Christians allude to as Christian fellowship. Aristotle, Greek philosopher, said, "Without friends no one would choose to live, though he had all other goods." John Donne, English poet and clergyman, said, "No man is an island."

For the most part, the most contented people in our society and in the churches come from the most contented and harmonious families; and the most discontented people in our society and in the churches have the worst childhood backgrounds.

There are many good, loving people in the churches. And we can be thankful for them. They are helping keep our troubled, fractured society glued together. However, for the most part, the most emotionally secure and most loving people are those who received the most love during childhood ... not because of their getting saved in the church.

This leads to an explanation of the cause of problems and friction in many churches. The teachings of many churches are influenced greatly by a misunderstanding of what the Apostle Paul said. It seems ironic that Christians praise and worship the man Jesus, yet they seem to pay more attention to the teachings of the Apostle Paul than what Jesus said. The influence of the Apostle Paul is so deeply ingrained that many give undue attention to what the Apostle Paul said, all the while ignoring — or at least glossing over — what Jesus said.

The Apostle Paul said: "As it is written, There is none righteous, no, not one. There is none that understandeth, there is none that seeketh after God. ... All have sinned, and come short of the glory of God" (Romans 3:10-23). At least a part of what the Apostle Paul said was based on his observation of the Jews and Gentiles; he said they were all under sin. And perhaps a part of what he said was based on a passage in "The Psalms." Note the phrase, "As it is written." Perhaps this refers to the following passage in "The Psalms": "The fool hath said in his heart, There is no God. They are corrupt, they have done abominable works, there is none that doeth good. The Lord looked down from heaven upon the children of men, to see if there were any that did understand, and seek God.

They are all gone aside, they are all together become filthy; there is none that doeth good, no, not one" (Psalms 14:1-3).

It seems that fundamentalists have surmised from the foregoing (or similar) statements that we are all sinners, we were born sinners, we are not perfect and never will be. Fundamentalists proclaim that "there is none righteous, no not one." Beliefs about how sinful we are have been drummed into us so thoroughly that an old gospel hymn relegates us to the category of a worm. Some Christians seem to believe that the only perfect person was Jesus, and that he was perfect because he was God in human flesh.

It is not reasonable and logical — and it is not consistent with anything in the Bible — that a perfect, intelligent, loving God created us sinful, evil, and imperfect. And to think that we are born sinners — evil and imperfect — is not consistent with: "God created man in his own image, in the image of God created he him; male and female created he them" (Genesis 1:27). And, "God created man, in the likeness of God made he him" (Genesis 5:1).

Many Christians seem to overlook, or not understand, the Scriptures that tell us that we are created in the image and likeness of God, which is perfect. And they seem to ignore or gloss over something that Jesus said: "Narrow is the way that leadeth unto life and few there be who find it" (Matthew 7:14), and "They that are whole have no need of the physician, but they that are sick; I came not to call the righteous, but sinners to repentance" (Matthew 9:13).

From this we realize that there are those who are saved without the teachings of Jesus. Who are they? There are at least two possibilities. People who were born and reared in a loving, happy, harmonious family environment — receiving the unconditional love of a loving, happy, contented mother — are saved. They have no underlying fear that is the hidden cause of suffering.

Remember that both Moses and Jesus said, "Love the Lord thy God with all your heart, and with all your soul, and with all your mind." We are saved when we love as they told us to love. And, how do we learn to love? For the most part, we learn to love by the experience of having been loved. For the most part, we learn to love by having been loved, mothered, and nurtured by a loving, happy, contented mother. The unconditional love of a loving mother — a mother who is pure is heart — is on par with the love of God; it is one and the same. A drop of ocean water is not the ocean; however, it has the attributes of the ocean water.

A mother's calling is the highest of all callings. Certainly a father has an influence; however, for the most part, it is the influence of our mother that determines how we believe and think in our heart ... how much we love and how much we hate. In the final analysis, the greatest of all human teachers is none other than a loving mother. A loving mother teaches us to love, and not from words, but by her love, mothering, and nurturing. Think about it! Adequate love would solve the problems of all those things that trouble us most.

For those who did not receive such a blessing — who did not receive unconditional love as a child — how can they to be saved? How are they to learn to love? The answer to this question is why Jesus preached the gospel. He was sent to save those who are lost; those who did not receive adequate love in their childhood environment. Fundamentalists seem to ignore the fact that Jesus was sent to save the sinners: "They that are whole have no need of the physician, but they that are sick; I came not to call the righteous, but sinners to repentance." Ignoring this — or at least glossing over it — has led to considerable confusion and problems in the churches.

In most churches there is a ritual that potential members go through before joining the church. Potential members include those who are already saved and those who are sinners. The problem is that both those who are saved and those who are sinners go through the same ritual. However, going through the ritual does not save the sinners ... the very people that Jesus was sent to save. Thus, the church ends up like a smelting pot: the saved and the sinners, the hypocrites and those who are pure heart, the stable and the unstable. There is no distinction made between the saved and the sinners, between the "sheep and the goats" ... between the stable and the unstable.

We know from the wisdom in a six-word statement by James, brother of Jesus and author of "The Letter of James," the cause of — and the solution to — the things that trouble us the most. And

Why Christians Leave Christianity

we know from this six-word statement what will save us. Incidentally, James was executed because of his teachings.

James said, "A double minded man is unstable in all his ways" (James 1:8). And, "Draw nigh to God, and he will draw nigh to you. Cleanse your hands, ye sinners; and *purify your hearts, ye double minded*" (James 4:8). Think about it! The cause of — and the solution for — all that troubles us most are found in a six-word statement in above passage: "Purify your hearts, ye double minded." We are saved when we purify our hearts. When we purify our hearts, we are unified with our true spiritual self ... the same thing as being unified with God ... the same thing as Jesus being one with his Father.

Thus, we know from this six-word statement the cause of — and the solution to — the things that trouble us the most: anxiety, depression, hatred, suffering, loneliness, restlessness, anger, guilt, jealousy, insecurity, divorce, shootings in the schools, crime, violence, psychosomatic illness (those illnesses that account for about 90 percent of the visits to doctors); fractured, troubled, dysfunctional families; the breakup of families, guilt, shame ... the list goes on. The cause is being double mind and unstable in all our ways. And the solution to those things that trouble us the most is purifying our hearts. ... the same thing as "cleaning the inside of the cup and the platter" and "casting the devils out of our heart." Purifying our heart is the same thing as obliterating the impurities from our mind as advocated by the Buddha.

Doubled-minded people, "unstable in all their ways," are guided by their false ego-self rather than their true spiritual self. They are alienated from God... alienated from their true spiritual self. Jesus said, "Wide is the gate and broad is the way that leadeth to destruction, and many there be who follow it." Those who follow the way to destruction are unstable in all their ways; they are not in harmony with truth, God, and nature.

People who are unstable in all their ways include those who lie, steal, cheat, and those who will "stab another in the back;" those who are selfish and greedy; those who suffer from psychosomatic illnesses; those whose marriage relationships are disastrous and chaotic; those who are fearful, religious fanatics; those who are neurotic; those who are getting therapy and taking tranquilizers and antidepressants; those who are angry and violent; those who have evil in their heart; those who are lunatics; and those who harbor devils and unclean spirits in their hearts.

Think about it! In a society in which about 90 percent of the families are dysfunctional, it is safe to assume that many church members are characterized by the traits mentioned above. And the people with these traits are integrated with those who are pure in heart. Church leaders do not seem to distinguish between the "sheep and the goats," between the saved and the sinners, between the stable and the unstable.

In addition, to add to the confusion, churches have liberals and conservatives. Both groups think they are right. With the hodgepodge of members, it is little wonder that there is friction and disagreements about beliefs. Why argue about many beliefs?

It is useless and misleading to interpret a passage in the "Gospel According to Matthew" to mean that Jesus (or a king) will separate the sheep and the goats after people are dead. Why argue about these types of things? The main thing is to be saved. Besides, the passage about the separation of the sheep and the goats is not the authentic words of Jesus, according to the previously quoted book, *The Five Gospels — What Did Jesus Really Say?*

The church is a great place for socialization and camaraderie, and it performs several useful, helpful functions. It's especially helpful to those who are already saved; there is no comparable organization. However, the teachings of Christianity are not saving sinners ... the people that Jesus was sent to save. According to a Chinese proverb, "The beginning of wisdom is to call things by their right names." Ministers do a grave disservice to sinners — and the very world itself — calling sinners Christians.

Note how matter-of-fact and straightforward that James said, "Purify your hearts, ye double minded." He did not pussyfoot around; he told the people directly that they were double minded. Can you imagine ministers telling hypocrites that they are sinners? Surely, ministers know church members who are hypocrites; "by their fruits, we know them." However, it seems that church leaders dare not tell hypocrites that they are not saved.

James also said: "Out of the same mouth proceedeth blessing and cursing. My brethren, these things ought not so to be." Isn't it easy to observe in many churches what James was speaking about? By their fruits, don't we know many that are not saved, who pretend to be saved ... who are hypocrites?

James also said, "But if ye have bitter envying and strife in your hearts, glory not, and lie not against the truth. ... For where envying and strife is, there is confusion and every evil work. ... The wisdom that is from above is first pure, then peaceable, gentle, and easy to be entreated, full of mercy and good fruits, without partiality, and without hypocrisy. And the fruit of righteousness is sown in peace of them that make peace" (James 3:10-18).

Many church members do not have peace and joy in their hearts. And to think that Jesus preached the gospel about 2,000 years ago so that the lost — the sinners — would be saved, and consequently, have peace and joy. For the most part, those "who are sick and in need of a physician" do not find what they are seeking in mainline churches ... thus, this is at least a part of the explanation for some Christians leaving mainline Christian churches.

Think of the problems that would be solved if churches were teaching sinners how to purify their hearts and become stable in all their ways ... what everyone wants. Love and truth are so powerful that only a comparatively small percentage of peaceful, loving people are enough to keep many churches, families, and a troubled society glued together. Think of what a difference it would make if all church members were saved ... were pure in heart. All would be peaceful, joyous, and contented.

As it is, double minded people — who are unstable in all their ways — stir up considerable friction, confusion, and trouble in the churches, in the families, and in our society. Many marriages are composed of two unstable people trying to live together. And one who is stable cannot form a stable relationship with one who is not stable. Single minded people — stable in all their ways — form stable relationships. Think of all the problems that would be solved if families were loving, harmonious, peaceful, and stable!

Moses said (and Jesus repeated several hundred years later), "Therefore shall a man leave his father and his mother, and shall cleave unto his wife; and they shall be one flesh" (Genesis 2:24). Double-minded people — unstable in all their ways — do not become one flesh.

"Purifying our heart" is consistent with Buddha's parable of the piece of cloth. When we have rid ourselves of the impurities in our heart, our heart is pure; we are in agreement with truth; we are in harmony with God ... we are stable in all our ways.

James also said, "If any of you lack wisdom, let him ask of God that giveth to all liberally ... and it shall be given him. ... Wherefore lay apart all filthiness and superfluity of naughtiness, and receive with meekness the engrafted word, which is able to save your souls" (James 1:5-21). Note what will save our souls. Also, note that James did not simply say "the word." He said, "the engrafted word." "Engrafted" means established firmly; implanted. The "engrafted word" — the same thing as the truth that rests in our heart — will save us. And we discover it by communing with our own heart. "Ask of God" is the same thing as "call upon the name of the Lord," a phrase used by the Apostle Paul.

Think about it! When we purify our hearts we are saved; we are unified with God. Thus, the church would provide the solution to untold suffering and problems in this world if they were teaching people how to purify their hearts ... all in agreement with the purpose for Jesus preaching the gospel.

How do we purify our hearts? Moses said, "Sanctify yourselves" ... the same meaning of what James said, "purify your hearts." The primary question is how does one purify his or her heart. This question was answered in Chapter 3, "The Truth about What Will Save Us." To reiterate, there is something we must do. As explained elsewhere in this book, there are ways of discovering the truth that will save us had we never heard of Jesus. One way of saving ourselves is by doing what David the Psalmist said to do: "Commune with your own heart." Communing with our own heart is the same thing as communion with God ... a form of prayer. What David said to do is the same thing that the Buddha taught: "Be ye lamps unto yourselves; seek salvation alone in truth" ... this would save us.

Why Christians Leave Christianity

Many people — those on the broad path to destruction — do not know the experience of being in agreement with truth ... the experience of being in harmony with God. They do not know what they are missing. They have no basis for comparison. For the most part, many Christians have not abided by what Jesus said. They have not:
- Discovered the truth that sets them free.
- Become as perfect as their Father who is in heaven is perfect.
- Cleaned the inside of the cup and the platter.
- Cast the devils from their subconscious minds.
- Become as free, humble, and truthful as little children.
- Learned to do the "will of the Father" ... a prerequisite for enjoying Heaven.
- Learned to pray to the Father who is in secret, the way that Jesus meant for us to pray. They have not learned to commune with their own heart, as alluded to by David, the Psalmist.

Many church members are confused about such significant concepts as heaven, hell, and Satan. They do not understand that heaven is within us. They are confused about what is required to be saved. They do not know the real reason for Jesus preaching the gospel. Many do not understand clearly that the "Father," as alluded to by Jesus, is the true spiritual self.

What this boils down to is that many Christians do not understand the message Jesus intended for us. They have not discovered the truth that sets them free. They have not discovered the "peace of God that passeth all understanding." They have not discovered the peace, joy, and righteousness characteristic of heaven.

The soothing, inspirational atmosphere of the church — including the misleading teachings of the church — is enough to keep many trapped in their comfort zone ... which is not comforting. Many leave the church in search of what they are searching for, which is a life in agreement with truth ... a life with meaning ... a life in agreement with the gospel that Jesus preached. Others remain in the church and work on perfecting their facade of being righteous, taking an active part in the church, and doing things to demonstrate that their mask is who they are ... all the while, basically, they are insecure, unhappy, restless, and discontented.

Jesus was not swayed by outer appearances of people who were seemingly successful and prosperous. Not all ministers and religious teachers are really Christian ... "by their fruits we know them." I am reminded of a Protestant Minister who was a participant in a very intense workshop. He was so deeply troubled that he was contemplating suicide. From *Buddha In The Palm Of Your Hand*, by Osel Tendzin, we learn: "It is not actually possible to help others properly until we stop creating pain for ourselves."

Jesus said, "...they be blind leaders of the blind. And if the blind lead the blind, both shall fall into the ditch."

If we pay close attention to what Jesus said, what matters is what's inside of us; it's the condition of our heart. A pure heart is a prerequisite for enjoying the kingdom of Heaven.

If we study and assimilate why Jesus "was sent" — why he preached the gospel of the kingdom of God — we realize that it was to help people overcome suffering and to have peace and joy ... the same explanation of why Buddha taught the Four Noble Truths and the Eight-fold Path to enlightenment ... the same explanation for the teachings of the saints of the Old Testament.

In order to enjoy the peace and joy of heaven, we must return to the purity, humility, and innocence with which we came into this world ... thus, Jesus' statement, "Except ye be converted and become as little children, ye shall not enter into the kingdom of Heaven" (Matthew 18:3).

Children are born equal in the spirit of truth ... created in the image and likeness of God. Children are born pure in heart ... a prerequisite for enjoying heaven. Children are naturally free, spontaneous, honest, humble, and truthful ... deep inside the soul of us, the way we all desire to be. ... as perfect as Jesus told us to be, "as perfect as our Father who is in heaven."

Jesus "was sent" to save the lost. A child is not born lost, but becomes lost when he or she is born into a family that is lacking in adequate love ... when he or she is reared in the world of the ego. We can be assured that a child who is rebellious, unruly, or a chronic crier (who does not have a physical cause of pain) is being forced to adapt to a hostile environment that is out of harmony with love and truth ... out of harmony with God and nature. He or she is not getting the love, mothering, and nurturing that a child is programmed to expect. His or her rebellious behavior and crying are a cry for love. A "spoiled brat" (a child who pitches temper tantrums, trying to get his or her way) is a child who is not getting adequate love, mothering, and nurturing. Children, who become problem children, have parents with problems ... parents who are out of harmony with truth, God, and nature.

From psychology we know that behavior is learned. We know that the hidden cause of psychological problems and mental suffering is acquired for the most part during early childhood. And it is all this stuff — the mental aberrations, the devils, the impurities — buried in our subconscious mind from which we desire to be saved. In other words, we desire to be saved from ourselves ... saved from our fearful, false ego-self ... the Satan within us.

Psychologists, psychiatrists, counselors, and therapists work regularly with patients, trying to help them overcome negative, false stuff buried in their subconscious mind that is causing them undue suffering, misery, and torment. It's safe to say that many patients have tried the church and many are church members. However, they do not understand and embody the gospel of the kingdom of God that Jesus preached.

Jesus taught us the basics. Let's remember that his ministry was cut short, to slightly more than three years. There are some important things that he taught, yet he did not teach us — or at least did not make clear — how to do what he said. For example, Jesus did not tell us clearly how to discover the truth that sets us free. In this regard, the Old Testament is a great help. We know from David, the Psalmist, that we can discover truth by "Communing with our own heart."

Psychologist Erich Fromm said, "... the real 'fall of man' is his alienation from himself, his submission to power, his turning against himself even though under the guise of his worship of God. ... Man will seek the haven of the church and of religions because his inner emptiness impels him to seek for some shelter. But professing religion does not mean being religious."

Our inner emptiness, restlessness, discontent, mental turmoil — and our inherent desire for inner serenity, peace, joy, happiness

— keep us searching, trying one religion and then another, reading self-help books galore, seeking the services of psychics, astrologers, therapists, counselors, and on and on and on ... trying to find meaning in life. We would have no need for all this seeking and searching if only we lived in agreement with truth ... if only we believed and comprehended the message that Jesus intended for us.

We do not want to burn the whole house to get rid of the rats or to throw the baby out with the bath water. Certainly our lives, our families, our society — the very nation itself — are better off because many people *attempt* to abide by the Ten Commandments. But think about the differences churches could make if they taught the gospel of the kingdom of God in a manner that we could understand and believe. Think of what a difference it would make if we were taught how to discover the truth that sets us free ... a prerequisite for being saved and, consequently, for enjoying heaven.

Because of our age-old concepts of hell, we do not think of hell as being mental suffering. We do not think of hell as being a troubled, tormented mind, but it is. There are many signs of a troubled, tormented mind ... many signs of hell: anger, hatred, depression, anxiety, restlessness, discontentment, frustration, dysfunctional families, tension headaches, psychosomatic illnesses, psychological stress, taking antidepressants and tranquilizers, violence, rape, crime, various addictions, various phobias, child abuse, spousal abuse, drug abuse ... and on and on and on ... all signs of a troubled mind ... all signs of hell on earth.

And we know from the teachings of the Buddha that suffering will arise again and again until one has rid him or her self from the impurities in his or her mind. If Christians really comprehended the gospel that Jesus preached, their suffering would cease. And they would not leave Christianity for Buddhism. Christians leave Christianity for Buddhism (and/or for other alternative ways of trying to find what they are seeking), because of the following primary weaknesses in the teachings of modern-day churches:

- The failure to teach the true teachings of Jesus in a clear, straightforward language that people can believe and understand.
- The failure to teach people how to "enter into the closet and shut the door" and pray to "our Father," who is in heaven. Trans-

Why Christians Leave Christianity 183

lated into our language, this means knowing how to be still, stop the chatter of the ego, and commune with our true, divine spiritual self.
- The failure to teach us how to do some of the things alluded to by Jesus if we are to enjoy the peace and joy that he envisioned for us; for example: How to discover the truth that sets us free; how to "clean the inside of the cup and the platter;" how to cast out devils; how to be converted and become as little children; how to be "born again," how to do the will of the true spiritual self.
- The failure to teach us to cherish, praise, love and worship our true, divine spiritual self, rather than praising and worshipping the man Jesus.

Acknowledging the greatest weaknesses in the teachings of the church helps us understand the greatest opportunity. Our ultimate goal in life is unity with God. The way to unify with God is by communing with our true, divine, spiritual self ... the same thing as communing with God. This is what David, the Psalmist, alluded to when he said, "Commune with your own heart." By communing with our own heart, we are able to arrive at the state of consciousness that Jesus envisioned for us, in his words, "that where I am there ye may be also" (John 14:3). He was in unity with his Father; in his words, "I and my Father are one." This is same thing as being in unity with God ... the goal of all great religions.

The emphasis of mainline churches is on preaching, teaching, reading, and studying; however, this does not save us if we do not learn to commune with our own heart and discover the truth that sets us free. We could read the Bible cover to cover and study it for a lifetime, and we could listen to sermons as long as we live and never discover the truth that sets us free. The truth that sets us free dwells within our own heart, and that's the only place we will ever discover it. By communing with our true, divine, spiritual self, we learn how to:
- Discover the truth that sets us free.
- "Clean the inside of the cup and the platter."
- "Knock, open, seek, and find."
- Cast the devils from our heart.
- Be as perfect as Jesus told us to be.

- Be converted, and become as little children, a prerequisite for enjoying Heaven.
- Do the will of the Father (our true spiritual self), which we will do quite naturally when we are living in harmony with truth and God.
- "Call upon the name of the Lord," realizing that this is the same thing as communing with our own heart ... the way we acquire the wisdom for knowing the truth that sets us free.
- "Be transformed by the renewing of our mind," as alluded to by the Apostle Paul.
- "Pray to your Father who is in secret," as Jesus taught us to pray.
- "Seek ye the Lord while he may be found; call ye upon him while he is near," as alluded to by Isaiah.
- "Commune with our own heart," as alluded to by David, the Psalmist.
- Find our way to God, which we accomplish by being still and communing with our true spiritual self ... there is no other way. Regardless of what path we might choose, if we are to be successful in unifying with God (the goal of all great religions), at some point we will commune with our own heart.

All the foregoing things are comparatively easy to accomplish ... if only we would be still and pay attention ... if only we would learn how to commune with our own heart ... the same thing as communion with God.

A vast portion of the Bible is based on communion with God. Yet, modern-day churches fail to teach us — or at least to make it clear — how to do this, thus, a great weakness in the teachings of mainline churches. Thus, one of the greatest opportunities for the churches is to teach us how to be still, calm our mind — in Jesus' words, "shut the door" — and commune with our own heart.

Clearly, something is missing in the churches; otherwise, there would not be more than 250 denominations in Christian churches, all with different beliefs ... and everyone thinking they are right.

If leaders of Christianity had been teaching the gospel of Jesus since his death about 2,000 years ago, there would not be so many different religious beliefs. Joseph Smith founded Mormonism because he thought that Christianity had been corrupted and the true gospel of Jesus needed to be restored. If leaders of Christianity were teaching the true gospel of Jesus in a manner that people can understand and embody, church members would not leave Christianity for Buddhism or for any alternative religious organization. Why would they? After all, what else is there to find once we have discovered the truth that sets us free and are unified with God? Life cannot get any more peaceful than living in harmony with God.

The Apostle Paul, who alluded to God as the God of peace, said, "Be of one mind; live in peace, and the God of love and peace shall be with you." Being of one mind is the same thing as being in unity with our true spiritual self, the same thing as being in unity with God. We are of one mind when we purify our hearts.

Why would anyone leave Christianity for an alternative religious teaching once they discover the truth that sets them free and enjoy the "peace that passeth all understanding" ... once they enjoy heaven? Mormonism, Islam, Christian Science, Religious Science, Unity, and other religions and religious cults would never have evolved had the gospel of Jesus been taught during the past 2,000 years in a manner that people believe, understand, and embody.

It is possible to find salvation by doing what the Buddha said: "Be ye lamps unto yourselves; seek salvation alone in truth. Those who shall not look for assistance from anyone beside themselves, it is they who shall reach the very topmost height." However, there is a way — an experience-based way of learning — that can be quite helpful. This method, involving participation in a properly conducted small group, could be quite appealing to many church members. Most definitely, it could be most rewarding.

This experienced-based learning is best accomplished in small, closed groups—coming together for the sole purpose of sharing, of being honest and truthful, of discerning falsehoods from that which is true, and consequently, discovering the truth that sets one free.

This method involves no reading, studying, and discussion of religion or psychology ... no discussion of anything outside the here and now. It is a method of learning to do by doing. It is a way of *seeing* behind the masks we wear and seeing ourselves as others see us ... a way of discerning truth from falsehoods.

To help accomplish the goal of unity with one's true self, a closed group provides an environment for people to recognize their fears, faults, and the masks they are wearing, and consequently, it provides a way of learning to be real. Because of the process of sharing and unfolding that gets underway in a group, it is disruptive for newcomers to enter the group; it is disruptive for people to come and go. Thus, for those interested in the group activity, they must join a group when it first begins, and participants must be committed to regular attendance for a specified time period.

If the group interaction goes the way it could and should go, the end result is that everyone in the group will become as one ... all in harmony with truth. Can you imagine what we, our families, and our society would be like if we were all in harmony with truth—unified with God? Jesus was unified with his Father, the same thing as being unified with God, and he had peace and joy. This is what Jesus wanted for us ... for all the world.

Thus, there are two additions that churches could add to their agenda that have the potential for helping people find salvation. One addition is sessions devoted to learning to calm the mind and meditating ... for communing with one's true spiritual self. Most of the Old Testament is based on communion with the God ... the same thing as communing with the true spiritual self. We, too, can — and must — do this. The only way we will ever become unified with God is by communing with our true spiritual self.

The other addition is making provisions for small groups in which participants are dedicated to discovering the truth that sets them free. After all, what is more satisfying than living in harmony with truth, God, and nature? What is more satisfying than enjoying heaven? Once one discovers the truth that sets him or her free — once one is unified with his or her true spiritual self (the same thing as being unified with God) — he or she would have no desire to leave the church for another religious teaching.

The goal of the group participation is to help one discover truth and to unify with God. We need not concern ourselves with life after we die. If we are unified God now, all is well. And, if we are not unified with God while we are alive on planet earth — regardless of the hereafter — we will never be unified with God

Exactly how to proceed in a small group to assure success of the group is beyond the scope of this book. However, I must add that the greatest risk of things not going the way they could and should go lies with the leader. If the leader is leading from the ego, rather than from the heart, the results can only be more hurtful than helpful. Because of the ego, many people want to be a leader. Perhaps someone is well learned, quite knowledgeable and impressive and he or she thinks this qualifies him or her to be a leader. He or she may have "learned the tricks, but not the trade." Those with strongest desire to be a leader should not be. The *strong desire* is a function of the ego. And, leading from the ego, rather than from the heart, spells certain disaster; it all becomes a farce ... perhaps the leader and others exploiting others. Such group activity is more destructive than helpful.

On the other hand, those in a spiritually led group (led by a qualified leader) can expect a spiritual high ... like "being born again." The spiritually led group has the potential for helping those with serious intentions to discover the truth that sets them free ... deep inside the soul of us what everyone wants.

Let us learn something from what Isaiah said: *"Hear the word of the Lord,* ye rulers of Sodom; *give ear unto the law of our God,* ye people of Gomorrah. To what purpose is the multitude of your sacrifices unto me? saith the Lord; I am full of the burnt offerings of rams, and the fat of fed beasts; and I delight not in the blood of bullocks, or of lambs, or of he goats. ... Bring no more vain oblations; incense is an abomination unto me ... *Come now, and let us reason together,* saith the Lord; *though your sins be as scarlet, they shall be as white as snow"* (Isaiah 1:10-18).

Sometimes when we read words that we don't quite understand, we tend to read on without taking time to resort to a dictionary to understand the meaning. "Abomination" is anything hateful and disgusting. "Oblation" is an offering of sacrifice. "Vain" things are of the ego and have no real value; they are worthless, empty, and idle. Instead of humility, vain things show an excessively high regard for one's self, looks, possessions and ability.

In our everyday language, Isaiah was fed up with people offering sacrifices of things to impress ... vain things people give when they are motivated by the ego. He knew that the people offering the sacrifices were not free of their sinful ways ... only pretending. He posed the question: What purpose is the multitude of your sacrifices? He was not delighted with them, and he wanted no more of them.

Does Isaiah's observation remind you of what is easily observable today? Does it remind you of many Christians who profess to believe on Jesus and who pretend to be righteous, but do nothing to discover the truth that frees them from their deeply held fears and false beliefs that rob them of peace and joy?

Rather than the vain, meaningless offerings, note what Isaiah said, "Come now, and let us reason together. ... and your sins will become white as snow." His descriptive language, "white as snow," means the same thing as being pure in heart, a prerequisite for enjoying heaven. This is what can happen in a properly conducted group where participants "reason together." The participants soon learn to distinguish between false things of the ego and true things of the heart. They become unified with their true spiritual self, and consequently, unified with one and another. They learn to embody the message Jesus intended for us ... deep inside the soul of us, what everyone craves.

And let us not lose sight of what it is that renders our "sins as white as snow." According to Isaiah, it is "hearing the word of the Lord ... give ear unto the law of our God, and coming together and reasoning together." In a group process of "reasoning together" (of sharing what the participants are experiencing — their feelings — in the present moment), all participants began at their present level of consciousness and understanding. As the group progresses, at some point the participants will be sharing from their true spiritual self (sharing the word of the Lord). The group interaction — combined with one's own personal meditations — soon lead to exquisite communion with God. It leads one to an understanding of the truth that sets one free.

Again, a leader serving from the level of love, honesty, humility, patience and understanding — rather than serving from the level of the ego, trying to impress — is a must. Most often, the best leaders are those who do and say the least; however, of the little that they do and say, it is of *extreme* importance.

Church leaders could do well to ask themselves the question: What is the goal of the church? If the answer is to help people find salvation — to help people find their way to God — sessions devoted to meditation and experience-based learning in small groups are two ways to help accomplish the goal.

Several years ago a deacon of a Baptist Church asked me: What can the church do to stem the tide of declining attendance? A goal of the church ought to be to help people unify with God ... to help people find salvation. The way to do this is by teaching the gospel that Jesus preached ... teaching in a manner that people can understand and embody. And, experience based learning in small groups can help understand and embody the teachings of Jesus. Helping people find salvation is a sure way to stem the tide of declining church attendance. After all, everyone wants to live in unity with truth, God, and nature ... and to have peace and joy.

In summary, the teachings of both Jesus and Buddha were to help us overcome suffering and to have peace and joy. Thus, many Christians who leave Christianity for Buddhism or other alternative religious teachings are attempting to overcome their mental suffering and to find peace, joy, inner serenity, and contentment.

Thus, many Christians are seeking and searching for the way of life they would experience if they comprehended the gospel that Jesus preached. Jesus' basic message of love and truth — the same message as that of the Buddha — is the message that everyone insatiably craves. And they will never be genuinely happy, satisfied, and contented until they get it. Deep inside, we insatiably desire to express life in harmony with truth, God, and nature ... we insatiably desire to have peace and joy ... we desire the abundant life that Jesus wanted for us.

When Christian teachers begin teaching the gospel that Jesus preached (teaching in a manner that people can believe and comprehend), instead of the problem of people leaving the church, the problem might be accommodating the flood of people. After all, deep inside the soul of us, the message Jesus intended for us is what everyone craves.

Chapter 8
The Power of God

For eons, people have known there is a God ... there is a force in the Universe. During biblical times, people thought that God was an angry, vengeful, jealous God, who punished them for their sins. Similarly, people have mistakenly believed (many people still do) in a Satan who has power over us. There is only one God and only one power, which is the power of God.

Many people believe in duality (two powers), the power of God and the Power of Satan. Actually, what is sometimes thought to be the power of Satan is the power of God working through us according to a negative, destructive, fearful, false, subconscious belief ... "It is done unto us as we believe."

The power and complexity of God is beyond comprehension. How could we possibly understand the power and complexity of God when we cannot understand the complexity of the subconscious mind, which is our spiritual channel to the power of God? Understanding something about the nature of our subconscious mind and also something about the nature of God's power can help us harmonize with God, which is the ultimate goal of religion.

There have been numerous articles and books about the power of the subconscious mind. Let's note what some distinguished people have said pertaining to the power of thoughts, beliefs, and the subconscious mind, and then let us note what Jesus and other biblical teachers said.

William James, philosopher and psychologist, said, "The power to move the world is in your subconscious mind. ... Believe that life is worth living and your belief will help create the fact."

Dr. Joseph Murphy, author of the book, *The Power Of Your Subconscious Mind*, wrote: "You can bring into your life more power, more wealth, more health, more happiness, and more joy by learning to contact and release the hidden power of your subconscious mind. You need not acquire this power; you already possess it. ... Within your subconscious depths lie infinite wisdom, infinite

The Power of God

power, and infinite supply of all that is necessary, which is waiting for development and expression. ... It is your right to discover this inner world of thought, feeling, and power, of light, love, and beauty. Though invisible, its forces are mighty. Within your subconscious mind you will find the solution for every problem, and the cause for every effect."

Clergyman and author of several books, including *The Power of Positive Thinking*, Norman Vincent Peale, said, "Change your thoughts and you can change anything."

The title of a book *The Power is Within You* by Louise L. Hay (a metaphysical lecturer and author of several best-selling books, including *You Can Heal Your Life*), says a lot. We are beginning the twenty-first century and many people do not know that the power is within us. According to the author, the way we connect with this power is by "going within." The author said, "The more you connect to the Power within you, the more you can be free in all areas of your life."

When we stop to think about it, "going within" is the same thing that Jesus did when he "went unto the Father," the same thing that the spiritual teachers of the Old Testament did when they communed with the Lord, the same thing as "calling upon the name of the Lord," as alluded to by the Apostle Paul, the same thing as communing with our own heart, as advocated by David the Psalmist. "Going within" is the same thing I alluded to in my first book, *Listening to Ourselves: The Key to Everything that Matters*. Being still, "going within," and listening to ourselves (communing with our own heart) is how we discover the truth that sets us free.

Incidentally, the title *You Can Heal Your Life* suggests that we are our own saviors, which we are; however, a truth teacher can be very helpful in guiding us on the pathway to truth.

To understand something about the power that is within us, note what Jesus said when the disciples ask him why he succeeded in curing a lunatic, but they could not. He said to them: "Because of your unbelief; for verily I say unto you, if ye have faith as a grain of mustard seed, ye shall say unto this mountain, remove hence to yonder place; and it shall remove; and nothing shall be impossible unto you" (Matthew 17:20).

Jesus did not say that only he had access to the power of God. The disciples had it. We all have access to the power, but the benefits that accrue to us are a pittance in comparison with the potential that it holds for us because of our unbelief. The power works through us according to the way we believe and think in our heart. Unfortunately, although not aware of it, many of our thoughts and beliefs are negative.

Jesus said, "All things, whatsoever ye shall ask in prayer, believing, ye shall receive" ... speaking about the power of belief.

When Jesus restored the sight of a blind man, Jesus said, "Go thy way; thy faith hath made thee whole" (Mark 10:52). It helps to know that faith is unquestionable belief, and the sight of the blind man was restored when his belief changed. Thus, according to the teachings of Jesus, the power is within everyone. And, "It's done unto us as we believe."

Clearly, biblical writers understood that there is more to us than just our conscious, thinking mind. James, author of "The Letter of James," spoke in terms of a double-minded man. The Apostle Paul spoke in terms of the natural man and the spiritual man. Jesus said, "I and my Father are one," speaking of two aspects of himself. When the spiritual teachers of the Old Testament spoke of the Lord, they were alluding to something within themselves. Isaiah said, "Seek ye the Lord while he is near" ... in our language, speaking of seeking the true spiritual self.

All the following statements by various biblical teachers mean essentially the same thing; all pertain to having a pure heart; all have the same result. In one manner or another, all the following statements involve the power of the subconscious mind. Remember that Jesus said: "The kingdom of God is within you." And we know from Jesus' teachings that our "Father" which is in heaven is the same thing as our true spiritual self. Also, bear in mind that the following are not simply things to read about; they are things we are to do if we are to purify our hearts ... if we are to be saved.

- Sanctify yourselves (Moses). [To sanctify is to save, to be made holy.]
- Wash thine heart from wickedness, that thou mayest be saved (Jeremiah). [The same thing as purifying our heart.]

The Power of God

- Seek ye the Lord while he is near (Isaiah). This is the same thing as seeking our true spiritual self, which is in heaven, which is within us. Our true spiritual self is perfect, created in the image and likeness of God.
- Seek ye first the kingdom of God (Jesus). ... the kingdom of God is within us, according to Jesus.
- Be converted, and become as little children (Jesus).
- Be ye transformed by the renewing of your mind (Paul).
- We are transformed by doing what James said to do: "Purify your hearts, ye double minded."
- Cleanse first that which is within the cup and platter, that the outside of them may be clean also (Jesus). [The same thing as purifying our heart.]
- "Cast the devils from your heart" (Jesus). This is the same thing as "cleaning the inside of the cup and the platter; the same thing as purifying our heart.
- "Those who call upon the name of the Lord shall be saved" (the Apostle Paul). "Calling upon the name of the Lord" (the true spiritual self) is how we commune with our own heart and discover the truth that sets us free ... it's how we purify our hearts.
- As for me, I will call upon God; and the Lord shall save me (Psalms 55: 16). [Same as the previous statement].
- "Call upon the Lord in truth. He will hear our cry and will save us" (Psalms 145: 17-19). [Same as the two previous statements].
- Love the Lord thy God with all your heart, with all your soul, and with all your mind (Moses and Jesus).
- Love thy neighbour as thyself (Jesus).

All of the above involves a change in the way we believe and think in our heart. Regarding the last two statements above, Jesus said that "On these two commandments hang all the law and the prophets" (Matthew 22:40). If we do any one of the foregoing, we are saved. If we love as both Moses and Jesus commanded us to love, we are saved; however, we cannot love as they commanded us to love if our heart is not pure ... if our feelings are tainted with fear and deeply held false beliefs we hold about ourselves. We cannot love freely and unconditionally if we harbor false beliefs that are contrary to our true perfection ... contrary to our true spiritual self.

We miss the meaning of Jesus' statement about "casting out devils" if we do not make allowance for the manner in which Jesus taught and the way he used personal pronouns. His exact words are: "If I cast out devils, then the kingdom of God is come unto you" (Matthew 12:28). From other things Jesus said, we realize that truth will obliterate the devils from our heart and that we can accomplish this by knowing the truth that sets us free. We also realize that we have the same access to the power that Jesus had.

Jesus said, "All power is given unto me in heaven and in earth. ...Verily, verily, I say unto you, he that believeth on me, the works that I do shall he do also; and greater works than these shall he do, because I go unto my Father" (John 14:12).

Jesus was speaking to his disciples. And the thing that set the disciples apart from the masses is that they were followers of the teachings of Jesus. Thus, what Jesus said is that we could do what he did ... if we believe the gospel that he preached. "Believeth on me" means to believe the teachings of Jesus. Think about it! Those who believe, understand, and embody the gospel that Jesus preached could do the things that Jesus did. Jesus did great works because he went unto the Father. We, too, can retreat to the Father within for wisdom, guidance, and understanding.

Think about it! The power of God is within us, and it works for our good, bringing us peace, love, joy, and happiness ... if only we purify our hearts ... if we transcend the ego, becoming unified with God. Purifying our hearts would bring us peace and joy, and consequently, would solve a host of problems for us, our families, our society, our nation—the very world itself.

The Psalmist suffered considerably before he discovered that quiet place within that he called the "secret place of the most high." He said: "I am poured out like water, and all my bones are out of joint; my heart is like wax; it is melted in the midst of my bowels. ... My strength is dried up like a potsherd; and my tongue cleaveth to my jaws; and thou hast brought me into the dust of death. ... I sought the Lord, and he heard me, and delivered me from all my fears" (Psalms 22:14-15, 34:4).

The Power of God

It is noteworthy that the Psalmist understood that his secret faults were within himself and that he discovered the answer to his suffering in that quiet place within, which he called the "secret place of the most high." It is noteworthy that the Lord who knew all about the Psalmist was an aspect of his subconscious mind. It is also noteworthy that both the Psalmist and Job were aware that fear was the underlying cause of their suffering. Job said, "For the thing which I greatly feared is come upon me" (Job 3:25).

Everything we believe is recorded in the subconscious mind. Thus, the subconscious mind knows all about us. The subconscious mind never ceases working (not even when we are asleep) to keep our vital organs functioning according to our body's needs. The subconscious mind acts with the speed of lightening to protect us when we are in danger.

If we touch our fingers to something that is hot, we do not have to think about withdrawing our fingers from the hot object. The speed of the signals from the subconscious mind that impels us to remove our fingers from the hot object is on par with the fastest of the fastest computers ... an example of little things we take for granted without being thankful for all our blessings.

The beliefs that create our reality have been programmed into our mind, and they are kept intact by our continually being reminded of them by our perception. Unfortunately for many of us, our early programming was tainted with fear, and from this fear, all manner of false beliefs became embedded in our subconscious mind. And for the most part, we have not bothered to reprogram ... we have not bothered to rid ourselves of our obscure, insidious fears and deeply held, false beliefs. We have not been transformed by the renewing of our mind as advocated by the Apostle Paul.

To help us understand the complexity and the power of the subconscious mind, it might help to think of a pail of muddy water. Clear water is in a pail of muddy water. When we clean the impurities from muddy water, the water must be clear. Similarly, if we obliterate unwarranted fears and false beliefs from our subconscious mind, what remains must be true. When we obliterate the impurities from our mind, then we know the difference between that which is true and that which is false.

The complexity and the power of the subconscious mind are awesome. Hypnosis provides a simple example of the power of the subconscious mind. Hypnosis, which involves a suggestion being planted in the subconscious mind, can be used to control pain. A hypnotized person can undergo surgery and dental work without a painkiller. Hypnosis also can be used in healing. However, keep in mind that the power is in our belief.

A well-trained hypnotist can plant a posthypnotic suggestion into the mind of a person, suggesting that he or she will do something when the hypnotist uses certain words. This ploy is used sometimes for entertainment purposes. The hypnotist plants a suggestion in the mind of a participant, sometimes a volunteer from an audience. The suggestion is something like, "When I say the word *sky* (or whatever word the hypnotist chooses to say that is a trigger for the hypnotic suggestion), then you will *crow like a rooster"* (or whatever the hypnotist chooses to suggest).

Then after the participant returns to his or her seat in the audience, the hypnotist continues with the program. Then during the program, the trigger word is incorporated into something the hypnotist says, at which point the participant arises in the midst of the audience and crows like a rooster. Thus, hypnosis involves planting a suggestion into the subconscious mind.

The hypnotist's use of posthypnotic suggestions helps explain something about us. Until we are awakened to truth, to a great extent we are living in a hypnotic state of mind, hypnotized by deeply held, false beliefs that are embedded in the subconscious mind. This is demonstrated when someone says something to us that triggers our anger ... something that triggers a belief suppressed in the subconscious mind. Subconsciously — with the speed of lightening and without us having any inkling of the cause of our reaction — we react angrily ... and most often we blame someone for making us angry. Actually, a person does not have to say anything to us to trigger our anger, which can be triggered by the way that a person looks at us.

The power of belief is also demonstrated by the use a placebo, an inert pill that has no healing properties. If a doctor gives a patient a placebo and the patient thinks the doctor is giving him or

The Power of God

her a pill to heal them, then in some cases the patient is healed ... because of the power of belief.

The power of the subconscious mind is also demonstrated in spiritual healing; the healing is the result of a belief that is sufficient to override a false belief that is the hidden cause of the disease. This is the secret to spiritual healing ... the power of belief.

During the time of Jesus' ministry, sick people (who believed that if they could only touch the hem of Jesus' garment, they would be healed), were healed by touching Jesus' garment. The power was in their belief, not in the garment.

When we understand how Jesus helped the blind to see and also understand the power of belief, then we understand the secret of performing miracles. According to the Scriptures, "Jesus spat on the ground and made clay of the spittle, and he anointed the eyes of the blind man with the clay. And said unto him, 'Go, wash in the pool of Siloam.' He went his way therefore and washed, and came seeing" (John 9:7).

The blind man went, believing that he would see when he washed the clay from his eyes. Thus, it was the power of belief that restored his eyesight. And God did not go into action doing anything that God is not always doing. Miracles occur when our faith and belief are strong enough — and when our wisdom and understanding are sufficient enough — to overpower subconscious, insidious fears and deeply held false beliefs.

The secret to Jesus' success in healing the sick resided in his unshakable, absolute, unconditional faith. He had no doubt; he knew that he knew that he knew. He knew the power of faith. His faith resided in his oneness with the Father ... with being in harmony with God. Jesus' faith was so absolute and unconditional that he engendered the sick to have the faith to believe, and as they believed, it was done unto them ... their faith "made them whole."

If we pay attention to the basic teachings of Jesus, we realize that access to the power of God is by way of a quiet mind ... the state of mind alluded to by the Psalmist when he said, "Be still, and know that I am God." When we (individually and collectively as a society) understand the message that Jesus intended for us, we realize that we hold the key — we have the power and the choice —

to save ourselves, to save our families, to save our society ... to save the very world itself. Believing and comprehending the gospel that Jesus preached — discovering the truth that sets us free — will save us. Believing what is fearful and false will cause us suffering and destroy us.

The Power of God works through us according to the way we believe and think in our subconscious mind, according to our faith and also according to our unwarranted fears ... according to what is programmed in our subconscious mind ... whether true or false.

Thomas Troward, author of *The Edinburgh Lectures on Mental Science,* said, "The subjective mind is entirely under the control of the objective mind. With the utmost fidelity it reproduces and works out to its final consequences whatever the objective mind impresses upon it."

What is faith, but belief? What is a thought, but a belief? What is fear, but belief? It is done unto us as we believe deep within our heart, not what our rational, logical mind might be telling us that we believe.

When we are in harmony with God, we have no mental turmoil and suffering. On the contrary, all is peace, love, joy, and happiness. When we know the truth that sets us free, we are in harmony with God. When we are in harmony with God, we experience heaven ... and life will never get any better than heaven.

If we study nature sufficiently, we realize that God is creating all the time, and the nature of this creative process is one of plenty, beauty, and perfection. What makes a difference between what we observe in nature and what we observe in the human population is that humans were given dominion over the Earth and were given the ability to choose. Many of our choices are negative and destructive ... influenced by fear ... influenced by our elephantine ego.

We choose heaven or we choose hell. If we choose hell, it will be a perfect hell ... with all the mental turmoil, anger, anxiety, jealousy, restlessness, discontent, and gnashing of teeth. If we choose a tension headache, we will get it, and it will be a perfect headache. Have you ever had a headache that was not a perfect headache? If we choose stress and tension, it will be perfect stress and tension ... with all the devastating, destructive ramifications.

The Power of God

On the contrary, if we choose heaven, it will be a perfect heaven, characterized by love, joy, happiness, peace of mind, and inner serenity ... things that matter most in life, and they are free!

Our choices are between good and evil, love and fear, and between that which is true and that which is false. If our choices are based on that which is fearful and false, then suffering will manifest in one manner or another. Consciously, we do not choose the specific form of our suffering. For example, there are many illnesses that are psychosomatic in origin, caused by negative, false beliefs. Consciously, we do not choose the specific form of our illness.

The power of God is everywhere and in everything. And it is always creating. We choose and God creates according to our choosing. Our choosing is done by the way be believe and think in our heart.

For clarification, we can think of the Power of God like we think of electricity. Electricity is the same, regardless of how we choose to use it. We can choose to use it for heating, cooling, cooking, killing, powering motors. God is always the same, and works for us according to our choosing ... according to the programming in our subconscious mind.

Similarly, a computer works on what is programmed into the computer, thus the expression "good in, good out" or "garbage in, garbage out" (GIGO). Our channel for choosing — our spiritual link to the power of God — is by way of the subconscious mind, according to our deeply held beliefs, whether true or false, whether fearful or loving, whether bringing health and happiness, or bringing mental turmoil and suffering.

Marcus Aurelius, Roman statesman, said, "Our life is what our thoughts make it." Our mind chooses what we do, what we say, and how we feel. We function mentally and physically under the direction and control of our mind. When we are driving an automobile, who or what is it that is turning the steering wheel to determine the direction we choose to go? If (without thinking) we slam on the brakes to avoid an accident, who or what is it that is slamming on the brakes? If we find ourselves impatient and filled with road rage, what is the cause, except our own mind?

Both our physical and mental life is a function of our mind. Just as our physical efforts are under the guidance and control of our mind, so are our moods and emotions. Nothing makes us angry, hostile, anxious, jealous, possessive, depressed, sad, or happy, loving, peaceful, joyous, and contented, but our mind.

Marcus Aurelius also said, "Those who do not observe the movements of their own minds must of necessity be unhappy." Herein lies the secret to achieving a breakthrough to awareness and discovering the truth that sets us free: observing the movements of our mind. We do this by doing what David, the Psalmist, said to do: "commune with your own heart."

By observing the movements of our mind, we can do what the Apostle Paul said to do about 2,000 years ago: "Be ye transformed by the renewing of your mind." We renew our mind by obliterating the impurities from our subconscious mind. Our mind is either clear or it is cluttered. It cannot be both at the same time. We have peace and joy when our mind is clear. We have a troubled mind — we suffer — when our mind is cluttered with fears and deeply held false beliefs.

In his book, *The Undiscovered Self,* the great psychiatrist, C.G. Jung, states: "Virtually everything depends on the human soul and its functions. It should be worthy of all the attention we can give it." We can surmise from Jung's discussion of the conscious, the unconscious, the inner man, the self, the spiritual and moral component of humans, the psyche, and the physical, that he was alluding to two aspects of one's self. Jesus alluded to two aspects of himself when he said, "I and my Father are one."

Jesus gave his Father "all the attention he could give it." Jesus attributed everything that matters most to his Father. If we give our true, spiritual self sufficient attention, we will discover the truth that sets us free ... we will be saved. ... we will have peace and joy.

We know from the teachings of Jesus that the only way to enjoy genuine peace and joy is by doing the will of the Father, the same thing as abiding by our true spiritual self. Unification of the divided self is the same thing as being one with our true spiritual self, which is the same thing as being unified with God ... the same

The Power of God

thing as Jesus and his Father being one. Unification of our divided self brings peace and joy.

R. D. Laing, author of *The Politics Of Experience,* said, "True sanity entails in one way or another the dissolution of the normal ego, that false self competently adjusted to our alienated social reality; the emergence of the 'inner' archetypal mediators of divine power, and through this death a rebirth, and the eventual reestablishment of a new kind of ego-functioning, the ego now being the servant of the divine, no longer its betrayer."

Note the part, "through this death a rebirth," noting also the use of the word "death." Remember, Jesus said, "Ye must be born again." And in some instances, when Jesus alluded to "death," he was speaking of being dead in spirit.

When we understand and embody the message Jesus intended for us, the ego will be a "servant of our true spiritual self, no long its betrayer."

Swami Vivekanandam, author of *What Religion Is,* said, "Conquer yourself, and the whole universe is yours. Until we give up the world manufactured by the ego, never can we enter the Kingdom of Heaven. None ever did, none ever will. ... This rascal ego must be obliterated."

We conquer ourselves by communing with our own heart ... by discovering the truth that sets us free. Truth obliterates the influence of the false ego-self.

Our false ego-self self chooses falsity over truth, death over life ... death of our spirit while our body is alive... and actually the physical death of our body by some dread disease, rather than surrendering to truth ... the same thing as surrendering to God. Our false ego-self is elusive, relentless, and determined to be right and to appear special and important. And there is no end to our suffering until we discover the truth that sets us free ... until we learn to cherish, embrace and worship our true spiritual self, what Jesus alluded to as worshipping the Father.

It helps to know that both Jesus and biblical writers of the Old Testament recognized the division in one's self ... the division in our psyche. They knew there was something within that causes suffering, and there is something within that brings joy and peace.

The spiritual teachers of the Old Testament knew that the Lord — and Jesus knew that the Father — brought peace and joy (*Lord* and *Father* being the true spiritual self).

An example of Jesus speaking of two aspects of himself is: "Jesus cried and said, He that believeth on me, believeth not on me but on him who sent me" (John 12:44). Jesus spoke of himself and the Father who sent him. In the foregoing statement, "me" alludes to Jesus' natural self (what the Apostle Paul calls the "natural man), and "him" alludes to Jesus' Father (his true, spiritual self). In addition, the phrase, "neither the Son, but the Father" (Mark 13:32), alludes to two aspects of Jesus (his natural self and his spiritual self).

Jesus also said: "I am come a light into the world, that whosoever believeth on me should not abide in darkness. For I have not spoken of *myself*, but of *the Father who sent me*; he gave me a commandment, what I should say and what I should speak. ... Whatsoever I speak, therefore, even as the Father said unto me, so I speak" (John 12:49-50). Jesus was guided by his true spiritual self (his *Father)* in most everything he said and did.

Jesus said, "My doctrine is not mine, but *his that sent me*. If *any man will do his will*, he shall know of the doctrine, whether it be of God, or whether I speak of myself. He that speaketh of himself seeketh his own glory; but he that seeketh his glory that sent him, the same is true, and no unrighteousness is in him" (John 7:16-18). Note the significance of this passage. *"His that sent me"* alludes to Jesus' Father. And, *"Any man will do his will"* alludes to following the guidance of the true spiritual self. And if any man do the will of their true spiritual self, he will know if the doctrine is of God. The doctrine that comes from the true spiritual self is true. And we, too, can commune with our true spiritual self and discern what is true and what is false.

Overcoming the false ego-self is the secret to enjoying the abundant life that Jesus promised when he said, "I am come that they might have life, and that they might have it more abundantly" (John 10:10) ... meaning life this very moment ... not after we are dead and gone.

The Power of God

Jesus and the writers of the Old Testament did not use the words and phrases we use today. They did not speak in terms of the conscious mind, subconscious mind, ego, true self, and false self. In our language, Jesus was speaking of the ego when he said, "Ye are from beneath; I am from above; ye are of this world; I am not of this world. ... I have overcome the world." Jesus was living in the world physically, but not living in the world of the ego.

Jesus said that his disciples had overcome the world ... meaning the world of the ego. Jesus said, "They are not of the world, even as I am not of the world." The disciples believed the gospel that Jesus taught, and they had overcome the world of the ego. We, too, can do this by understanding and believing the gospel as taught by Jesus and, consequently, doing as he himself did ... which is retreating to the Father within for wisdom and understanding.

Let us remember that the disciples were human like we are. Jesus was human, too, but there are those who have stretched the Scriptures to make it seem that Jesus was God in human flesh. The primary thing that set Jesus apart from the masses is that he abided by the will of his Father (the true spiritual self). What a difference that makes! How many people do you know who abide by that which is true, rather than acquiescing to the dictates of the false ego-self?

Speaking to the Jews, Jesus said, "I have many things to say and to judge of you; but he that sent me is true; and I speak to the world those things, which I have heard of him. ... I do nothing of myself; but as my Father hath taught me, I speak these things. And he that sent me is with me; the Father hath not left me alone; for I do always those things that please him. ... If ye continue in my word, then ye are my disciples indeed; and ye shall know the truth, and the truth shall make you free. ... If the Son therefore shall make you free, ye shall be free indeed" (John 8:26-36).

Note the parts, "the truth shall make you free" (verse 32) and "If the Son therefore shall make you free" (verse 36). In this instance, "Son" means the same thing as "truth." The truth that rests within our heart sets us free. Truth is forever ... it is changeless.

And we know from Jesus that "the Spirit of truth proceedeth from the Father" (John 15:26).

Jesus also said, "I can of mine own self do nothing; as I hear, I judge; and my judgment is just; because I seek not mine own will, but the will of the Father which hath sent me. If I bear witness of myself, my witness is not true. There is another that beareth witness of me; and I know that the witness which he witnesseth of me is true" (John 5:30-32). Our spiritual self is characterized by truth. Again, note that Jesus spoke of two aspects of himself. "the Father" (his true spiritual self), and the other aspect of himself, which he alluded to as "I," "mine own self," "me," and "mine own will." And in the passage above, "he" alludes to his "Father." Note that the witness of "myself" is not true; however, the witness of the Father is true. From this, we realize that Jesus was a human being.

Similarly, we realize that Jesus was speaking of two aspects of one self when he said, "My Father is greater than I" and "I and my Father are one." The Father is the true, divine, spiritual self. Jesus did not use the word ego; however, in our language, the "I" alluded to by Jesus is (in our language) the ego-self. In our language, Jesus was speaking of the true self and the false self.

From studying and assimilating related passages concerning the "Father," we realize that the "Father" was in Jesus, the "Father" sent Jesus, the words of truth that Jesus spoke came from the Father, Jesus did everything to please his Father, Jesus' Father was true, and we know that a prerequisite for enjoy heaven is doing the will of the Father.

We also realize that (in our language), the Father is our true divine spiritual self. Following the guidance of our true spiritual self brings peace and joy, which was Jesus' purpose for preaching the gospel. Acquiescing to the false ego self brings suffering in myriad ways. The suffering, discontent, restlessness and the social problems so prevalent in our society (anxiety, depression, hate, anger, guilt, shame, stress, tension headaches, emotional insecurity, divorce, dysfunctional families, drug, child, and spousal abuse, psychosomatic illnesses, crime, violence ... the list goes on) evolve from our false ego-self.

The Power of God

The Apostle Paul makes the distinction between the things that are of the natural man (the ego self) and the things that are of the spirit of God. The Apostle Paul said: "Eye hath not seen, nor ear heard, neither have entered into the heart of man, the things which God hath prepared for them that love him. But God hath revealed them unto us by his Spirit; for the Spirit searcheth all things, yea, the deep things of God. For what man knoweth the things of a man, save the spirit of man, which is in him? Even so the things of God knoweth no man, but the Spirit of God. Now we have received, not the spirit of the world but the spirit which is of God, that we might know the things that are freely given to us of God; which things also we speak, not in the words that man's wisdom teacheth but that the Holy Ghost teacheth, comparing spiritual things with spiritual. But the natural man receiveth not the things of the Spirit of God, for they are foolishness unto him; neither can he know them because they are spiritually discerned" (1 Corinthians 2:9-14).

We discover the "deep things of God" by being still and paying attention. Our false ego-self knows things of our false ego-self, but it is alienated from our true spiritual self and, consequently, does not know truth. The phrase, "spirit of the world," alludes to the world of the ego. Spiritual things ("the spirit which is of God") permeate the Universe — in and through everything — programmed into us by an all-loving, all-knowing, all-perfect God. We need search no further than within ourselves for the truth that sets us free ... it's already within us. We need search no further than within ourselves for spiritual things ... for heaven.

Note the part by the Apostle Paul, "The natural man receiveth not the things of the Spirit of God, for they are foolishness unto him." Our false ego-self has no inkling of what genuine peace and joy is. Until we experience genuine peace and joy, we have no basis for comparison.

Thus, "Eye hath not seen, nor ear heard, neither have entered into the heart of man, the things that God hath prepared for them that love him" (1 Corinthians 2:9). Spiritual things — heavenly things — are already prepared for us; Jesus has not gone to prepare them. The things that are already prepared for us are ours to enjoy when we know, love, and accept our true spiritual self and, consequently, abide by the truth that is already within us.

We cannot understand spiritual things without transcending the insidious fears and false beliefs characteristic of the false ego-self and discerning that which is true from that which is fearful and false. We cannot transcend insidious, obscure fears and deeply held, false beliefs without "shutting the door" and calming the chatter of our false ego-self.

We find in "The Proverbs": "The wisdom of the prudent is to understand his way; but the folly of fools is deceit. ... There is a way which seemeth right unto a *man*, but the end thereof are the ways of death" (Proverbs 14: 8-12), "man" being the false ego-self.

When we have learned to discern spiritual things from things "savored by man" (savored by our false ego-self) and, consequently, abide by the truth that proceeds from our true spiritual self, we can truly call ourselves Christian. When we are truly Christian, we enjoy peace and joy. When we, as a society, enjoy peace and joy, our families, our society, our nation — the very world itself — will be peaceful and harmonious.

William James, author of *The Varieties of Religious Experience,* included a lecture titled: "The Divided Self, And The Process Of Its Unification." He relates varied experiences of others and the mental turmoil they endure before being converted and unifying the divided self. Although using different words and phrases, the author writes about the experience that we experience when we understand and embody the gospel that Jesus preached. Unification of the divided self must be the same thing that Jesus alluded to when he said, "I and my Father are one."

James, author of the "Letter of James," wrote about two aspects of ourselves. He said, "A double-minded man is unstable in all his ways. ... Humble yourselves in the sight of the Lord, and he shall lift you up" (James 4:10). James used the word "Lord" the same way that the writers of the Old Testament used it. The "Lord" is our spiritual self ... and we are lifted up when we surrender to truth and abide by our true spiritual self.

The following words and phrases allude to the true spiritual self: Lord, Father, thine heart, thy ways, acknowledge him, he shall

The Power of God

direct thy paths, thou wilt keep him in perfect peace, and stayed on thee. All these words and phrases allude to the true spiritual self, that place within us where we "live and move and have our being" ... that place within us that knows what is true and what is false ... that place within us where we discover the truth that sets us free.

Note how the foregoing words and phrases are used in the following few passages. In the Book of Proverbs we find, "Trust in the Lord with all thine heart and lean not unto thine own understanding. In all thy ways acknowledge him, and he shall direct thy paths" (Proverbs 3:5).

If we abided by this wisdom ("in all thy ways acknowledge him, and he shall direct thy paths"), no doubt we would have peace and joy. Similarly, if we abided by the wisdom of Isaiah, we would have peace and joy. Isaiah said, "Thou wilt keep him in perfect peace whose mind is stayed on thee" (Isaiah 26:3). In our language, we will have perfect peace (the purpose for Jesus preaching the gospel) if we keep our mind focused on things of our true spiritual self ("whose mind is stayed on thee"), rather than acquiescing to the dictates of the ego. Keeping our "mind stayed on thee" and abiding by the truth that proceeds from our true spiritual self is the same thing as "doing the will of the Father," which according to Jesus is a prerequisite for enjoying heaven.

If we study and assimilate what Jesus and the Apostle Paul said pertaining to things of the flesh, we realize that they were speaking of worldly things ... things of the world of the ego. Things of the flesh are characteristic of our false ego-self. Things of the spirit of God are characteristic of the true spiritual self. All things sinful and evil evolve from the false ego-self. All things loving, peaceful and truthful evolve from our true spiritual self.

A majority of people suffer a troubled mind as long as they live; they are on the "broad path the leads to destruction." Most of the time when Jesus and biblical writers used the phrases, "eternal life" and "life everlasting," they were speaking of life as long as one lives on planet earth.

In Jesus' time, people had difficulty understanding what Jesus said. Jesus told Nicodemus, "Except a man be born again, he cannot see the kingdom of God." Nicodemus wanted to know what it meant to be born again; he made his question clear. Although Nicodemus understood the language of that time, he was confused about the word "born" as used by Jesus. Nicodemus ask, "How can a man be born when he is old? Can he enter the second time into his mother's womb and be born?" Although Nicodemus' question was clear, Jesus' answer was not.

Jesus talked of being born of water and Spirit, that which is born of flesh is flesh, and that which is born of spirit is spirit, and "The wind bloweth where it listeth, and thou hearest the sound thereof, but cannot not tell where it cometh and whither it goeth; so is every one that is born of the Spirit" (John 3:5-8).

Obviously Jesus knew that he was not answering Nicodemus' question in a clear, straightforward manner. After skirting around it, he said to Nicodemus, "If I have told you of earthly things and you believe not, how shall you believe if I tell you of heavenly things?" Heavenly things are things like love, joy, happiness and peace of mind ... the kingdom of Heaven, which is within us.

In the foregoing passage, the manner in which Jesus used the word "flesh" is the same way that the Apostle Paul and others used it several times. The Apostle Paul said, "For they that are after the flesh do mind the things of the flesh; but they that are after the Spirit the things of the Spirit. For to be carnally minded is death; but to be spiritually minded is life and peace. ... So then they that are in the flesh cannot please God."

Note the phrase, "spiritually minded is life and peace," in the above passage. Paul was speaking of people who are alive; thus, "life" alludes to the life of the Spirit. Those who "are in the flesh" are abiding by the ego, rather than abiding by the guidance of the true spiritual self. Jesus did all things to please his Father ... the same thing as pleasing God. And the Apostle Paul was speaking of the present. Again, Jesus taught the gospel that we might have peace, that we might have life and have it more abundantly ... so that we would be fully alive in the spirit of truth.

The Apostle Paul goes on to say, "This I say then, walk in the Spirit, and ye shall not fulfill the lust of the flesh. For the flesh lusteth against the Spirit, and the Spirit against the flesh; and these are contrary the one to the other; so that ye cannot do the things

The Power of God

that ye would. ... Therefore, brethren, we are debtors, not to the flesh, to live after the flesh. For if ye live after the flesh, ye shall die; but if ye through the Spirit do mortify the deeds of the body, ye shall live" (Romans 8:13).

Note that the Apostle Paul said, "ye shall live." Again, he was speaking to people who are alive as we think of being alive. Thus, he was speaking of living in the spirit of truth ... not living as we typically think of living.

The Apostle Paul clarifies the ways of the Spirit and the flesh in the following. Bear in mind that the ways of the Spirit bring peace and joy, and the ways of the flesh bring suffering. Paul said: "Now the works of the flesh are manifest, which are these: Adultery, fornication, uncleanness, lasciviousness, idolatry, witchcraft, hatred, variance, emulations, wrath, strife, seditions, heresies, envyings, murders, drunkenness, revellings, and such like. ... As I have also told you in time past, that they which do such things shall not inherit the kingdom of God" (1 Corinthians 6:9-11).

These are things of the flesh, things that evolve from our false ego-self. None of this evolves from the true spiritual self. And we may note that the Apostle Paul used words different from what we typically use in our everyday language. For example, "wrath" is intense anger, rage, fury. "Variance" is conflict with another. "Strife" is vying with another; it involves bitterness, quarreling, conflict. "Heresies" include false religious beliefs. "Revellings" include boisterous festivity. "Emulations" include ambitious rivalry and envious dislike. ... all characteristic of the ego ... all inharmonious with truth.

Things of the flesh include things of the false ego-self. About the things that evolve from our true spiritual self, the Apostle Paul said, "But the fruit of the Spirit is love, joy, peace, long-suffering, gentleness, goodness, faith, meekness, temperance; against such there is no law. ... If we live in the Spirit, let us also walk in the Spirit. Let us not be desirous of vain glory, provoking one another, envying one another. For he that soweth to his flesh shall of the flesh reap corruption; but he that soweth to the Spirit shall of the Spirit reap life everlasting. ... For as many as are led by the Spirit of God, they are the sons of God" (Romans 8:14).

Note that the Apostle Paul said that those who are led by the Spirit of God are the sons of God. Thus, Jesus was not the only son of God. Being led by the Spirit of God is the same thing as abiding by our true spiritual self, which is the same thing as Jesus doing the will of his Father ... a prerequisite for enjoying peace and joy ... a prerequisite for enjoying heaven.

And note the part, "Let us not be desirous of vain glory." Let us not do and say those things that we subconsciously think will make us appear special and important. Let us not do things to brag and boast about and to gloat over. "Vain" and "vain-glory" include those things that are conceited, boastful, having no real value, empty, worthless, idle, hollow, and things having or showing an excessively high regard for one's self, looks, possessions, ability; things that are not genuine, truthful, and sincere. Vain-glory includes those things that David, the Psalmist, hated. He said, "Therefore I esteem all thy precepts concerning all things to be right; and I hate every false way" (Psalms 119:128).

John, author of "The First Letter of John," said, "For all that is in the world, the lust of the flesh, and the lust of the eyes, and the pride of life, is not of the Father, but is of the world" (1 John 2:16). Let us remember that the Bible is composed of material that was written a few thousand years ago. In our language, what John said is that evil, sinful things do not come from our true spiritual self, but from our false ego-self. ... from the world of the ego.

The ego approach to being satisfied brings us attention, praise, and adulation; and that is our reward, which does not satisfy the soul. Thus, we keep trying to get more attention, praise, and adulation. Life becomes hectic, stressful, and meaningless. We become alienated from our true self, alienated from God ... and that is hell.

If we assimilate what David the Psalmist said, we realize that he had overcome the world of the ego, "I hate every false way. ... I delight to do thy will." By overcoming the world of the ego, he overcame a serious affliction. David worshipped the Lord and chose to abide by the will of the Lord ... similar to what Jesus did. Jesus worshipped the Father and he did the will of the Father.

When we stop and ponder what David said, we understand why he said "I hate every false way." False ways are an inherent

The Power of God

factor in all mental suffering, unhappiness, evil, hypocrisy, crime, violence, problems in relationships, divorce, the masks we wear to hide the way we believe and think in our heart. False ways are an inherent part of all that is ugly and deplorable.

Isaiah said, "Let the wicked forsake his way and the unrighteous man his thoughts; and let him return unto the Lord, and he will have mercy upon him; and to our God, for he will abundantly pardon. For my thoughts are not your thoughts, neither are your ways my ways saith the Lord. For as the heavens are higher than the earth, so are my ways higher than your ways, and my thoughts than your thoughts" (Isaiah 55:8).

Isaiah was speaking about two aspects of one self: The real, true, spiritual self, which he calls the Lord, and "your ways," alluding to another aspect of oneself (in our language, the ego-self). Clearly, the ways and the thoughts evolving from our true self are higher than those of the ego-self ... what Jesus alluded to as the "world" when he said that his disciples were not of the world, "even as I am not of the world."

Jesus was motivated by — and followed the guidance of — his true self (the Father within him, who *sent him*). And he taught according to the wisdom and guidance that he received from his Father (his true self). And a most significant thing about this whole scenario is that we, too, have the Father within us (in our language, our true spiritual self). We discover the truth that sets us free *only* by communing with our true spiritual self.

What all the foregoing about the divided self, the true self and the false self boils down to is that our power — our channel to the Almighty — is our subconscious mind (what biblical writers often called the "heart"). Our subconscious mind is quite complex; thus, Jesus' statement, "In my Father's house are many mansions."

About 3,000 years ago, Zephaniah saw a need for a "pure language, so that all may call upon the name of the Lord, to serve him with one consent" (Zephaniah 3:9). Still today, there is a need for a common language. Many spiritual teachers have alluded to the same thing, using different words ... and sometimes not being specific. Jeremiah said wash your heart [the subconscious mind] from wickedness. James, author of "The Letter of James," said "purify your hearts, ye double minded." The Apostle Paul said, "Be ye therefore transformed by the renewing of your mind." Although Jesus was not specific, he spoke in terms of "cleaning the inside of the cup and the platter" and "casting out devils." He also said, "Blessed are the pure in heart [the subconscious mind]." The Buddha spoke in terms of ridding ourselves of the impurities in our mind. What all this boils down to is in the wisdom of the Proverb, "As a man thinketh in his heart [the subconscious mind] so is he," and also what Jesus said, "It is done unto us as we believe (as we believe in our subconscious mind, not our logical, rational, analytical mind). Our outer expression of life is a reflection of what is repressed in our subconscious mind. The power of God works through us according to the way we believe and think in our heart (our subconscious mind).

The Apostle Paul said, "Know ye not that your body is the temple of the Holy Ghost which is in you, which ye have of God, and ye are not your own" (1 Corinthians 6:19)? This reminds me of something that David, the Psalmist said, "Bless the Lord, O my soul, and all that is within me." Think about it! All that is within us! The truth, the true spiritual self, the God within us, the power, heaven, life, ... all that is needed to enjoy peace and joy now. Think about all the good that comes to us when we "clean the inside of the cup and the platter." When we believe and comprehend the true teachings of Jesus, we love, worship, and praise the God that is within us ... our true divine spiritual self. And we have peace and joy ... the purpose for Jesus preaching the gospel.

In summary, the power of God works through us according to what we believe and think in our heart ... whether true or false, good or evil, fearful or loving, positive or negative. As Jesus said, "It is done unto us as we believe." We have the choice of surrendering to truth and choosing heaven, or following the dictates of our false ego-self and choosing hell. It's all within us. We choose our reality by the way we believe and think in our heart.

Chapter 9
Wisdom and Understanding

We find in "The Proverbs," "Wisdom is the principal thing; therefore, get wisdom; and with all thy getting, get understanding" (Proverbs 4:7). Also, we find, "The fear of the Lord is the beginning of knowledge; but fools despise wisdom and instruction" (Proverbs 1:7). And from the dictionary, we find "fool" defined as "A person lacking understanding, judgment, or common sense."

The ultimate wisdom is knowing the truth that sets us free. How do we get wisdom and understanding? Knowledge alone is not the answer. We could study the Bible for a lifetime (some people do) and never arrive at the truth that sets us free. We could be a walking encyclopedia of knowledge and still be unwise and foolish. There are many special reference materials (commentaries, concordances, dictionaries, etc.) to help people understand the Scriptures. However, these do not help us to understand the true teachings of Jesus as long as we cling to false teachings that cause us to distort what we read and study. It is not a lack of knowledge that renders us foolish and unwise; it is believing things that are not true. We gain wisdom and understanding by being still and communing with our true spiritual self. ... by doing what David, the Psalmist said to do: "Commune with your own heart."

Knowledge can be powerful if we use it along with common sense and the power of reasoning to guide us in the steps we need to take to gain wisdom and understanding. If our mind is set with false beliefs about such significant things as heaven, hell, Satan, and also false beliefs about what Jesus said, much of our reading and studying the Bible is useless. We distort and misinterpret what we read and study, trying to make it seem consistent with our false beliefs. Thus, we do not come to an understanding, appreciation, and an acceptance of the truth that sets us free.

The Apostle Paul said, "The wages of sin is death." We commit sin — we miss the mark — when we think thoughts that are contrary to truth. Thoughts precede action. When we think negative thoughts that evolve from our false self, death of both our physical body and our spirit — the life within us while we are alive — begins. Clearly, we desire the wisdom and understanding to replace fearful, false thoughts with true thoughts.

We either are in agreement with truth or we are not. If we are not in agreement with truth, we are living a lie; and our life is fraught with isolation, anxiety, depression, frustration, unhappiness, dissatisfaction, and loneliness.

Ralph Waldo Emerson, American essayist and poet, said, "Every violation of truth is not only a sort of suicide in the liar, but is a stab at the health of human society." Wearing a mask (almost everyone does) is a violation of truth. From observing our society, it is clear that we are in violation of that which is true and, consequently, do not possess the wisdom and understanding to bring us peace, love, joy, and happiness.

It seems that at some point in time logic and common sense will emerge. If we do not gain the wisdom and understanding that will bring us love, joy, happiness, peace, and contentment while we are alive, we are not going to accomplish this after we die. A primary thing we need to be clear about is that it's all within us ... the source of our love, joy, happiness, and peace of mind ... in brief, heaven is within us. And it is also helpful to know that the source of our hate, anger, revenge, evil ... in brief, the source of our suffering — the source of hell — is within us. It all depends on how we believe and think in our heart ... "it is done unto us as we believe."

To get wisdom and understanding it helps to bear in mind that Jesus used the term, "Father," in the same sense that biblical authors of the Old Testament used the word "Lord." And it helps to know that Jesus and authors of the Old Testament gained wisdom and understanding from within by being still and listening to themselves ... by listening to their inner voice. We, too, can do what they did. Note the following:

- For the Lord giveth wisdom; out of his mouth cometh knowledge and understanding. He layeth up sound wisdom for the righteous (Proverbs 2:6-7).
- Behold, happy is the man whom God correcteth; therefore despise not thou the chastening of the Almighty (Job 5:17).

Wisdom and Understanding

- For whom the Lord loveth he correcteth; even as a father the son in whom he delighteth (Proverbs 3:12).
- Evil men understand not judgment; but they that seek the Lord understand all things. Better is the poor that walketh in his uprightness, than he that is perverse in his ways, though he be rich (Proverbs 28:5-6).
- For God giveth to a man that is good in his sight wisdom, and knowledge, and joy (Ecclesiastes 2:26).

Note that the word "God" and the word "Lord" as used in the above are synonymous. And, it's helpful to know that what corrects us is something within us; it's our own true spiritual self. We gain wisdom and understanding by communing with our spiritual self ... our own heart.

Remember, when Jesus taught his followers to pray, he said to "pray to *our* Father who is *in secret*" ... "in secret" being in our mind. He also said, "The words that I speak unto you, I speak not of *myself*; but the *Father that dwelleth in me*, he doeth the works" (Italics added for clarification). Note that he was speaking of two aspects of himself. In our language, "myself" is our logical, conscious thinking mind, and the Father that dwelleth within, is our deeper, true, spiritual self ... that self within us from which flows wisdom and understanding ... that self within us who knows the truth that sets us free.

The importance of *wisdom* and *understanding* is emphasized in the Bible; however, it is most important to be clear that the understanding we are seeking comes from the "heart" ... from a quiet place within ... never from the chatter evolving from our conscious, rational, logical mind ... never from the chatter evolving from our false ego-self ... not from sermons ... not from reading and studying ... not from some mystical being up in the sky someplace. We gain wisdom and understanding from within ourselves by "shutting the door" and listening to ourselves ... by doing what David, the Psalmist, said to do: "Commune with your own heart."

Understanding will deliver us from our sins and deliver us from our suffering; however, it must be our own understanding. Regardless of how much psychiatrists or anyone else understand about us — or regardless of anything outside ourselves — it is our own understanding that evolves from our deeper, inner, true self that frees us from our insidious fears and deeply rooted false beliefs ... if only we would be still, pay attention, and listen to ourselves, and consequently, surrender to truth.

Surrendering to truth is the same thing as surrendering to God ... the only thing that will bring us genuine joy, peace, and happiness. We are never as humble, honest, and free as little children until we transcend the influence of the ego and express life in harmony with our true spiritual self, which brings us peace, joy, and happiness.

The simple *secret* to finding happiness is found in "The Proverbs": "Happy is the man who finds wisdom and the man who gets understanding" (Proverbs 3:13), and "Wisdom resteth in the heart of him who hath understanding" (Proverbs 14:33). And, in a nutshell, here is the secret to finding happiness: "Whoso trusteth in the Lord, happy is he" (Proverbs 16:20). You need look no further for a way to find happiness; this is the simple *secret* to being happy. If you trust in your true spiritual self and abide by the truth that proceeds from within, you will be happy. Do this seriously and conscientiously, and you are assured of happiness.

David the Psalmist said, "He that dwelleth in the secret place of the most High shall abide under the shadow of the Almighty. I will say of the Lord, He is my refuge and my fortress, my God; in him will I trust" (Psalms 91:1-2). Think about it! "In him will I trust" is the secret to finding happiness.

Dwelling in the "secret place of the most High" is the same thing as being under the guidance of our true spiritual self, and this is our channel to the "Almighty." When we trust our true spiritual self and abide by its guidance (the same thing as doing the will of the Father, a prerequisite for enjoying heaven), we are in harmony with the Almighty God. This is the ultimate of peace, joy, and happiness ... this is heaven.

Think about it! Think about how simple the process for finding happiness is in comparison to all the seeking and searching in which people engage: seeking help from therapists, seeking help from psychics and astrologers, reading self-help books galore, and on and on and on. All one has to do to find happiness is to be still

Wisdom and Understanding

and commune with his or her own heart ... and trust their true spiritual self.

David, the Psalmist, said, "The Lord is nigh unto all them that call upon him in truth. He will hear their cry, and will save them" (Psalms 145:17-19). We are happy when we are saved. We are saved by doing what David said to do. "Communing with our own heart" is the same thing as calling upon the Lord. This is how we learn to trust in the Lord (the true spiritual self), a prerequisite for being peaceful, joyous, and happy.

We also know from the teachings of Jesus what will bring us peace, joy, and happiness. Jesus' sole purpose for preaching the gospel is that we might have peace and joy. When we have peace and joy, we are happy; when we are happy, we have peace and joy. We have peace and joy and we are happy when we are saved ... when we believe and embody the gospel that Jesus preached.

Jesus said, "Except ye be converted, and become as little children, ye shall not enter into the kingdom of Heaven" (Matthew 18:3) ... you will not have peace, joy and happiness. When we "clean the inside of the cup and the platter" — obliterating subconscious, insidious fears and deeply held false beliefs — we are as truthful, honest, humble and pure in heart as little children. When we are pure in heart, we have peace and joy and we are happy. To purify our hearts, we must trust in the Lord (our true spiritual self) and discover the truth that sets us free.

About 500 years BC, Sophocles, a Greek Writer, said, "There is no happiness where there is no wisdom." Wisdom and understanding are prerequisites for knowing the truth that sets us free. Wisdom and understanding obliterate unwarranted fears and false beliefs ... freeing us from the world of the ego ... freeing us to live in agreement with the truth that "resteth in our heart."

Everyone wants to be happy, rather than wearing his or her mask pretending to be. In all simplicity, we are happy when we abide by the truth that "resteth in our heart." We are happy when we are expressing life in harmony with that which is true ... which is our purpose for being on planet earth.

Our greatest struggle in life is not for power, prestige, adulation, riches, fame, and fortune; it is not our struggle for success; it is not our struggle in our relationships with others. By far, our greatest struggle is with ourselves. We have an inherent, never-ending desire to express life in harmony with truth, God, and nature. Our greatest struggle is with the false ego-self, which is relentless in leading us astray and (paraphrasing the words of Buddha) compelling us to think that delusion is better than truth. We will never realize how much of our thoughts, time, and energy are devoted to following the dictates of the ego until we achieve a breakthrough to awareness and discover the truth that sets us free.

We learn from the Buddha that "People are in bondage because they have not yet removed the idea of the ego. ... The thought of your ego stands between your reason and truth; banish it, and then will you see things as they are. He who thinks correctly will rid himself of ignorance and acquire wisdom." (*Sayings of Buddha* by The Peter Pauper Press).

Vannevar Bush said, "It is man's mission to learn to understand." William Blake said, "Men are admitted to Heaven ... because they have cultivated their understanding."

We seem to gloss over the wisdom of "The Proverbs." Even though it states that "Wisdom is the *principal thing*; therefore, get wisdom; and with all thy getting, get understanding," we seem to give this very little attention. The significance of getting wisdom and understanding is that it leads us to knowing the truth that sets us free, and this will save us. Instead of focusing our attention on something as important as this, we focus undue attention on the myth of the virgin birth.

Even if the myth were true, it does not alter what we must do to gain the wisdom and understanding for knowing the truth that sets us free. Teachings about the virgin birth have been pounded into us so thoroughly that it is like the myth is etched in stone and is not to be questioned. And it seems that Christians praise and worship Jesus, rather than understanding and believing what he taught ... rather than gaining the wisdom and understanding for knowing the truth that sets us free.

Logic, reason, and common sense do not support the myth about the virgin birth, and the myth is not supported by the Holy Scriptures. On the one hand, it seems that there are those who say

Wisdom and Understanding

that Jesus is our example. On the other hand, it seems that they say that Jesus was God in human flesh, suggesting that it is humanly impossible to achieve the level of consciousness of Jesus. Jesus achieved the level of consciousness of being at one with his Father, the level of consciousness that brings peace and joy. That is what Jesus wanted for us, "... that where I am, there ye may be also" (John 14:3). Jesus wanted us to live in harmony with our true spiritual self so that we would enjoy peace and joy.

As it is, we seem to believe the myth about the virgin birth and, consequently, preclude the possibility of achieving the level of perfection that Jesus told us to achieve. Jesus said, "Be ye therefore perfect, even as your Father who is in heaven is perfect." Thus, we gloss over much of what Jesus said ... all the while assuming that Jesus was God in human flesh and that what he did is humanly impossible. Jesus abided by the will of his Father, which set him apart from the masses of people. He abided by that which is true, which is the simplest — and yet the most rewarding — thing we will ever do.

Perhaps the most popular biblical passage accounting for the myth of the virgin birth is in "The Gospel According to Matthew." The account of the virgin birth by Matthew is not supported by the account given by Luke, author of "The Gospel According to Luke." Matthew suggests that Jesus' birth is the fulfillment of a prophecy by Isaiah. Luke does not suggest this.

Matthew alludes to the following passage by Isaiah: "Behold, a virgin shall conceive and bear a son, and shall call his name Immanuel." Isaiah was comforting Ahaz, who was troubled by conflicts among the leaders of the nations. Ahaz said, "Ask thee a sign of the Lord thy God."

If we study and assimilate the teachings of Isaiah — particularly his use of the word "Lord" — we realize that what he said about a virgin conceiving a child is not related to Jesus' birth.

In the hundreds of uses of the word "Lord" by the spiritual teachers of the Old Testament, they were not alluding to the man Jesus. They were speaking of following the guidance of the Lord within themselves ... and trying to help the people at that time in history. When Isaiah said, "Seek ye the Lord while he may be found; call ye upon him while he is near. ... For ye shall go forward with joy and be led forth with peace," he was speaking about seeking the Lord (the true spiritual self) *then and there* ... not speaking about seeking a Lord that was to born several hundred years later.

The crux of Isaiah's message was to hear and follow the word of the Lord. Although Isaiah is often referred to as a prophet, his purpose for teaching was not to prophesy future events. "Prophet" is defined as a divinely inspired, spiritual teacher. This definition applies to Isaiah. There is no justification for believing that Isaiah was prophesying the birth of Jesus, which occurred several hundred years later.

Note what Isaiah said in the following passage and then note what Jesus said, which is essentially the same thing that Isaiah said. The fact that Jesus was reading from the writings of Isaiah seems to have been glossed over. The passage by Jesus is in "red" letters in red-letter editions of the New Testament, although Jesus was reading from something that Isaiah said. Those who heard Jesus reading fastened their eyes on him, and they "wondered at the gracious words that proceeded out of his mouth" ... words of Isaiah.

Isaiah said: "The spirit of the Lord God is upon me, because the Lord hath anointed me to preach good tidings unto the meek. He hath sent me to bind up the brokenhearted, to proclaim liberty to the captives and the opening of the prison to them that are bound, to proclaim the acceptable year of the Lord and the day of vengeance of our God, and to comfort all that mourn" (Isaiah 61:1-2). Isaiah was speaking about the present.

Reading from the passage by Isaiah, Jesus said: "The Spirit of the Lord is upon me because he hath anointed me to preach the gospel to the poor; *he hath sent me* to heal the brokenhearted, to preach deliverance to the captives and recovering of sight to the blind, to set at liberty them that are bruised ... to preach the acceptable year of the Lord" (Luke 4:18-19).

Isaiah's message was not about the man Jesus. It is important to understand that Isaiah was "sent" for the same purpose that Jesus was "sent" ... that we might have peace. Isaiah was anointed for the same reason Jesus was anointed.

Wisdom and Understanding

The passage in "The Gospel According to Matthew," which seems to support the belief of a virgin birth, is not clear enough to support the belief, especially in view of the passage in "The Gospel According to Luke" (explained below). The lack of clarity begins with Matthew 1:18. If we read from the beginning of this chapter, we realize that this particular verse of scripture is the completion of the genealogy of Jesus: "When as his mother Mary was espoused to Joseph, before they came together, she was found with child of the Holy Ghost."

This genealogy of Jesus does not mention the fact that the account of Jesus' birth was based on a dream by Joseph, which is explained in the next few verses of that passage of scripture. In the following verses (Matthew 1:19-21), we find Joseph's dream: "Then Joseph, her husband, being a just man, and not willing to make her a public example, was minded to put her away privily. But while he thought on these things, behold the angel of the Lord appeared unto him in a dream, saying, Joseph, thou son of David, fear not to take unto thee Mary, thy wife, for that which is conceived in her is of the Holy Ghost. And she shall bring forth a son and thou shalt call his name Jesus, for he shall save his people from their sins."

Regardless of how we might twist the Scripture — adding to it and taking from it — a dream is not reality. And the Holy Ghost is something within our subconscious; it has to do with our spirituality; it has to do with the way we believe and think in our heart. When we are fully alive in the spirit of truth, we are filled with the Holy Ghost.

"Espoused" means married. And we note the phrase, "Joseph, her husband." So, Mary and Joseph were married "before they came together." In the genealogy, we find the clause, "before they came together." In the dream we find: "fear not to take unto thee Mary thy wife." Following Joseph's dream, we find: "Then Joseph, being raised from sleep, did as the angel of the Lord had bidden him and took unto him his wife. And knew her not till she had brought forth her firstborn son, and he called his name Jesus."

In the passage of scripture by Matthew, we also find, "Now all this was done that it might be fulfilled which was spoken of the

Lord by the prophet, saying, 'Behold, a virgin shall be with child and shall bring forth a son, and they shall call his name Emmanuel, which being interpreted is, God with us.'"

Let's face it! We do not know what all this means. Isaiah was skilled in using beautiful, descriptive language. Sometimes it is clear what he meant and sometimes it is not. However, it is not consistent with his teachings to think that what he said about "a virgin shall conceive" alludes to the birth of Jesus several hundred years later. Why wrangle with this passage of Scripture, twisting it and exaggerating it, trying to make it seem that Isaiah was prophesying the coming of the Messiah and that Jesus was *the* Messiah? Regardless of what Isaiah meant, we need not let it deter us from what is most important. Remember that Jesus said that those who believe the gospel would be saved. Thus, the important thing is to believe and understand and do what Jesus said.

Luke, author of "The Gospel According to Luke," does not claim that the birth of Jesus is the fulfillment of a prophecy by Isaiah. In addition, Luke alludes to Joseph as being the father of Jesus.

Luke's genealogy of Jesus begins with Chapter 3, verse 23, of "The Gospel According to Luke:" "And Jesus himself began to be about thirty years of age, being (as was supposed) the son of Joseph." Luke traces the genealogy back to Adam: "... which was the son of Adam, which was the son of God." The word "supposed" seems to raise questions about the account of Jesus' birth. And note that Adam was called "the son of God" (Luke 3:38). Also, note that Mary alludes to Joseph as the father of Jesus (Luke 2:48).

When we stop to think about it, the background, life, teachings, and death of John the Baptist were strikingly similar to that of Jesus. An angel (Gabriel) came to Zacharias, a priest and the husband of Elisabeth, the mother of John the Baptist, foretelling the birth of a very special son, whose name would be John. And, an angel (Gabriel) came to Mary, the mother of Jesus, foretelling the birth of a very special son, whose name would be Jesus.

As foretold by the angel, John became a great teacher. When John began talking, people ask, "What manner of child shall this be!" When he began teaching, there were those who wondered if he

Wisdom and Understanding

were the Christ. John the Baptist and Jesus grew and waxed strong in spirit, filled with wisdom. John was filled with the Holy Ghost; he was the first to preach, "The kingdom of Heaven is at hand."

Thus, there were similarities in the life and teaching of both John and Jesus. In addition, there was a similarity in the cause of their death. John would not have been imprisoned and then beheaded had he not been preaching the gospel ... the same explanation of why Jesus was killed, because he was preaching the gospel.

Both Jesus and John the Baptist were filled with the Holy Ghost. Elisabeth, the mother of John, was filled with the Holy Ghost before John was born. And, Gabriel, the angel, told Mary, "Thou art highly favoured; the Lord is with thee."

The parents of John the Baptist "were righteous before God, walking in all the commandments and ordinances of the Lord, blameless." Note the use of the word "Lord." This was before Jesus was born. After Jesus' birth, some people called him Lord.

Regardless of the actual events surrounding the birth of Jesus, it does not alter what we must do to comprehend the message Jesus intended for us ... it does not alter what we must do to be saved. Let us not forget that the principle thing is to get wisdom and understanding. The myth of the virgin birth seems to divert the focus of attention from getting wisdom and understanding; it diverts attention from the message Jesus intended for us to the man Jesus. If during the time since the death of Jesus (about 2,000 years), had religious teachers been teaching the gospel of Jesus — in a manner we can comprehend — we, our families, our society — the very world itself — would be in harmony with truth, God, and nature ... all would be peaceful.

Think of what a difference it will make in our lives, families, society, nation — the very world itself — when we begin worshipping our true spiritual self and expressing life in harmony with truth, rather than worshipping and praising Jesus and continuing to follow the dictates of our false ego-self. When we believe and comprehend the message Jesus intended for us, peace and joy will reign ... that will be the end of the world of the ego.

When we stop to think about how things might have been about 3,000 years ago, we can have a special appreciation for what the spiritual teachers of the Old Testament said and did. There is no way we can know the exact conditions of that time in history; however, we know that the spiritual teachers of the Old Testament did not have the resources for studying and learning we have today. They did not have telephones, televisions, radios and the Internet. They did not have the many reference materials we have today such as commentaries, dictionaries, and encyclopedias; they did not have the King James Version of the Bible. They did not have the benefit of the teachings of Jesus.

However, the spiritual teachers of the Old Testament had the ultimate source of wisdom: the God within them. We, too, have this source of wisdom, but pitifully and painfully, we seldom use it. The spiritual teachers of the Old Testament learned to go within themselves and commune with their own heart (what Jesus called going to the Father) to gain wisdom and understanding. They did what we must do if we are to discover the truth that sets us free. ... free to express life in harmony with truth, God, and nature.

When we acknowledge and understand our obscure, insidious fears and deeply rooted false beliefs — the hidden cause of our suffering and unhappiness — we are delivered from them ... then we are in agreement with truth. Understanding leads to the discovery of the truth that sets us free.

Heraclitus, philosopher, said, "Much learning does not teach understanding." Knowledge is not wisdom; however, we can use our knowledge — along with common sense — to help us gain the wisdom and understanding for knowing the truth that sets us free.

In summary, the essence of peace, joy, happiness and tranquillity of mind is wisdom and understanding. We gain wisdom and understanding — we discover the truth that sets us free — by doing what Jesus and the spiritual teachers of the Old Testament did; they communed with their own heart. We, too, can do this. We must "commune with our own heart" if we are to unify with God and have peace, joy, and happiness.

Chapter 10
Prayer that Never Fails

Often when we think of prayer, we think in terms of praying for something. Webster's New World College Dictionary has two definitions of prayer: "A humble and sincere request, as to God" and "Any spiritual communion, as with God."

By far, the most often used form of prayer by spiritual leaders of biblical times was communion with God. A vast portion of the entire Bible is based on communion with God.

By far, the most widely used form of prayer that we hear today is a request for something. But many times the request is not sincere and humble. Instead, it is in the vein of what Jesus said not to do: "Use not vain repetitions, as the heathen do."

The manner in which Jesus taught us to pray is a way of affirming life as it is meant to be, which is joyous and peaceful ... heaven on earth.

Let's think about prayer for a moment. How often do you pray? Who taught you to pray? When you pray, are you pleading for God to do something? It might help with your prayers to know that when you pray God does not go into action doing anything differently than God has always done and always will be doing. Regardless of how much we pray or what we do, we do not alter what God is doing.

Successful prayers require changes within ourselves ... not changing what God is doing. The creating power of God is creating all the time, and it creates for us according to our deeply held fears, beliefs, and desires. We make the choices and God creates accordingly. Jesus said, "It is done unto us as we believe."

Three things Jesus said are of utmost significance if we are to understand Jesus' prayer. These appear only once in the New Testament. Is not one time enough if we really trust Jesus and believe and understand what he said? If we do not really grasp the significance of these three statements, we will not grasp and understand Jesus' manner of praying. Here are the statements: "Shut the door," "the Spirit of truth, which proceedeth from the Father," and "The kingdom of God is within you."

Not understanding any one of those statements could impede us from praying as Jesus taught us to pray ... could impede us from discovering the truth that sets us free ... could impede us from unifying with God, the goal of all great religions.

Although Jesus did not tell us specifically that the Father is within us, we know this from inference, logic, and common sense ... from the many ways in which Jesus used the word "Father." Jesus said so much with so few words that it helps immensely to be clear about what and where the Father is ... to know without a doubt that the Father is within us. Thus, the foregoing statements by Jesus are a must. And it helps to remember some of the other things that Jesus said, such as, "Be ye therefore perfect, even as your Father who is in heaven is perfect."

With the foregoing in mind, let us take a look at Jesus' prayer, but before proceeding with the prayer that Jesus taught us, let's note what he said *not to do*: "When you pray, do not be like the hypocrites. They love to pray standing in the synagogues and in the corners of the streets, that they may be seen of men ... do not use vain repetitions as the heathen do, for they think they will be heard for their much speaking." The hypocrites and heathen were functioning from the ego, wanting to appear special and important, thinking that they would be "heard for their much speaking."

Now, let's note what Jesus said *to do*. If you miss this instruction, you will never pray an effective prayer ... you will not pray as Jesus taught. Jesus said, "When you pray, enter into the closet; and when you have *shut the door*, pray to the Father who is in secret and the Father who seeth in secret shall reward you openly."

"In secret" alludes to an aspect of our subconscious mind; the same place alluded to by the Psalmist when he spoke of the "secret place of the Most High." Using logic and common sense, where is "the Father who is in secret?" Let's be realistic and face it: The Father to whom we are praying is within us ... not somewhere up in the clouds. The "Father" is our true, spiritual self.

"Entering into the closet and shutting the door" was Jesus way of saying, be still, calm your mind, and transcend the chatter of

Prayer that Never Fails

your conscious, thinking mind. In effect, Jesus was saying to listen to our heart, not our head ... to transcend the chatter of our mind that is dominated by our false ego-self and to listen to our inner voice and hear the truth that proceeds from our true spiritual self (what Jesus called the Father).

If we do not "shut the door" and block out the chatter typical of our conscious thinking mind — and particularly all that stuff that evolves from our false ego-self — we will never pray as Jesus taught us to pray ... and we will never discover the truth that sets us free.

The manner in which Jesus taught us to pray follows, with comments of explanation following what Jesus said:
- "Our Father which art in heaven, Hallowed be thy name. Thy kingdom come; Thy will be done in earth, as it is in heaven."

Jesus had already told us that heaven is within us. Thus, both heaven and our Father (our true divine, spiritual self) are within us. And when Jesus said, "Thy kingdom come," he was speaking of the Father's kingdom. Thus, when we have "shut the door" and stopped the chatter of the ego (transcending all fearful, false thinking, which is the source of all mental turmoil) the kingdom is where we are in consciousness. "Thy will be done" alludes to the will of the Father. And the will of the Father is to express life in harmony with love and truth. Remember, Jesus said that his way of life is simple. In all simplicity, "Thy will be done in earth as it is in heaven" is an affirmation of life as it is meant to be. Our behaviors — our actions and our reactions — are to be in agreement with the will of the Father, which is in agreement with love and truth.

"Our Father [hallowed be thy name] who art in heaven," is our true, perfect self that is created in the image and likeness of God. "Hallowed" is defined by Webster, "Made holy or sacred." Our true spiritual self is holy; it is sacred; it is perfect. Our true spiritual self is in agreement with truth, in agreement with nature ... in harmony with God ... and that is heaven ... all within us.

And in Jesus' manner of praying, he was affirming that our outer expression reflects our innermost being ... all aspects of our mind (whatever we wish to call them) being in agreement with truth ... thus, our conscious mind and our subconscious mind being in

agreement with truth and love. You may note that Jesus was not pleading for anything, but simply stating that it will be done.
- "Give us this day our daily bread."
Note that Jesus was not praying for material possessions, only for "our daily bread."
- "And forgive us our debts, as we forgive our debtors."
Let us let go of old hurts, old grudges and resentments, and let us live in the moment and enjoy the joy and peace that we enjoy once we free ourselves from fear and false beliefs and, consequently, are living in agreement with truth.
- "And lead us not into temptation, but deliver us from evil; for thine is the kingdom, and the power, and the glory, forever. Amen."

Note how Jesus began his prayer and note that it is the Father (the spiritual self) that forgives. He began his prayer, "Our Father which art in heaven." And, he said, "And forgive us our debts, as we forgive our debtors. ... For if ye forgive men their trespasses, your heavenly Father will also forgive you" (Matthew 6:9-14). Similarly, we find in "The Gospel According to Mark" that the Father (again, the true spiritual self) forgives: "And when ye stand praying, forgive, if ye have ought against any; that your Father also which is in heaven may forgive you your trespasses" (Mark 11:25).

In addition, let us note that Jesus said, "pray to your Father who is in secret and your Father who seeth in secret shall reward you openly." In another passage, Jesus said, "Fear not, little flock; for it is your Father's good pleasure to give you the kingdom" (Luke 12:32). Speaking of the kingdom, Jesus was speaking of the kingdom of Heaven; he was speaking about peace and joy.

Jesus also said that the "kingdom of God is within us" (Luke 17:21). And we know from the Apostle Paul that the kingdom of God is righteousness, peace, and joy. Note that it is our *Father* who rewards us openly, and it is our *Father's* good pleasure to give us the kingdom (the *Father* being our true spiritual self).

Speaking about rewards, Jesus was not speaking of materialistic things. He was speaking about spiritual things, heavenly things; he was speaking about peace, love, and joy. Thus, when we pray to our Father (our true spiritual self) in the manner in which

Prayer that Never Fails

Jesus taught, we are rewarded with the peace and joy of heaven ... the heaven that is within us.

Jesus said, "Therefore I say unto you, What things soever ye desire, when ye pray, believe that ye receive them, and ye shall have them" (Mark 11:24). Pause and note what Jesus said. Do you believe what he said? If we pray as Jesus taught us to pray, our prayers will be answered. And it's important to keep in mind that Jesus' message is about spiritual things ... things like love, peace, joy ... things that are in harmony with truth, God, and nature.

Think for a moment about the parable of the rich man and Lazarus. What is the value of riches to the person who is "tormented by this flame"? To the person who is living in hell? To the person who is alienated from God, troubled by such things as anxiety, fear, depression, loneliness, guilt, worry, hate, anger, shame and whose inner emptiness demands that he or she appears special and important? In brief, what is the value of riches to the person who does not have peace and joy ... who is not happy?

Praying as Jesus taught us to pray is the same thing that David, the Psalmist, advocated: "Commune with your own heart." This is how David was rewarded with untold benefits. Communing with our own heart is the same thing as praying to the Father who is in secret ... thus, the state of consciousness for praying as Jesus taught us to pray.

More about this in Chapter 11, "The Essential Teachings of Jesus," but for now note the similarity of something that David, the Psalmist said: "Bless the Lord, O my soul and all that is within me, bless his holy name. ... and forget not all his benefits; Who forgiveth all thine iniquities; who healeth all thy diseases" (Psalms 103:1-3). And, "Look upon mine affliction and my pain; and forgive all my sins" (Psalms 25:18). And, "For thou, Lord, art good, and ready to forgive; and plenteous in mercy unto all them that call upon thee" (Psalms 86:5).

Thus, we are forgiven of our sins by communing with our true divine spiritual self, by "calling upon thee" ... the same thing as communion with God. Fundamentalists believe that Jesus took away our sins. Jesus did not teach this; he taught the forgiveness of sins. Jesus taught that those who believe the gospel are saved. When we are saved, our sins are forgiven.

Let us not be swayed by the thoughts that evolve from our false ego-self, which always brings restlessness, discontent, suffering, and unhappiness, but deliver us from evil. All evil evolves from our false ego-self. The evil that tortures us mentally is the evil that is within us.

A God of love does not cast us into hell. We do it to ourselves by our thoughts that evolve from subconscious fears and false beliefs. Our thoughts create our reality ... "It is done unto us as we believe." "Thine" refers to our "Father," which is in heaven ... which is within us. And we know from the Apostle Paul that the kingdom of Heaven is characterized by joy, peace, and righteousness ... all that is in agreement with truth and love.

Jesus said, "Be ye therefore perfect, even as your Father who is in heaven is perfect." We will never enjoy heaven until we are as perfect as Jesus told us to be. And when we are as perfect, "even as your Father who is in heaven is perfect," we are saved, a prerequisite for enjoying heaven.

When we have "cleaned the inside of the cup and the platter," when we have "cast the devils from our mind," when we discover the truth that sets us free, then we are as perfect as Jesus told us to be. Then we are in harmony with truth ... the same thing as being in harmony with God.

When our outer expression of life is in agreement with our true innermost being — when we are as perfect as Jesus told us to be — we experience the "peace that passeth all understanding. This is "Letting thy will be done in earth as it is in heaven" ... and this is heaven. Heaven is a peaceful, harmonious state of mind, with all aspects of our mind being in agreement with truth ... a mind in harmony with God and nature. This is the state of mind of Jesus, thus, his statement, "I and my Father are one."

Keeping in mind that Jesus used the word "Father" in the manner that the writers of the Old Testament used the word "Lord," we note a similarity between the words in Jesus' prayer and something that King David, the father of Solomon, said as it appears in "The First Book of the Chronicles": "Blessed be thou, Lord God of

Prayer that Never Fails

Israel our father, forever and ever. Thine, O Lord, is the greatness and the power and the glory and the victory and the majesty, for all that is in the heaven and in the earth is thine. Thine is the kingdom, O Lord, and thou art exalted as head above all. Both riches and honour come of thee and thou reignest over all, and in thine hand is power and might, and in thine hand it is to make great and to give strength unto all. Now, therefore, our God, we thank thee, and praise thy glorious name. ... for all things come of thee" (1 Chronicles 29:10). Note that King David alluded to the Lord God of Israel as "our father." And he said, "... for all things come of thee."

What Jesus said about praying is in agreement with what the spiritual writers of the Old Testament said. David, the Psalmist, said:

- I acknowledged my sin unto thee, and mine iniquity have I not hid. I said, I will confess my transgressions unto the Lord; and thou forgavest the iniquity of my sin (Psalms 32:5-6).
- The Lord is righteous in all his ways, and holy in all his works. The Lord is nigh unto all them that call upon him in truth. He will hear their cry, and will save them" (Psalms 145:17-19). Note that the Lord (the true spiritual self) will save them.
- As for me, I will call upon God; and the Lord shall save me. Evening, and morning, and at noon, will I pray, and cry aloud; and he shall hear my voice" (Psalms 55:16-17).
- Make me to hear joy and gladness. ... and blot out all mine iniquities. Create in me a clean heart, O God; and renew a right spirit within me. Cast me not away from thy presence; and take not thy Holy Spirit from me. Restore unto me the joy of thy salvation; and uphold me with thy free spirit (Psalms 51:7-12).

David used the words "God" and "Lord" synonymously. And, note that "the Lord shall save me" (the "Lord" being the true spiritual self).

An example of a prayer similar to what Jesus taught us is in "The First Book of the Kings" (author unknown). The author was praying to the Lord, the same thing as Jesus praying to the Father. And if we are to pray as Jesus taught us to pray, we will pray to our true, divine, spiritual self ... God within us.

The author of the subject book (1 Kings 8:28-44), said, "Have thou respect unto the prayer of thy servant, and to his supplication, O Lord my God, to hearken unto the cry and to the prayer, which thy servant prayeth before thee to day ... hear thou in heaven thy dwelling place; and when thou hearest, forgive. ... hear thou in heaven, and forgive the sin of thy servants, and of thy people Israel, that thou teach them the good way wherein they should walk."

According to Webster, to "hearken" is to listen carefully. And, "Supplication" is to ask for humbly and earnestly, as by prayer. And, note that the author said, "hear thou in heaven thy dwelling place." "Thou" and "thee" refer to the Lord (in our language, the true spiritual self). And note that the dwelling place of the Lord (the true spiritual self) is in heaven (in Jesus words, the Father, which is in heaven). And, we know from the teachings of Jesus that heaven is within us.

A considerable portion of the Old Testament is based on communion with God, a form of prayer. For example, in "The Book of Exodus," we find: "And the angel of the Lord appeared unto him [Moses] in a flame of fire out of the midst of a bush; and he looked, and, behold, the bush burned with fire, and the bush was not consumed. ... God called unto him out of the midst of the bush, and said, Moses, Moses. And he said, Here am I" (Exodus 3:2-4). Note that it was an angel that appeared unto Moses. Also, note that the words "Lord" and "God" are used interchangeably.

No one has ever seen God or heard a physical voice of God. Angels appear to us in our inner vision; angels are a way of communing with God. Moses did not literally see or hear anything outside himself; it was all a vision ... mental activity. Thus, the "angel of the Lord" was something within Moses. The many references to the phrases "angel of God" and "angel of the Lord" and phrases such as "hear ye the word of the Lord" and "saith the Lord" allude to visions and communion with God. When Moses spent forty days and forty nights with the Lord and wrote the Ten Commandments, he was in communion with Lord within him. ... his true divine spiritual self.

There is a similarity between visions and dreams. Both occur in a quiet state of mind. Most dreams occur in a light state of sleep.

Prayer that Never Fails

Some of the things we see in visions and dreams are symbolic. There are messages in both visions and dreams, if only we know how to interpret them. A clue for helping one understand dreams and visions is to be still and pay attention, letting the mind go to where it needs to go for us to understand the symbolic meaning of images that appear.

I'm reminded of a group exercise in which the participants "made up" a dream for another participant. A participant was selected from among all the participants to receive the dream. He was asked to leave the room while we, the remaining participants, made up a dream for him. To reveal further information about how we "made up" the dream would spoil the use of this exercise for those teachers who use it. Thus, I will add only that the exercise demonstrated something about how the mind works ... the way it works when people see visions.

In all simplicity, we are saved when we discover the truth that sets us free. We discover truth by communion with our true spiritual self, the same thing as communion with God. We do not gain the wisdom for knowing the truth that sets us free by reading the words of others or by listening to sermons. We gain wisdom by doing what Jesus and the spiritual teachers of the Old Testament did; they communed with their own heart ... the same thing as communing with God.

Mainline churches do not teach us clearly how to calm the mind, see visions, let angels appear unto us, how to commune with God (at least they do not make it clear), and consequently, they do not teach us how to discover the truth that sets us free.

When Jesus "went unto the Father," he was in communion with God. The Apostle Paul said, "For whosoever shall call upon the name of the Lord shall be saved." When we call upon the name of the Lord, we are in communion with God, the only way we will ever be saved. "Calling upon the name of the Lord" is a form of communion with God, a form of prayer.

All the following words and phrases allude to a communion with God: Hear ye the word of the Lord, thus saith the Lord, the Lord said unto me, call upon the name of the Lord. The pronouns "he" or "him" (where the antecedent of the pronoun is Lord, God, or Lord God, or angel) allude to communion with God.

The Bible, from cover to cover, includes many visions, which are a form of communion with God, a form of prayer. Most all (if not all) of the "The Revelation to John" is based on visions. We tend to gloss over a huge portion of the Bible (from "Genesis" to "The Revelation to John") and miss the potential that the Bible holds for us. We read about visions and angels, and we tend to gloss over these things as if seeing visions and angels was something unique for people of biblical times, but that it is not something for us to do.

A huge portion of the Bible (from cover to cover) is composed of information obtained from communion with God. When we commune with God, we can have visions; we can see angels. By communion with God, we can gain the wisdom and understanding for knowing the truth that sets us free. A fact is that we will never find what we are seeking until we do what the spiritual teachers of the Old Testament did; they communed with God, which is a form of prayer.

A calm mind — entering into the closet and shutting the door (the language of Jesus) — is an absolute prerequisite for seeing angels and communing with God. David, the Psalmist, said, "Be still ... commune with your own heart." To be still we must calm the chatter of the ego-self.

An overriding benefit from communion with God is guidance. Remember that Jesus said that only those who do the will of the Father (those who abide by the truth that proceeds from one's own true spiritual self) will enjoy heaven. We get guidance in communion with our true spiritual self. Many times, the guidance comes in the form of visions, images, and angels. Communion with God is all mental activity. One does not actually "see" or "hear" anything. Everything "seen" or "heard" in visions is within oneself. It's all mental activity.

Some visions can seem weird and bazaar. Actually, many are gems of wisdom, if only we know how to interpret them. Some people who have studied "The Book of Ezekiel" think that Ezekiel was troubled with schizophrenic paranoia. An example of one of

Prayer that Never Fails

Ezekiel's visions begins with Chapter 8. Note that he said, "The hand of the Lord God fell there upon me." This is only one of the many words and phrases that have been used to describe a state of mind necessary for seeing visions and communing with God.

Beginning with verse 4 of chapter 8, we find, "Behold, the glory of the God of Israel was there, according to the vision that I saw. ... Then said he unto me, Son of man, lift up thine eyes now the way toward the north. ... Then said he unto me, Son of man, hast thou seen what the ancients of the house of Israel do in the dark, every man in the chambers of his imagery?" (Ezekiel 8:4-12).

This vision is quite lengthy. I allude to it here to explain something about the nature of visions. The pronoun "he" as used throughout this vision alludes to the Lord (Ezekiel's deeper, innermost being, his true spiritual self). The Lord was Ezekiel's guide. Ezekiel did not actually "see" or "hear" anything outside himself. Again, a vision is all mental activity.

In the New Testament, we note that the Apostle Paul saw visions and followed the guidance of the Lord, similar to what Ezekiel did. In "The Acts of the Apostles" we find, "Then spake the Lord to Paul in the night by a vision, Be not afraid, but speak, and hold not thy peace; For I am with thee" (Acts 18:9-10).

And, in "Acts" 22:6-18, we find where Paul said, "And it came to pass, that, as I made my journey, and was come nigh unto Damascus about noon, suddenly there shone from heaven a great light round about me. And I fell unto the ground, and heard a voice saying unto me, Saul, Saul, why persecutest thou me? And I answered, Who art thou, Lord? And he said unto me, I am Jesus of Nazareth, whom thou persecutest. ... And I said, What shall I do, Lord? And the Lord said unto me, Arise, and go into Damascus; and there it shall be told thee of all things which are appointed for thee to do. ... And it came to pass, that, when I was come again to Jerusalem, even while I prayed in the temple, I was in a trance; and saw him saying unto me, Make haste, and get thee quickly out of Jerusalem." Note that Paul was in a trance, a state of mind for seeing visions.

Whereas Ezekiel used the pronoun "he," alluding to the Lord, Paul used the pronoun "him." And sometimes, it was as if Paul were speaking with Jesus ... all in a vision. The exact same phrase used by Paul, "The Lord said unto me," is used several times in the Old Testament. It is mental activity in the form of guidance; for example: "And the Lord said unto me, Arise, get thee down quickly from hence; for thy people which thou hast brought forth out of Egypt have corrupted themselves" (Deuteronomy 9:12). And, "Then the Lord put forth his hand, and touched my mouth. And the Lord said unto me, Behold, I have put my words in thy mouth" (Jeremiah 1:9).

Whereas the spiritual writers of the Old Testament communed with angels and the Lord, Jesus communed with the Father (same thing, but different words). ... the same thing as communion with God. And, we may note that although Jesus taught us to pray as explained above, when he "went to pray," he was seeking guidance. Fundamentalists believe that Jesus was God in human flesh. It's illogical to think that God would need to seek guidance. Let's face it! Jesus was human. Thus, when Jesus led Peter, John, and James up into a mountain to pray, Jesus was seeking guidance concerning the Ascension. He received guidance in the form of visions.

In "The Gospel According to Luke" (9:28-32), we find, "And it came to pass about eight days after these sayings, he [Jesus] took Peter and John and James, and went up into a mountain to pray. And as he prayed, the fashion of his countenance was altered, and his raiment was white and glistering. And, behold, there talked with him two men, which were Moses and Elias; who appeared in glory, and spoke of his decease which he should accomplish at Jerusalem. But Peter and they that were with him were heavy with sleep; and when they were awake, they saw his glory, and the two men that stood with him."

The two men (Moses and Elias) "spoke of his decease which he should accomplish at Jerusalem," thus, providing guidance. Clearly, it was a vision; Moses had been dead for several hundred years. We may also note that "Peter and they that were with him were heavy with sleep," a state of mind receptive to seeing visions.

Prayer that Never Fails

Similarly, we may note that when Peter went upon the housetop to pray that he did not pray for something as we typically think of praying. Instead, his communion with God was through visions. His vision provides an example of something that is important for us to know about visions.

Let us take a look at Peter's vision. "Peter went up upon the house top to pray ... he became very hungry, and would have eaten; but while they made ready, he fell into a trance, and saw heaven opened, and a certain vessel descending unto him, as it had been a great sheet knit at the four corners, and let down to the earth; wherein were all manner of fourfooted beasts of the earth, and wild beasts, and creeping things, and fowls of the air. And there came a voice to him, 'Rise, Peter; kill, and eat'" (Acts 10:9-13).

Some people proclaim that every word in the Holy Scriptures is the inspired word of God. Although the vision by Peter might have been inspired by God, unless Peter explained the symbolic meaning of what he saw and heard, there is no way we will ever know, regardless of how much we read and study. The sheet, the vessel, the fourfooted beasts, and the creeping things are symbolic. They had a very specific meaning for Peter. And, most likely he knew in a flash what they meant. But, unless he explained the meaning of them, we will never know.

This does not mean that we cannot get an understanding of some of the visions reported in the Bible. Clearly, we can; it all depends upon the particular circumstances and the manner in which the vision is reported. However, what we are not likely to ever know is the symbolic meaning of such things as the "fourfooted beasts and creeping things" as reported by Peter (if he did not explain the meaning). We are not likely to ever know the symbolic meaning of many of the images reported by the apostle John in "The Revelation to John" (The Apocalypse). Religious teachers do people a disservice if they interpret the visions of John to mean something that is contrary to the gospel that Jesus preached.

Many images are flashbacks to images in a childhood scene. And without being aware of the childhood scene and how something in the scene impacted the one seeing the symbolic image, we don't know the meaning of the image. If the one seeing the image in his or her inner vision and observes it in the stillness of the mind, then he or she will understand the symbolic meaning, which is only meaningful to the one seeing the image.

What can be helpful to others is the wisdom that one acquires from understanding the meaning of his or her images and shares the wisdom with others. And the wisdom shared with others is helpful mostly to the extent that others use it as a guide as to what they must do to know the truth that sets them free. In the final analysis, what we must do is commune with our own true spiritual self ... the same thing as communing with God.

Webster's definition of "angel" is: "a messenger of God, a supernatural being, either good or bad, to whom are attributed greater than human power, intelligence." I wonder about the "bad." ... A bad messenger of God? Possibly, this alludes to images that a deeply troubled person gets when he or she has not calmed the mind sufficiently enough to transcend fear thoughts. Or, it could allude to seemingly negative images, which have a message in them if only we pay sufficient attention to understand the message. In this case, the seemingly negative image is a positive, beneficial message.

For example, in our meditations — communing with our inner most being in the stillness of our minds — we can get an image that is seemingly negative; there is something about it that is troubling. If we pay close attention, the image is symbolic of something that has had a false influence on us in almost everything we have said or done since we were a child. Once we understand the hidden meaning of the image — which is quite easy to do, if only we pay attention — then we can say with honesty, meaning, and understanding, "Get thee behind me, Satan; thou art an offense unto me." Then we are free from a false influence that has been robbing us of peace and joy. Thus, the seemingly "bad" angel has been positive, helping us to understand the truth that sets us free.

Two instances in which Jesus saw visions involved a ship in a storm and his disciples fearful of perishing. One instance he saw a vision of himself walking on water. In the other instance he saw a vision of himself rebuking the wind. In one instance, he remained on land and *went to pray*. Remember that Jesus told us to enter the closet and shut the door when we pray. Entering into the closet and

Prayer that Never Fails

shutting the door is a way of calming the mind and stopping the chatter typical of the ego. It's the state of mind for praying and seeing visions.

In the other instance in which Jesus saw a vision involving a ship, he was asleep on the ship. In both instances he was in a state of mind for seeing visions. A dreamy state of mind similar to a light sleep is a prerequisite for communing with God ... is a prerequisite for seeing visions. A calm state of mind is what David the Psalmist alluded to when he said, "Be still."

In "The Gospel According to Matthew" we find, "And when he [Jesus] had sent the multitudes away, he went up into a mountain apart to pray; and when the evening was come, he was there alone. But the ship was now in the midst of the sea, tossed with waves; for the wind was contrary. And in the fourth watch of the night Jesus went unto them, walking on the sea. And when the disciples saw him walking on the sea, they were troubled, saying, It is a spirit; and they cried out for fear. But straightway Jesus spake unto them, saying, Be of good cheer; it is I; be not afraid. And Peter answered him and said, Lord, if it be thou, bid me come unto thee on the water. And he said, Come. And when Peter was come down out of the ship, he walked on the water, to go to Jesus. But when he saw the wind boisterous, he was afraid; and beginning to sink, he cried, saying, Lord, save me. And immediately Jesus stretched forth his hand, and caught him, and said unto him, O thou of little faith, wherefore didst thou doubt? And when they were come into the ship, the wind ceased" (Matthew 14:23-32).

Note that this happened during "the fourth watch of the night" and that Jesus' disciples "saw him walking on the sea." Jesus' disciples did not actually see Jesus walking on the sea; Jesus saw all of this in his vision.

In the other vision by Jesus, we find, "And when he [Jesus] was entered into a ship, his disciples followed him. And, behold, there arose a great tempest in the sea, insomuch that the ship was covered with the waves; but he was asleep. ... And his disciples came to him, and awoke him, saying, Lord, save us; we perish. And he saith unto them, Why are ye fearful, O ye of little faith? Then he arose, and rebuked the winds and the sea; and there was a great calm. But the men marvelled, saying, What manner of man is this, that even the winds and the sea obey him!" (Matthew 8:23-27). Note that Jesus was asleep, a state of mind for seeing visions. Fundamentalists believe that Jesus literally walked on the water and calmed the wind. They believe that Jesus could do this because they believe that he was God in human flesh. I am not sure how fundamentalists justify Peter walking on water. Perhaps they believe that Jesus gave him the power. These passages of Scriptures are based on visions.

Jesus' teachings are easier to grasp once we realize that he was human. In instances when Jesus went to pray, he was seeking guidance. And sometimes he received guidance in the form of visions. When Jesus had sent the multitudes away and went up into a mountain apart to pray, he was troubled because his disciples were troubled. After all, they were embarking on an unusual journey, following Jesus' instructions: "Go ye therefore, and teach all nations ...teaching them to observe all things whatsoever I have commanded you" (Matthew 28:19).

Jesus knew, and the disciples knew, that they would be rejected, hated, imprisoned, and persecuted (perhaps executed) for teaching the gospel. Jesus said to his disciples, "Behold, I send you forth as sheep in the midst of wolves; be ye therefore wise as serpents, and harmless as doves" ... ye shall be hated of all men for my name's sake" (Matthew 10:16,22). In our language, the disciples would be hated for teaching the truth.

Jesus knew that if his disciples were fearful they would falter. Thus, in his prayer, Jesus had visions of a boisterous storm and a ship and the disciples afraid that they would perish. Thus, Jesus was seeking guidance for buoying up the faith and spirits of his disciples. Thus, in his prayer (in his communion with the Father within), the cause of his disciples' concern became clear to Jesus. It was a lack of faith, expressed in the words of Jesus: "Why are ye fearful, O ye of little faith"?

In a similar vein, note the guidance that Joshua received in a vision after the death of Moses. In The Book of Joshua, we find: "Now after the death of Moses the servant of the Lord it came to pass, that the Lord spake unto Joshua ... saying, Moses my servant

Prayer that Never Fails

is dead; now therefore arise, go over this Jordan, thou, and all this people, unto the land which I do give to them, even to the children of Israel. ... Only be thou strong and very courageous, that thou mayest observe to do according to all the law, which Moses my servant commanded thee; turn not from it to the right hand or to the left, that thou mayest prosper whithersoever thou goest. This book of the law shall not depart out of thy mouth; but thou shalt meditate therein day and night, that thou mayest observe to do according to all that is written therein; for then thou shalt make thy way prosperous, and then thou shalt have good success. Have not I commanded thee? Be strong and of a good courage; be not afraid, neither be thou dismayed; for the Lord thy God is with thee whithersoever thou goest" (Joshua 1:1-9). ... all mental activity.

If we compare some visions throughout the Bible, we notice some common words and phrases. Following the baptism of Jesus, Matthew said, "And Jesus, when he was baptized, went up straightway out of the water; and, lo, the heavens were opened unto him, and he saw the Spirit of God descending like a dove, and lighting upon him; And lo a voice from heaven, saying, This is my beloved Son, in whom I am well pleased" (Matthew 3:16-17).

Jesus' experience was similar to the experience of Ezekiel, who called it a vision. Visions are something we see with our inner vision; it's all within us. Ezekiel said, "... the heavens were opened, and I saw visions of God" (Ezekiel 1:1). Clearly, this was a vision; no one has seen God.

John, author of "The Revelation to John" (The Apocalypse), said, "I looked, and, behold, a door was opened in heaven; and the first voice which I heard was as it were of a trumpet talking with me." "A door was opened in heaven" is similar to what Peter saw, "heaven opened" and similar to what Jesus saw, "the heavens were opened unto him."

We know that neither Peter nor John literally saw heaven opened. The phrases "a door was opened in heaven" and "saw heaven opened" allude to a state of mind that is receptive to seeing visions. When Paul "fell unto the ground," he was in a state of mind for seeing visions.

Note that Peter "went *up upon* the house top to pray." The word *up* must have a special meaning; otherwise the way it is used ("up upon") is suplerous. Before Moses wrote the Ten Commandments, he "... went into the midst of the cloud, and gat him *up into* the mount." When Jesus taught the beatitudes, "he went *up into* a mountain and when he was set." *Up* as used in these examples mean a high state of conscious awareness. Whether Jesus or Moses actually went up into a mountain (as we think of going to the mountains), the important thing to know is that they were in a calm state of mind, a state of mind in which one blocks out distractions and stops the chatter of the ego. In the examples of Peter and the Apostle Paul, they were in a trance.

It is also significant that Jesus told Peter, James and John as they came down from the mountain, "Tell the vision to no man." Visions can be seemingly weird; reactions from others could be myriad and varied. Some time ago, a devout Christian accused me of engaging in Satan worship, because I practiced Transcendental Meditation® (TM), which is a way of calming the mind ... which is a prerequisite for discovering the truth that sets us free.

However, I must explain that I added an additional step to TM. The instructions in TM were to repeat a mantra. I used the mantra, as I was instructed, to calm my mind. However, I added the step of letting my mind take me to where it needed to go for providing guidance and understanding. Exploring our inner selves in the quietness of our minds to discover the truth that sets us free is an especially helpful adjunct to praying as Jesus taught us to pray, affirming the expression of life as it is meant to be.

The Saints of the Old Testament time communicated with the Lord within themselves ... gaining wisdom, understanding, and guidance. Similarly, Jesus "went unto the Father." Similarly, the Apostle Paul communicated with the Lord, sometimes as if he were communicating with Jesus. All this constitutes a form or prayer, a communion with God.

When we are in communion with our true divine spiritual self, we are in communion with God. That's where and how we learn the greatest lesson life has to offer. We do not learn this lesson from sermons, reading, studying and arguing. Although these things

Prayer that Never Fails

might inspire and motivate us, they do not bring us what we desire, which is peace and joy, which is heaven ... which is the kind of life that Jesus wanted for us. To find the kind of life that Jesus wanted for us, there is something we must do besides reading, studying, and listening to sermons.

- We must do what David, the Psalmist, said to do: "Commune with your own heart," the same thing as communion with God.
- We must do what Isaiah said to do: "Seek ye the Lord while he may be found; call ye upon him while he is near. ... For ye shall go forward with joy and be led forth with peace." We only find the Lord (our true spiritual self) by communing with ourselves in the stillness of our mind.
- We must do what the Apostle Paul said to do: "Call upon the name of the Lord." When we do this, we are in communion with God. We find salvation by communing with God.
- We must do what Jesus said to do: "Enter into your closet, and when thou hast shut thy door, pray to *your* Father which is in secret." He also said, "Seek, and ye shall find." The only place to seek is within ourselves, and the only way to seek is in the stillness of our mind, by communing with God, which is a form of prayer.

In the final analysis, we can find everything we need to know to overcome our suffering and to find peace and joy — to enjoy heaven — by communing with our true spiritual self ... the same thing as communion with God ... by doing the same thing that spiritual leaders did during biblical times.

What Jesus said ("Enter into the closet and when you have shut the door, pray to your Father who is in secret."), means doing the same thing that David the Psalmist said: "Stand in awe, and sin not; commune with your own heart upon your bed, and be still" (Psalms 4:4). Herein lies the *secret* (using the word "secret" loosely) to prayer that never fails, the *secret* to discovering the truth that sets us free, the *secret* to purifying our heart, the *secret* to unifying with God ... the *secret* to being saved.

Thus, being still and communing with our own heart is a form of prayer that never fails. Communing with our own heart is consistent with Jesus' manner of praying: "Pray to your Father which is in secret; and your Father which seeth in secret shall reward you openly" (Matthew 6:6). This form of prayer guides us to a purification of our heart; it guides us to unification with God; it guides us to an understanding of the truth that sets us free; it guides us to the narrow path to life that few find. This form of prayer saves us.

We are always guided by both love and truth or by fears and falsehoods. Love and truth bring joy, peace, and happiness. Fear and falsehoods bring suffering, restlessness, discontent, depression, anxiety, anger, and on and on and on ... all that negative stuff that saps us of the life of our spirit.

Jesus said to the Pharisees: "Ye are they which justify yourselves before men; but God knoweth your hearts; for that which is highly esteemed among men is abomination in the sight of God." Remember that Jesus sometimes used the words "Father" and "God" interchangeably. The God that knoweth our hearts is the God within us ... our true, divine, spiritual self (what Jesus called the Father).

In one way or another, Jesus' manner of praying and all of his teachings are aimed toward the abundant life ... toward enjoying peace and joy ... toward enjoying heaven. When Jesus spoke about casting out devils, he was speaking about getting rid of something within us that is contrary to truth. Likewise, when Jesus spoke about cleaning the inside of the cup and the platter so that the whole cup and platter would be clean, he was speaking about getting rid of something within us that is contrary to truth. Likewise, when Jesus said, "Repent. The kingdom of Heaven is at hand," he was speaking of changing our ways ... changing something within us ... changing our deep-down beliefs. Thus, Jesus' teachings are aimed at helping us to rid ourselves of fearful, false thinking — all negativity in our mind — so that we can enjoy heaven here and now.

When Jesus said, "You shall know the truth and the truth shall make you free," he was speaking in terms of freeing ourselves from something within us that is contrary to truth ... that something being the hidden source of all our mental suffering, all our unhappiness, and all restlessness and discontent. He was speaking about having a pure heart and abiding by the truth that rests within our heart. He was speaking about harmonizing with God ... the same thing as harmonizing with our true self ... at which point we enjoy heaven ... at which point we naturally do the will of "our Father which art in heaven" ... at which point we naturally "do unto others as we would have others do unto us."

In Jesus' manner of teaching and praying, he was trying to get us to follow the guidance we get from listening to our inner voice — our true spiritual self — as opposed to following the whims of our false ego-self and doing things to appear important and to gain attention, recognition, and adulation.

Once you master the art of being still and communing with your own heart, you will get an inner knowing and understanding that will allow to you discern that which is true from that which is false. At this level of knowing, you will know that you know that you know. Then you will realize that you have reached the level of understanding that the Psalmist alluded to when he said: "I have more understanding than all my teachers; for thy testimonies are my meditation. I have refrained my feet from every evil way, that I might keep thy word. I have not departed from thy judgments; for thou hast taught me" (Psalms 119:99-102).

Think about what David said! By far, the greatest teacher for those who are lost is none other than their own true spiritual self. Think about it! The Old Testament is filled with profound gems of wisdom, which the spiritual teachers of the Old Testament got from within themselves. We, too, can do what they did.

This passage by David coincides with the teachings of Jesus. David was taught by — and did the will of — the Lord. Jesus was taught by — and did the will of — the Father. Both David and Jesus retreated within themselves — to the God within — for wisdom, guidance, and understanding ... the same thing alluded to by Isaiah when he posed the question: "Should not a people seek unto their God?"

Jesus said, "Take heed that ye do not your alms before men, to be seen of them; otherwise ye have no reward of your Father who is in heaven. Therefore, when thou doest thine alms, do not sound a trumpet before thee, as the hypocrites do in the synagogues and in the streets, that they may have the glory of men. Verily I say unto you, they have their reward. But when thou doest alms, let not thy left hand know what thy right hand doeth, that thine alms may be in secret; and thy Father who seeth in secret himself shall reward thee openly" (Matthew 6:1-6).

We will not enjoy heaven until we are truthful and honest. Recall some of your past behavior, some of the things you did and some of the gifts you gave. Was all this simply from the love and the goodness in your heart? Or, did you secretly expect something in return? Or, at some level, did you secretly want others to notice what you were doing? Were you really striving for ego gratification, trying to appear righteous, loving, good, special, and important? If so, you got your reward; but it is not what you really want, which is the peace and joy you experience when you follow the guidance of your inner voice ... the guidance coming from your true self.

Our ultimate reward in heaven is when we are as perfect as Jesus told us to be: "Be ye therefore perfect, even as your Father who is in heaven is perfect." If the word "perfect" tends to baffle you, bear in mind the simplicity of Jesus' message. Jesus was simply telling us to love and to be truthful and honest ... to abide by the truth that proceeds from our true spiritual self. When we "clean the inside of the cup and the platter, we are perfect."

When we discover the truth that sets us free, we are free from the devils in our mind ... free of falsehoods ... free of anything that is contrary to truth. A peaceful state of mind is free from obscure, insidious fears and deeply rooted, false beliefs and, consequently, free from evil, guilt, hate, anger, jealousy, possessiveness, insecurity ... free from all psychological neuroses ... free from all that robs us of love, joy, peace of mind, and inner serenity.

It is significant to note that Jesus' teachings do not include anything about enjoying heaven after we die. He was speaking about the present moment ... here and now. Let us remember that Paul described heaven as peace and joy. Our true nature is love, peace, and joy ... what we experience when we are in agreement with truth ... in harmony with God.

Swami Satchidananda said, "The aim of all spiritual practices is to know your real Self, to know the knower." Who is "the knower" except our true self? Who knows our secret faults but we ourselves? Who knows our subconscious, unwarranted fears (the hidden cause of our suffering) but we ourselves? Who knows the

Prayer that Never Fails

way we believe and think in our heart but we ourselves? Who knows the truth that will save us (the truth that rests within our heart) but we ourselves? Who can discover the truth that will set us free except we ourselves? Who can discover the kingdom of God for us except we ourselves? Who will save us except our true spiritual self?

In the book, *How to Know God - The Yoga Aphorisms of Patanjali* (translated with a commentary by Swami Prabhavananda and Christopher Isherwood), the author explains that the first stage for acquiring perfect knowledge of the true Self is: "The realization that the source of all spiritual wisdom is inside ourselves, that the Kingdom of Heaven is within us. As Swami Vivekananda says: 'After long searches here and there, in temples and in churches, in earths and in heavens, at last you come back, completing the circle from where you started, to your own soul and find that He, for whom you have been seeking all over the world ... on whom you were looking as the mystery of all mysteries shrouded in the clouds, is nearest of the near, is your own self, the reality of your life, body, and soul.'"

We as a society are so far alienated from our true self (out of harmony with truth, God, and nature) that it is elusive for us to find and harmonize with our true spiritual self. We do not know what genuine peace is, and we do not know what we are seeking ... and we do not know what we are missing. We will not know what peace is until we experience it. No one can describe peace to us so that we will know what it is; we will only know from the experience.

We do not know what it is like being free from the *need* to appear special and important. We do not know what life is like free of our masks, pretending to be something we are not. Consequently, we do not know the genuine joy, peace, and inner serenity that is characteristic of our true, spiritual, perfect self. ... the self of us (our inner most being) who is "as perfect even as your Father who is in heaven is perfect" ... as perfect as Jesus told us to be.

And let us remember that Isaiah said, "Thou wilt keep him in perfect peace whose mind is stayed on thee" (Isaiah 26:3). "Whose mind is stayed on thee" (stayed on our true spiritual self) equates with "doing the will of the Father" ... a prerequisite for enjoying heaven, according to Jesus ... a prerequisite for enjoying genuine inner serenity, peace, and joy.

And as Isaiah said, when we find our true self, we will go forth with peace and joy. And notice the beautiful, descriptive language of Isaiah: "... the mountains and the hills shall break forth before you into singing, and all the trees of the field shall clap their hands." ... this must be heaven!

It's incomprehensible what our lives and our society will be like when the masses of people find their true spiritual self and "go forth the with peace and joy." Planet earth will be a utopia ... peaceful and joyous ... like "a new heaven and a new earth." Think about it! When we discover our true, spiritual self, it is like "being born again." We recapture the purity of heart, the innocence, the humility — the freedom and spontaneity! — with which we were born.

And let's remember that Jesus said: "Except ye be converted and become as little children, ye shall not enter into the kingdom of Heaven" (Matthew 18:3). And, "Except a man be born again, he cannot see the kingdom of God" (John 3:3). "Being converted and becoming as little children" and "being born again" mean the same thing; both lead to the peace and joy of heaven.

Thinking of the words of Isaiah reminds me of an opportunity and a pleasure that I experienced several years ago while being in the presence of two holy men from India, two disciples of a Yoga master. Their life was the epitome of peace and joy; they radiated a peace and contentment that is rare in our society.

The instructions for meditating that one of them gave me remind me of the words of Isaiah. The Holy Man from India instructed me something like, "You might feel as though you will float to the ceiling; do not be afraid; just let go." ... the secret: "Do not be afraid; just let go."

Think about it! At all times we could enjoy the life that Isaiah described ... if only we would let go and surrender to truth ... if we sought and lived in agreement with our true self. Just imagine what our lives, our families, and our society would be like if we prayed as Jesus taught us to pray: "Thy will be done in earth as it is in heaven," which is to express life in agreement with truth ... in

Prayer that Never Fails

agreement with our true self; that is the will of our Father; that is the will of God. That is our purpose on planet Earth. Deep inside, that is what every one of us wants.

Imagine what our lives and our society would be like if everyone (carpenters, merchants, doctors, mechanics, lawyers, teachers, truck driver, farmers, clergy, wives, husbands, fathers, mothers — butchers, bakers, candlestick makers — in brief, everyone!) performed their duties from the center of truth and love. Deep inside, it is what every one of us wants to do. It is incomprehensible what planet Earth would be like ... like a "new heaven and a new earth."

If we give in to our ego, it will find all sorts of things to keep us busy and divert us from discovering truth, which obliterates the influence of our false ego-self ... the one thing our false ego-self will resist to the bitter end. And the one thing we insatiable desire more than anything else is freedom from the world of the ego and consequently the freedom to enjoy heaven here and now.

In summary, a most significant aspect of Jesus' prayer is an affirmation of life as it is meant to be, which is in harmony with truth, which brings peace and joy. ... "Thy will be done in earth as it is in heaven." ... heaven being characterized by peace and joy.

Often when we think of prayer, we think in terms of pleading to God for help. A form of prayer often over looked — a form of prayer used extensively by biblical teachers — is communion with God. This is the same thing that David the Psalmist advocated when he said: "Commune with your own heart."

Communing with our own heart is a form of prayer that guides us to a purification of our heart. It guides us to unification with God; it guides us to an understanding of the truth that sets us free; it guides us to the narrow path to life that few find. Communing with our own heart is a form of prayer that does not fail.

When we, as a society, have learned to commune with our own heart and discover the truth that sets us free, we will be saved. We will have learned the greatest lesson life has to offer ... all will be joyous and peaceful.

Chapter 11
The Essential Teachings of Jesus

Understanding what Jesus said helps us understand what the spiritual teachers of the Old Testament said. And understanding what the spiritual teachers of the Old Testament said helps us understand what Jesus said. The spiritual teachers of the Old Testament taught the most essential teachings of Jesus. From their teachings we know what would save us. Knowing this helps us shift our focus of study from the man Jesus to his teachings.

A significant difference between Jesus' teachings and those of the writers of the Old Testament is that they repeated again and again the phrases, "I am the Lord," and "I am the Lord your God." The Old Testament is saturated with phrases such as, "Thus saith the Lord" and "Hear ye the word of the Lord," and there are several references to "angel of God" and "angel of the Lord." It is significant to know that these phrases allude to communion with God ... to gaining wisdom, understanding, and guidance from within themselves. ... the same thing that Jesus did when he "went unto the Father."

One of the things that helped me considerably with assimilating and understanding the teachings of Jesus and the spiritual teachers of the Old Testament is searching for key words and key phrases by the use of a computer that has the Bible on it. I searched using several key words and phrases; e.g., Father, word of the Lord, saith the Lord, hell, heaven, peace, call upon the name of the Lord, eternity, etc. Searching the Bible for the phrases "thus saith the Lord" and "Word of the Lord" led to my understanding that the word "Lord" as used by the spiritual teachers of the Old Testament and the word "Father" as used by Jesus mean the same thing. And, in our language, "Lord" and "Father" are the same thing as our true spiritual self.

Here is an example of what I discovered, searching for the phrase, "call upon the name of the Lord." The Apostle Paul said, "For whosoever shall call upon the name of the Lord shall be

The Essential Teachings of Jesus

saved" (Romans 10:13). Obviously, "calling upon the name of the Lord" is important; this will save us. However, fundamentalists seem to think that calling upon the name of the Lord is calling upon the name of Jesus. In the subject statement, the Apostle Paul used the word "Lord" in the same manner that the spiritual teachers of the Old Testament used it.

I searched the entire Bible for the phrase, "call upon the name of the Lord." I found that the statement was first used in "The Book of Genesis": "... then began men to call upon the name of the Lord" (Genesis 4:26).

Zephaniah, author of "The Book of Zephaniah," said: "For then will I turn to the people a pure language, that they may *all call upon the name of the Lord*, to serve him with one consent" (Zephaniah 3:9). Thus, Zephaniah was alluding to the need of a pure language about 3,000 years ago "that they may all call upon the name of the Lord, to serve him." "Him," as alluded to here, is in our language the true spiritual self. In the language of Jesus, "to serve him" is the same thing as doing the will of the Father, a prerequisite for enjoying heaven.

David the Psalmist, said, "I will take the cup of salvation, and call upon the name of the Lord." In the following passages, although David did not use the exact phrase, "call upon the name of the Lord," what he said, means the same thing. David said: "The Lord is righteous in all his ways, and holy in all his works. The Lord is nigh unto all them that call upon him in truth. He will hear their cry, and will save them" (Psalms 145:17-19). And, "As for me, I will call upon God; and the Lord shall save me" (Psalms 55:16). Note that the "Lord shall save me" ... the true spiritual self.

David used the words "Lord" and "God" synonymously. "Calling upon the Lord" and "calling upon God" mean the same thing. In our language, both phrases mean the same thing as calling upon our true divine spiritual self; this will save us. Calling upon our true spiritual self is how we discover the truth that sets us free.

David also said, "The Lord will hear when I call unto him. ... Put your trust in the Lord. ... Commune with your own heart. ... Teach me thy way, O Lord, and lead me in a plain path. ... Unto thee, O Lord, do I lift up my soul. O my God, I trust in thee. ...

Show me thy ways, O Lord; teach me thy paths. Lead me in thy truth, and teach me; for thou art the God of my salvation. ... Good and upright is the Lord; therefore he will teach sinners in the way."

Who or what is it that David called upon to "Show me thy ways, O Lord; teach me thy paths," and who "will teach sinners in the way," except the true, divine, spiritual self? And, what is it that is "nigh unto all them that call upon him" except the true spiritual self? What is the "Lord" that knows "thy truth," and what is the "God of my salvation," except the true spiritual self? Where did David get his guidance — "thy truth" — for the plain path, except from the truth within himself ... from "the secret place of the most high" ... from his true spiritual self, the Lord within him"? David's relationship with the Lord was similar to Jesus' relationship with the Father. ... just different words.

Did David possess any ability that we do not have the potential to develop? We, too, can retreat to the "secret place of the most high, commune with our own heart," and discover the truth that sets us free. If we overcome the world of the ego, truth will guide us on the right path.

Thus, to understand the meaning of the Apostle Paul's statement, "For whosoever shall call upon the name of the Lord shall be saved," it helps if we assimilate what Jesus, the Apostle Paul, and the spiritual teachers of the Old Testament said—keeping in mind that the spiritual teachers of the Old Testament spoke of the "Lord" in the same manner that Jesus spoke of the "Father" ... in our language, the true spiritual self.

Although Isaiah did not use the same wording as the Apostle Paul, he said the same thing. Isaiah said, "Seek ye the Lord while he may be found, *call ye upon him while he is near.*" And note what Isaiah said that we would enjoy when we find the Lord (the true spiritual self): "For you shall go forth with joy and be led forth with peace." When we are abiding by the truth that proceeds from our true spiritual self — the same thing as Jesus doing the will of the Father — we are saved. When we are saved, we have peace and joy.

In our language, we are saved when we call upon our true spiritual self (the "name of the Lord") and discover the truth that

The Essential Teachings of Jesus

sets us free. The only place to discover the truth that sets us free is within us. We discover truth — we are saved — by doing what David, the Psalmist, said to do: "Be still ... commune with your own heart. ... Put your trust in the Lord." In our language, we are to be still, commune with our own heart, and trust our true spiritual self. We have the ability to do what David did.

Jesus said, "Ask, and it shall be given you; seek, and ye shall find; knock, and it shall be opened unto you. For every one that asketh receiveth; and he that seeketh findeth; and to him that knocketh it shall be opened. ... How much more shall your Father which is in heaven give good things to them that ask him"?

We know from the teachings of Jesus that "Every one that asketh receiveth; and he that seeketh findeth." And we know from what Jesus said that the Father would give good things to them that ask him. Deep inside the soul of us, we all want peace and joy, which is characteristic of heaven. And, we know from the teachings if Jesus that "It is your Father's good pleasure to give you the kingdom" ... to give us peace and joy.

Instead of fear, mental turmoil, confusion, hatred, anger, resentment, jealousy, anxiety, emotional insecurity, guilt, shame, depression, pretension — wearing our masks pretending to be righteous and happy — we can have genuine peace, joy, and happiness ... all ours for seeking and asking.

This raises the questions: How do we seek? How do we ask? How do we discover the truth? How do we find the "plain path"? David, the Psalmist, left us a simple, straightforward answer: "Be still. ... Commune with your own heart."

The Apostle Paul said, "How then shall they call on him in whom they have not believed? how shall they believe in him of whom they have not heard? how shall they hear without a preacher? And how shall they preach, except they *be sent*? ... The word is nigh thee, even in thy mouth, and in thy heart; that is, the word of faith, which we preach."

Note that the *word* — the truth — is already in us. Also, we might notice that Paul uses the word "sent" in the same manner that Jesus and the spiritual teachers of the Old Testament used it. The spiritual teachers of the Old Testament were "sent" by the Lord. Jesus was "sent" by the Father ... same thing, just different words.

In "The Book of Deuteronomy," we find, "For this commandment which I command thee this day, it is not hidden from thee, neither is it far off. It is not in heaven, that thou shouldest say, 'Who shall go up for us to heaven and bring it unto us, that we may hear it and do it?' Neither is it beyond the sea, that thou shouldest say, 'Who shall go over the sea for us and bring it unto us, that we may hear it and do it?' But the word is very nigh unto thee, in thy mouth and in thy heart, that thou mayest do it. ... I command thee this day to love the Lord thy God, to walk in his ways and to keep his commandments and his statutes and his judgments" (Deuteronomy 30:11-14). ... the same thing as doing "the will of the Father"... in our language, the same thing as following the guidance of our true, spiritual self.

Thus, to discover the word — to discover truth — people began calling upon the name of the Lord early in the history of biblical times, first mentioned in the fourth chapter of "Genesis," the first book of the "Old Testament." Thus, "calling upon the name of the Lord" (our true spiritual self) — communing with our own heart — will save us. There is no other way to reap the benefits derived from living in harmony with truth, God, and nature than abiding by the truth that proceeds from our true spiritual self.

We find in "The Second Book of the Chronicles" (possibly written by Ezra), "As the Lord liveth, even what my God saith, that will I speak" (2 Chronicles, 18:13). We find in "The First Book of the Kings" (author is unknown), "As the Lord liveth, what the Lord saith unto me, that will I speak" (1 Kings, 22:14). Jesus said, "I do nothing of myself, but as my Father hath taught me, I speak these things."

Moses said, "I cannot go beyond the word of the Lord my God, to do less or more" (Numbers 22:18). And, "The word that God putteth in my mouth, that shall I speak" (Numbers 22:38). Also, "And Moses said, Hereby ye shall know that the *Lord hath sent me* to do all these works; for I have not done them of mine own mind" (Numbers 16:28).

Note that Moses was sent by and followed the guidance of the Lord. Similarly, Jesus was sent by and following the guidance of the Father. Moses also spoke in terms of the Lord thy God and the Lord your God. We might also note that Moses spoke of two aspects of himself: "mine own mind" and the Lord.

The point is that the spiritual teachers of the Old Testament used the words "God" and "Lord" similar to the way Jesus used the word "Father." Jesus said: "I speak that which I have seen with my Father, and I speak to the world those things which I have heard of him. ... The words that I speak unto you I speak not of myself; but the Father that dwelleth in me."

A significant thing for us to know is that we can call upon our true spiritual self (what David alluded to as communing with your own heart) and discover the truth that sets us free ... to find joy and peace ... to discover heaven here and now.

The lack of understanding about this one thing (that calling upon our true spiritual self will save us) has undoubtedly contributed to a belief in the Trinity (the Father, Son, and the Holy Spirit). We know from Jesus' teachings that there is one God ... "and him only shalt thou serve." So, why complicate things?

Webster defines "trinity": "The union of the three divine persons (Father, Son, and Holy Spirit)." It is misleading to think in terms of three divine persons as something separate from ourselves. Father, Son, and Holy Spirit allude to an aspect of something within us. The word "trinity" is not in the Bible.

We know that Jesus was committed to doing the will of his Father. Similarly, Moses and other spiritual leaders of the Old Testament era were committed to doing the will of the Lord.

Note what Balaam said: "If Balak would give me his house full of silver and gold, I cannot go beyond the commandment of the Lord, to do either good or bad of mine own mind; but what the Lord saith, that will I speak" (Numbers 24:13). Balaam was committed to do the will of the Lord. Similarly, Jesus was committed to do the will of his Father.

Spiritual leaders of the Old Testament era had learned the lesson that Jesus intended for us. The only thing that will bring us genuine joy, peace, and inner serenity is following the guidance of our true spiritual self. There is no substitute. Different people might use different words and phrases, but it all boils down to one thing: abiding by that which is true. Anything other than abiding by truth is a sham. If we are not living in agreement with truth, we are living a lie ... we are on the broad path that leads to destruction. We try to fill the emptiness by pretending to be special and important. We do those things we can gloat over ... all the while feeling empty, restless, and discontented ... always seeking for something to render us peaceful, happy, and contented. All the while, we are striving for unification with our true spiritual self, what Jesus alluded to when he said, "I and my Father are one" ... the same thing as living in harmony with that which is true.

The phrase, "The word of the Lord came unto me," appears several times in the Old Testament. In all simplicity, this means that the truth came to the spiritual teachers of the Old Testament from that place within where truth dwells. Whatever we call it (Lord, Father, or the true spiritual self), there is something within us that knows what is true and what is false. And the way to discern between that which is true and that which is false is by being still and communing with our own heart.

Hesiod, a 9th century BC Poet, said, "We know how to speak many falsehoods that resemble real things, but we know, when we will, how to speak true things" ... if only we would be still and pay attention.

Thus, from doing several searches with various words and phrases, it became clear to me that the spiritual teachers of the Old Testament gained wisdom, understanding, and guidance from the Lord within themselves in the same manner that Jesus received wisdom, understanding, and guidance from the Father within. And one of the most important things for us to know is that we can do what Jesus and the spiritual teachers of the Old Testament did. In fact, we must do what they did if we are to discover the truth that sets us free ... if we are to find salvation.

From "The Proverbs" we know, "Wisdom resteth in the heart of him that hath understanding." Wisdom and understanding are prerequisites for knowing the truth that sets us free. We gain wis-

The Essential Teachings of Jesus

dom and understanding — we discover the truth that sets us free — by being still and communing with our own heart.

God is no different today than during the Old Testament time. God did not do anything differently during the Old Testament time than what God is doing today ... and will always be doing. And the writers of the Old Testament and Jesus did not possess any special qualities that we do not have the potential to develop.

Thus, we can do what both the writers of the Old Testament and Jesus did. We can — and we must — retreat within ourselves for wisdom and understanding if we are to discover the truth that sets us free. Within us is the only place where we will ever discover the truth that sets us free ... the only place where we will discover the truth that will save us, our families, our society ... the very world itself.

We have the same access to truth and guidance — the same access to the "word of the Lord" — that both Jesus and the spiritual teachers of the Old Testament had ... if we learned to do what Jesus said, which is to "shut the door." "Shutting the door" is more than just closing the eyes. It is being still and transcending the chatter of our false ego-self.

If we study and ponder what both Jesus said and what the writers of the Old Testament said, we realize that they were speaking of the differences between the life we experience when we are functioning from the false ego-self and the life we experience when we are functioning from our true, spiritual self ... that self of us that is perfect, created in the image and likeness of God ... that self of us that is as perfect as Jesus told us to be: "Be ye therefore perfect, even as your Father who is in heaven is perfect."

The spiritual teachers of the Old Testament spoke in terms of the "Lord." Jesus spoke in terms of the "Father," same thing, just a different word. Some of the spiritual teachers of the Old Testament alluded to themselves as Savior. Jesus attempted to save people by preaching the gospel ... and "those who believe shall be saved, and those who do not believe will be damned."

Whereas the spiritual teachers of the Old Testament said, "I am the Lord" and "I am the Lord thy God," Jesus said, "I am the way, the truth, and the life; no man cometh unto the Father, but by me" (John 14:6).

Again, Jesus' purpose for preaching the gospel was that his followers might have peace and joy. We have peace and joy when we are unified with God. Once we understand the teachings of both the saints of the Old Testament and the teachings of Jesus, we realize that no one is unified with God, but by truth (same meaning as Jesus' words, "no man cometh to the Father, but by me").

Jesus' use of the personal pronouns of "I" and "me" has caused some misunderstanding about what Jesus said. For example, Jesus said, "These things I have spoken unto you, that *in me* you might have peace." This would have been easier to grasp had Jesus either omitted the phrase "in me" or used another phrase such as, "through my truth teachings." We know that we have peace when we believe, understand, and embody the teachings of Jesus ... the gospel that Jesus commanded his disciples to preach.

Ralph Waldo Emerson (poet, essayist), said, "Nothing can bring you peace but yourself." We bring ourselves peace by communing with our true spiritual self.

When the Jews were about to stone Jesus, they told him, "For a good work we stone thee not, but for blasphemy; and because that thou, being a man, makest thyself God." Jesus answered them, "Is it not written in your law, I said, Ye are gods?"

According the David the Psalmist: "They know not, neither will they understand; they walk on in darkness; all the foundations of the earth are out of course. I have said, Ye are gods; and all of you are children of the most High" (Psalms 82:5-6). Think about it! We are gods and children of the most High! ... if only we knew the truth that sets us free.

In "The Gospel According to John" we find, "In the beginning was the Word, and the Word was with God, and the Word was God. The same was in the beginning with God. All things were made by him; and without him was not any thing made that was made" (John 1:1-3). The "word" alluded to by the spiritual teachers of the Old Testament is truth. And, truth was in the beginning, and truth endures forever.

Confucius said, "With truth, everything done is right. ... Absolute truth is indestructible. Being indestructible, it is eternal."

There is a unity, harmony, and rhythm that permeate the Universe. This is the unity, harmony, and rhythm of God. When we are in harmony with our true divine spiritual self, we are in harmony with God. If we (everyone) were unified with God, we would be one spiritual body. However, those who are alienated from God are not in harmony with God and not in harmony with those who are.

If we, as a society, were one spiritual body, unified with God, there would be no unwarranted fears, insecurity, jealousy, envy, hatred, distrust; no drug, child, and spousal abuse; no lying, cheating, stealing; no violence. All would be peace and joy ... the kind of life — the kind of world — Jesus wanted for us. That's the kind of life we would enjoy if the gospel had been preached to all nations as Jesus commanded his disciples to preach.

If we, as a society, were unified with ourselves — unified with God — and consequently unified one with another, quite naturally, we would "do unto others as we would have others do unto us." Quite naturally, everything we did would be for the good of all. When unified as one spiritual body, what is good for a part is good for the whole; what harms a part, harms the whole. When we are in harmony with God, we harbor no evil in our heart. Thus, there is no evil among those who are in harmony of God. Instead of evil, there is peace and joy.

The Apostle Paul said, "And we know that all things work together for good to them that love God" (Romans 8:28). Think about it! Think about what our families, our society, our nation would be like if we love God ... if we love our true spiritual self with all our heart, and with all thy soul, and with all our might. ... "all things would work together for good."

Moses said, "I am the Lord your God; ye shall therefore sanctify yourselves, and ye shall be holy; for I am holy" (Leviticus 11:44). Aren't we inclined to gloss over statements such as this as if they are not applicable to us? What Moses said is quite significant, and it is as applicable today as it was about 3,000 years ago.

Webster defines "sanctify" "To make holy ... to make free from sin; purify." "Holy" is defined as "spiritually perfect or pure; untainted by evil or sin; sinless."

Moses was holy; he was sinless, and he wanted the Israelites to sanctify themselves and be free from sin ... to be holy. Moses wanted the Israelites to enjoy the sinless life that he himself enjoyed. When we are holy, we have peace and joy ... we enjoy the "peace that passeth all understanding." ... that is heaven.

Although Jesus did not use the same words and language that Moses used, he wanted us to sanctify ourselves and to be holy, to be sinless. Jesus said, "I and my Father are one." He was unified with God; he was holy; he was sinless. Jesus wanted us to be, "that where I am, there ye may be also" (John 14:3). When we are unified with our true spiritual self, we are in harmony with God; we are holy. When we are holy, we are as perfect as Jesus told us to be, "even as your Father who is in heaven is perfect" ... untainted by evil or sin; sinless" ... the way Jesus wanted us to be, so that we might have peace and joy.

Let's face it! If we are to be a true Christian, we must be holy, we must be sinless ... a prerequisite for enjoying heaven. We might twist the Holy Scriptures — add to and take from them — but there is no justification in the Bible for believing that Jesus' death on the cross had any bearing on the salvation of the spiritual teachers of the Old Testament. When Moses told the people of Israel to "sanctify yourselves," he was speaking of the present ... he was speaking of being saved then and there.

Jesus said, "Before Abraham was, I am." Fundamentalists make this statement seem like Jesus has always been in existence in some form and will always be in existence ... and that he was born as God in human flesh to save the world. From the following, note how words can be misleading if we do not take the time to study and understand what Jesus said: "For had ye believed Moses ye would have believed me, *for he wrote of me*. But if ye believe not his writings, how shall ye believe my words?"

From Jesus' question, we realize that he was speaking of believing the writings of Moses. And if the people did not believe what Moses wrote, they would not believe the words of Jesus.

The Essential Teachings of Jesus

Thus, Moses did not write about Jesus. Moses wrote about the truth and wisdom (the words) he got from the Lord within himself ... the Lord he was with forty days and forty nights when he gained the wisdom and understanding to write the Ten Commandments. Moses wrote about truth teachings, not about the man Jesus. Jesus' phrase, "my words," alludes to the words of truth and wisdom Jesus received from his Father within himself ... the same way Moses received truth and wisdom from the Lord within himself.

Thus, in effect, Jesus said that both he and Moses taught the words of the Lord (the truth they received from within themselves), and if the people did not believe what Moses said, they would not believe what Jesus said. If (a huge "if") we, individually and collectively as a group, communed with our own heart and followed the guidance of our true spiritual self, we would be in harmony with the same truth, and consequently, in harmony with one another and with ourselves ... the way Jesus wanted us to be.

The following are a few selected passages of Scriptures from the Old Testament. If you read these passages slowly — pondering as you read — you will recognize some striking similarities between what Jesus said and what the spiritual teachers of the Old Testament said several hundred years before Jesus' ministry. The saints of the Old Testament wrote about the present ... not a prophesy of the coming of Jesus several hundred years into the future. Fundamentalists seem to believe that the Old Testament is about Jesus. Instead, Jesus borrowed heavily from the teachings of the saints of the Old Testament.

Jeremiah said, "Then the word of the Lord came unto me, saying, 'Before I formed thee in the belly, I knew thee; and before thou camest forth out of the womb, I sanctified thee, and I ordained thee a prophet unto the nations.' Then said I, 'Ah, Lord God! behold, I cannot speak, for I am a child.' But the Lord said unto me, 'Say not, I am a child, for thou shalt go to all that I shall send thee, and whatsoever I command thee thou shalt speak. Be not afraid of their faces, for I am with thee to deliver thee,' saith the Lord. Then the Lord put forth his hand, and touched my mouth. And the Lord said unto me, 'Behold, I have put my words in thy mouth'" (Jeremiah 1:4-9).

Who ordained Jeremiah? Who put the words in his mouth, except his deeper, true inner-self? We may note that what the Lord told Jeremiah to do is similar to what Jesus told his disciples to do: "take no thought how or what ye shall speak, for it shall be given you in that same hour what ye shall speak. For it is not ye that speak, but the Spirit of your Father who speaketh in you."

Jeremiah also said, "Behold, I am the Lord, the God of all flesh; is there any thing too hard for me? ... O Jerusalem, wash thine heart from wickedness, that thou mayest be saved. How long shall thy vain thoughts lodge within thee? ... Heal me, O Lord, and I shall be healed; save me, and I shall be saved, for thou art my praise."

Note that Jeremiah said, "wash thine heart from wickedness." Jeremiah also said, "The heart is deceitful above all things, and desperately wicked." Several hundred years before the ministry of Jesus, Jeremiah told us what will save us: "Wash thine heart from wickedness." We "wash our heart" — we purify our heart — by discovering the truth that sets us free ... and this will save us.

Jesus said, "Cleanse first that which is within the cup and platter, that the outside of them may be clean also." When we do this, we have "washed our heart from wickedness," and we are saved. Jesus said it clearly: "Blessed are the pure in heart, for they shall see God." Our heart is pure when we wash it from wickedness ... when we "clean the inside of the cup and the platter."

The word "vain" sheds light on the nature of the false ego-self. Vain thoughts are characterized by undue admiration for oneself ... characterized by our ego's unending need to appear special and important. Vain thoughts are showy, conceited, worthless, and empty ... with no real basis of worth.

"O Lord, thou art my praise" alludes to the true, spiritual self. ... the God within us. Our channel for communing with the universal God is our true spiritual self. When we are unified with our true self, we are unified with God. When we are unified with God, we are in agreement with truth and nature. When we are in harmony with truth, we are in harmony with God ... and vice versa ... all one and the same. Life does not — cannot — get any better than living in agreement with truth, God, and nature.

The Essential Teachings of Jesus

Jeremiah also said: "Truly in vain is salvation hoped for from the hills and from the multitudes of mountains; truly in the Lord our God is the salvation of Israel." Thus, it is useless to try to find salvation anyplace, except within ourselves. All efforts to find salvation outside ourselves are in vain. And it might help to keep in mind that salvation is being saved from evil and destruction; it is the deliverance from sin and from the penalties of sin.

Whereas Jeremiah said that salvation is found in the Lord our God, we know from Jesus' teachings that salvation is found in the Father within (same thing, just different wording). We know from Jesus that we are sanctified by truth, which "proceedeth from the Father. Jesus said, "... through thy truth; thy word is truth" (John 17:17). Remember that Moses said, "sanctify yourselves, and ye shall be holy." This implies that we can save ourselves.

What Jeremiah said is that we can find salvation only within ourselves. Within ourselves is where we discover the truth that will save us. This is consistent with what Jesus said in regards to what will save us. This is also consistent with something that Paul said when he was in prison and consequently not available personally to his followers. He said, "But now much more in my absence, work out your own salvation." We are saved when we work out our own salvation. We work out our own salvation — we discover truth — by being still, "shutting the door," and communing with our true spiritual self.

The Apostle Paul also said, "Take heed unto thyself, and unto the doctrine; continue in them; for in doing this thou shalt both *save thyself*, and them that hear thee" (1 Timothy 4:15-16). Also, we know from James, author of the "Letter of James," that we can save ourselves: "Purify your hearts, ye double minded." When we purify our hearts, we are saved.

Paul's statement reminds me of what the Buddha said: "Be ye lamps unto yourselves; seek salvation alone in truth. Those who shall not look for assistance from anyone beside themselves, it is they who shall reach the very topmost height."

What the Buddha said to do is what the writers of the Old Testament did to discover truth and find salvation. They discovered the word of the Lord — which is truth — within themselves ... the same way that Jesus discovered the truth "that proceeds from the Father." We, too, can do what Jesus, the Buddha, and the writers of the Old Testament did. We can be still, commune with our own heart and discover truth that sets us free; this will save us.

Before Moses wrote the Ten Commandments, he went into the mount: "And Moses went into the midst of the cloud, and gat him up into the mount; and Moses was ... there with the Lord forty days and forty nights; he did neither eat bread, nor drink water. And he wrote upon the tables the words of the covenant, the Ten Commandments." Who or what was the Lord that Moses was with for forty days and forty nights, except his deeper, innermost being, his true self?

When we study and assimilate what both Jesus and the spiritual teachers of the Old Testament said, we realize that the Lord thy God is something that is within us (what I am calling our true spiritual self). Sometimes when religious teachers speak of Moses being with the Lord, they leave off a significant phrase of the Scripture. The Scripture is: "And the angel of the Lord appeared unto him [Moses] in a flame of fire out of the midst of a bush; and he looked, and, behold, the bush burned with fire. ... And when the Lord saw that he turned aside to see, God called unto him out of the midst of the bush, and said, Moses, Moses. And he said, Here am I" (Exodus 3: 2-4). What appeared to Moses was an angel. Angels appear in our inner vision. Also note that Moses used the words "Lord" and "God" interchangeably.

In "The Gospel According to John" we find: "Then Jesus said unto them, Verily, verily, I say unto you, Moses gave you not that bread from heaven; but my Father giveth you the true bread from heaven. For the bread of God is he which cometh down from heaven, and giveth life unto the world. Then said they unto him, Lord, evermore give us this bread. And Jesus said unto them, I am the bread of life; he that cometh to me shall never hunger; and he that believeth on me shall never thirst" (John 6:32-35).

Jesus also said, "This is the bread which cometh down from heaven, that a man may eat thereof, and not die. I am the living bread, which came down from heaven; if any man eat of this bread, he shall live forever; and the bread that I will give is my flesh,

The Essential Teachings of Jesus

which I will give for the life of the world. ... Then Jesus said unto them, Verily, verily, I say unto you, except ye eat the flesh of the Son of man, and drink his blood, ye have no life in you. Whoso eateth my flesh, and drinketh my blood, hath eternal life" (John 6:50-54).

Notice how difficult it was for the people of that time and place in history — who understood the language — to understand what Jesus said. After hearing what Jesus said, "The Jews therefore strove among themselves, saying, how can this man give us his flesh to eat?" (John 6:52).

Jesus clarified some of the Old Testament teachings; however, his manner of teaching created some confusion. The passage about "bread from heaven" mentioned in the Old Testament is easier to grasp than what Jesus said. In The Book of Nehemiah, we find: "Thou art the Lord the God, who chose A'bram ... Thou camest down also upon mount Sinai, and spakest with them from heaven, and gavest them right judgments, and true laws, good statutes and commandments ... and gavest them bread from heaven for their hunger, and broughtest forth water for them out of the rock for their thirst ... thou art a God ready to pardon, gracious and merciful, slow to anger, and of great kindness" (Nehemiah 9:7-17).

We know that the Lord did not literally come down from heaven and give the people bread and water. "Bread" and "water" as used here are idioms alluding to something that will satisfy the hunger and thirst for truth ... the hunger and thirst for being in harmony with God ... the hunger and thirst for peace and joy. *Truth satisfies the hunger and thirst for truth.*

"Heaven" is that special place within us where truth dwells. It's the place that David, the Psalmist, called the secret place of the most high. It's the place that Jesus alluded to when he said, "pray to your Father who is in secret" and "our Father which art in heaven."

Jesus said, "It is the spirit that quickeneth; the flesh profiteth nothing; the words that I speak unto you, they are spirit, and they are life" (John 6:63). Jesus alluded to "the words that I speak unto you that are spirit and life" as bread and flesh. And in the foregoing, he spoke of bread coming down from heaven. We know from the teachings of Jesus that heaven is within us. And we know from assimilating what Jesus and the spiritual teachers of the Old Testament said that truth comes from our true spiritual self ... not from our false ego-self. Thus, when Jesus was speaking of bread coming from heaven, he was speaking about the truth that proceeds from the Father ... from the true spiritual self.

And in the foregoing, where Jesus said, "not die" and "shall live forever," he was not speaking of dying and living as we typically think of dying and living. No one lives forever. Jesus was speaking of those who believe, understand, and embody his truth teachings; they will be fully alive in the spirit of truth as long as they live. They will not suffer the mental turmoil of anxiety, depression, resentment, anger, hate, jealousy, guilt, shame, worry, and the desire to do and say those things that make people seem to appear special and important. In brief, they will not be plagued with any of that negative, life draining stuff that comes from the false ego-self.

Jesus also said, "It is written, man shall not live by bread alone, but by every word that proceedeth out of the mouth of God" (Matthew 4:4). In this case, it seems that Jesus alludes to "bread" as food that is required by our physical body. Every word that proceedeth out of the mouth of God is true, and truth is the life of our spirit.

It's easier for us to grasp a practical meaning and understanding of what Jesus said when we know that our true, divine, spiritual self is the "mouth of God." The "mouth of God" is the same place from which Moses got the Ten Commandments, the same place the writers of the Old Testament and Jesus got wisdom, guidance, and understanding, the same place Buddha discovered truth ... the place we could discover the truth that sets us free—if only we would be still, calm our mind, and do what David, the Psalmist, said to do, "commune with your own heart" ... the "heart" being the same thing as the "mouth of God."

Let's remember that Jesus also said "truth proceedeth from the Father." While food is necessary for the physical body, our spirit thrives on the word of truth, which comes from the true self. As Jesus said about the Father (his true spiritual self), "Thy word is truth." And, Jesus said, "The word which ye hear is not mine, but the Father's which sent me" (John 14:24).

The Essential Teachings of Jesus

Thus, Jesus got the word of truth from his Father. The spiritual teachers of the Old Testament got the word of truth from the Lord ... same thing just different words. The significant thing for us to know is that however we wish to describe it, the word of truth that will save us dwells within us ... with our true spiritual self. The words that come from our true self are true; they are the life of our spirit while we are alive.

When we are living in agreement with the spirit of truth, we are fully alive, not the kind of life we live when under the influence of the bloated nothingness of the elephantine ego-self. If we discover the truth that sets us free and, consequently, are living in harmony with God, we "shall never hunger and thirst" for peace, joy, and righteousness ... all is within us.

By studying "The Psalms," we find several passages of Scriptures that are similar to what Jesus said. For example, Jesus said, "Blessed are the meek; for they shall inherit the earth" (Matthew 5:5). In "The Psalms," we find:
- The wicked borroweth, and payeth not again; but the righteous showeth mercy, and giveth. For such as be blessed of him shall inherit the earth (Psalms 37:21-22).
- For evildoers shall be cut off; but those who wait upon the Lord, they shall inherit the earth (Psalms 37:9).
- The meek shall inherit the earth; and shall delight themselves in the abundance of peace (Psalms 37:11).

"Meek" is defined as "humble." Remember that Jesus said, "Except ye be converted, and become as little children, ye shall not enter into the kingdom of Heaven." And, note that the humble "shall delight themselves in the abundance of peace." As a reminder, Jesus' sole purpose for preaching the gospel is that we might have peace.

From the following selected passages by Isaiah, we realize that Isaiah taught the essential teachings of Jesus and for the same purpose, which is to help people find peace and joy. And, although many Christians believe that Jesus is the Savior of the world, Isaiah spoke in terms of being savior and redeemer.

Isaiah said, "I am the Lord, and there is none else. ... Thus saith the Lord, your redeemer ... For I am the Lord thy God, the

Holy One of Israel, thy Saviour. ... I am the Lord, your Holy One ... I am the first and I am the last; and beside me there is no God. ... Look unto me, and be ye saved, all the ends of the earth; for I am God, and there is none else .... a just God and a Saviour; there is none beside me. ... And now, saith the Lord that formed me from the womb to be his servant. ... The Spirit of the Lord God is upon me, because the Lord hath anointed me to preach good tidings unto the meek; he hath *sent me* to bind up the brokenhearted, to proclaim liberty to the captives, and the opening of the prison to them that are bound ... to comfort all that mourn ... Thus saith the Lord, thy Redeemer, the Holy One of Israel; I am the Lord thy God which teacheth thee to profit, which leadeth thee by the way that thou shouldest go. ... And I will bring the blind by a way that they knew not; I will lead them in paths that they have not known; I will make darkness light before them, and crooked things straight. ... The meek also shall increase their joy in the Lord, and the poor among men shall rejoice. ... These things will I do unto them. ... Hear, ye deaf, and look, ye blind, that ye may see. ... Seeing many things but thou observest not, opening the ears but he heareth not ... I have blotted out, as a thick cloud, thy transgressions, and, as a cloud, thy sins; return unto me, for I have redeemed thee. ... for the Lord shall be thine everlasting light, and the days of thy mourning shall be ended. ... For the Lord is our judge, the Lord is our lawgiver, the Lord is our king; he will save us. ... the Lord shall give thee rest from thy sorrow and from thy fear, and from the hard bondage wherein thou wast made to serve ... I will trust and not be afraid; for the Lord is my strength and my song; he also is become my salvation. ... He giveth power to the faint, and to them that have no might he increaseth strength. ... In repentance and rest shall ye be saved; in quietness and in confidence shall be your strength."

If we ponder what Isaiah said — and if we ponder and assimilate what Jesus said — we realize that the essence of the teachings of Jesus are in the above words by Isaiah: "The Lord will save us and give us rest from our sorrows and our fears" (Sorrow is defined as mental suffering). Remember that Jesus said, "Learn of me, and you shall find rest unto your souls." It is noteworthy that

The Essential Teachings of Jesus

both the writers of the Old Testament and Jesus were speaking of the present ... not finding rest after we die. We "find rest unto our souls" when we are saved ... when we are living in harmony with truth.

Let us not gloss over what Isaiah said. In our language, our true spiritual self (what Isaiah called the Lord) will save us and give us rest from mental suffering and our fears. When we are saved from our fears and mental suffering, we have peace and joy ... the purpose for Jesus' preaching the gospel. We are free — we are saved — when we know that truth that sets us free from our obscure, insidious fears and deeply held false beliefs.

If we notice and pay attention, the Lord who "anointed and sent" Isaiah is the same thing as the Father who "sent" Jesus—the true spiritual self. And Jesus was sent to do the same thing that Isaiah was sent to do. When we allow for the idioms, language, and the manner of teaching, we realize Jesus had the same mission Isaiah had ... that we might have peace. Isaiah spoke of redeeming us, saving us, opening the prison to them that are bound, comforting all that mourn. Isaiah said, "Seek ye the Lord while he may be found, call ye upon him while he is near. ... For you shall go forth with joy and be led forth with peace; the mountains and the hills shall break out before you into singing, and all the trees of the field shall clap their hands" ... not hampered by obscure, insidious fears from expressing life fully.

Isaiah was speaking about going forth with joy and peace *now*, not after we die. Also, note that Isaiah described a way of life similar to the Apostle Paul's description of heaven, which is peace and joy. Isaiah was speaking of joy and peace that we experience when we find our true self. Isaiah's description must be the type of life that Jesus envisioned for us when he said, "I have come that they might have life and have it more abundantly."

Can you imagine? Can you comprehend what it would be like going through life with peace and joy? And "the mountains and the hills shall break forth before you into singing, and all the trees of the field shall clap their hands." The only requirement is living in agreement with truth, God, and nature ... the simplest thing we could ever do ... and the one thing we all desire to do.

Is not living in harmony with truth far better than being stressed, depressed, anxious, uptight, fearful, sad, lonely, worried, troubled, uneasy, angry, bored, hateful, resentful, restless, discontented, jealous, suspicious, possessive, aggressive, envious, and being relentless in our efforts to gain attention, praise, adulation, and recognition? Is not living in harmony with truth far better than being burdened with guilt and shame, suffering from an inferiority complex, or suffering from tension headaches or a host of other psychosomatic illnesses? Is not it far better to live in agreement with truth, rather than being engulfed with all that negative, life-draining stuff that comes from our false ego-self?

The preponderance of evidence points to a simple fact: Both Jesus and the writers of the Old Testament were speaking about us finding peace *now*. We have peace when we abide by the truth that proceeds from our true spiritual self. However, fundamentalists (in spite of overwhelming evidence) are prone to seek out some verse of Scripture that is not absolutely clear to anyone and take from and add to the Holy Scriptures to make them seem to support their erroneous beliefs about such significant things as heaven and hell.

We find in "The Book of Exodus": "And God said unto Moses, 'I am that I am'; and he said, 'Thus shalt thou say unto the children of Israel, I AM hath sent me unto you.'" It helps to keep in mind that just as the Father sent Jesus (the Father within himself), it was something within Moses that sent him. Both Jesus and the spiritual teachers of the Old Testament abided by the guidance they received from their true spiritual self.

Note that just as the Father was everything of a spiritual nature to Jesus, the Lord was everything of a spiritual nature to spiritual teachers of the Old Testament ... redeemer, savior, healer, the source of wisdom and guidance. Similarly, our true spiritual self could utterly transform our lives, and consequently, transform our families, our society, our nation ... the very world itself ... if only we learned to be still and commune with our own heart.

In understanding the Holy Scriptures, we must keep in mind the time periods and the different usage of words. Isaiah said, "Seek ye the Lord while he may be found, call ye upon him while he is near." In "The Acts of the Apostles" (possibly written by Luke), we

The Essential Teachings of Jesus

find, "That they should seek the Lord, if haply they might feel after him, and find him, though he be not far from every one of us; for in him we live, and move, and have our being" (Acts 17:27-28). Luke uses the word "Lord" in the manner that the spiritual teachers of the Old Testament used it. In both passages, the authors are speaking in terms of seeking and finding the true spiritual self. And notice what Isaiah said that we experience when we find our true self. Isaiah said, "For ye shall go forward with joy and be led forth with peace."

When we are living in agreement with truth — when we are expressing life from the center of our true spiritual self — we have peace and joy. We are not concerned with being accepted or being rejected ... not concerned about seeming special and important ... not concerned about being right or being wrong. When we are expressing life from the center of love and truth, we do no wrong ... thus, there is nothing to restrict our freedom to be free.

The only rejection that troubles us is self-rejection. The acceptance that matters most is self-acceptance. When we experience total freedom to be free, there is no resistance, no determined stance, no assertiveness, no indifference (which is on par with the worst hatred), no demands, no expectations, and no egotistic desire for attention and recognition ... simply, genuine peace, joy, and contentment.

What more could we ask than what we experience when we follow the guidance of the true thoughts that come from our true self, rather than the vain thoughts that come from our false ego-self? When we overcome the world of the ego, we become fully alive. Using Jesus' terminology, that is when we discover eternal life ... meaning being fully alive in spirit while we are alive.

Jesus told us some very important things to do, but he did not explain — or at least make clear — how to do them. Jesus said, "Ye shall know the truth and the truth shall make you free"; however, if he told us how to discover truth, he did not make it clear for the masses. We find in "The Psalms" the secret to discovering the truth that sets us free ... easy to grasp and understand. Actually, the Psalmist said everything we need to know to find salvation — to be saved — if only we ponder, assimilate, and understand what he said. We also find helpful clues for "cleaning the inside of the cup and the platter," for casting out devils, for becoming as perfect as Jesus told us to be. Also, studying and pondering some of the things that David the Psalmist said, helps us realize that we are our own healer, teacher, and savior.

The Psalmist used the word "precepts" about 20 times in "The Psalms." Thus, it helps to be clear about what a precept is. "Precept" is defined by Webster as "a commandment or direction meant as a rule of action or conduct. ... a rule of moral conduct."

"Precept" is closely related to the following words and phrases as used by the Psalmist: "thy word," "thy law," "thy truth," and "thy statutes." With the foregoing in mind, note the following comments by the Psalmist.

David the Psalmist, said: "I waited patiently for the Lord, and he inclined unto me and heard my cry. ... Through thy precepts I get understanding; therefore, I hate every false way. Thy word is a lamp unto my feet and a light unto my path. ... I delight to do thy will, O my God; yea, thy law is within my heart. ... Bless the Lord, O my soul, and all that is within me, bless his holy name. ... The Lord is my strength and song, and is become my salvation. ... the truth of the Lord endureth forever. Praise ye the Lord. ... For the word of the Lord is right, and all his works are done in truth. ... The Lord knoweth the thoughts of man, that they are vanity. ... Bless the Lord, O my soul, and forget not all his benefits ... who forgiveth all thine iniquities ... who healeth all thy diseases ... who redeemeth thy life from destruction ... who crowneth thee with lovingkindness and tender mercies ... who satisfieth thy mouth with good things, so that thy youth is renewed like the eagle's."

Who heard the Psalmist's cry, except some aspect of himself? When Jesus taught us to pray, he said, "Pray to thy Father who is in secret; and thy Father who seeth in secret shall reward thee openly." Where is the Father that is in secret, except within us? Who or what rewards us, except our communion with the true spiritual self ... our channel to the universal God.

Vain thoughts come from our false ego-self. The Psalmist hated the false ways of the ego, and he cherished the truth that he

The Essential Teachings of Jesus

discovered within himself ... saying, "the truth of the Lord endureth for ever. Praise ye the Lord" (Psalms 117:2).

Jesus said something very similar about truth enduring forever. Jesus said, "Heaven and earth shall pass away, but my words shall not pass away" (Matthew 24:35). The words that Jesus got from his Father are true, and truth endures forever.

Isaiah said the same thing, only the words and language are different. Again, the essential teachings of Jesus are in the Old Testament. Isaiah said, "My words which I have put in thy mouth, shall not depart out of thy mouth, nor out of the mouth of thy seed, nor out of the mouth of thy seed's seed, saith the Lord, from henceforth and for ever" (Isaiah 59:21).

Who or what is it that knows our thoughts better than we do ... better than our deeper, inner true self ... that place within us that knows what is true and what is false ... the place within us that the Psalmist called the "secret place of the Most High?"

Our understanding of what David the Psalmist was alluding to about hating every false way is scant until we achieve a breakthrough to awareness and gain insights into the influence of our ego. Then we realize how much of our energy, thoughts, and actions evolve around that which is fearful and false ... around that which brings disharmony and discord into our lives ... around that which brings about stress, struggle, and strain ... around that which causes mental turmoil ... around that which causes hell.

It's indescribable! It's incomprehensible what we, our families, our society — the very world itself — will be like when our thoughts, energy, and actions evolve from that which is true rather than from that which evolves from our false ego-self.

And notice the part by the Psalmist, "... so that thy youth is renewed like the eagle's." In ancient times the golden eagle, known for its superb aerial skills, was regarded as a symbol of courage and power. In Greek mythology, the eagle was the god of the sky. In Roman myths, the eagle is associated with a principal deity, having a divine nature or status. Think about it! When we abide by the truth that dwells within us, we will be fully alive in the spirit of truth ... for as long as we shall live ... "thy youth is renewed like the eagle's."

More comments by the Psalmist follow, but for now let's pause and note the significance of what the Psalmist said and how it is consistent with what Jesus taught several hundred years later ... only said differently ... keeping in mind that Jesus used the word "Father," whereas the Psalmist used the word "Lord."

We know that the "law" and "truth" are one and the same. And we know from Jesus' teachings that the truth resides within the Father ... resides within our own "heart." We are saved by the truth that rests within our own heart.

Thus, the potential for our salvation lies within us. Note that the Psalmist said, "Bless the Lord, O my soul, and all that is within me." Remember that Jesus said, "the kingdom of God is within you." Everything we need to save us — everything we are searching for — is within us. And we know that all the works of the Father are done in truth and that truth endures forever ... the one thing that never changes. We cannot alter truth ... we cannot add to truth or take from truth.

Surely we do not wish to gloss over what the Psalmist said about the benefits derived from following the guidance coming from our true, spiritual self ... from letting our true, spiritual self be (in the words of the Psalmist) "a lamp unto my feet and a light unto my path."

When we worship our true, spiritual self and abide by the guidance coming from it, quite naturally we do what Jesus alluded to when he spoke of doing the "will of my Father." And according to Jesus, doing the "will of my Father" is a prerequisite for enjoying heaven. Very simply, if we do not do the will of the Father — if we do not abide by the guidance of our true, divine spiritual self — we will never enjoy heaven. And let's remember that the Psalmist said, "I delight to do thy will, O my God" ... the same thing as Jesus doing the will of the Father.

The "will of my Father, which is in heaven" is the same for everyone. The will of our true divine self is to express life in agreement with truth ... is to abide by the guidance that comes from our true, spiritual self — the place within us that knows what is right and what is wrong, that knows what is good and what is evil, that knows what is true and what is false ... the place within us that knows "thy precepts" — rather than being guided by the influence of our false ego-self.

Note the significance of what the Psalmist said about the Lord: "Who redeemeth thy life from destruction." The truth that proceeds from our true, spiritual self redeems us from all that showy, destructive stuff evolving from our bloated ego ... all that stuff that robs us of genuine love, joy, and happiness and that causes all our unhappiness, mental suffering, restlessness, and discontent.

The truth that sets us free — the truth that lies within our heart — redeems us from our hatred, anger, jealousy, resentment, envy, emotional insecurity, anxiety, psychological fear ... all that negative, false, showy stuff that robs us of life while we are alive and causes all sorts of suffering, sickness, sorrow, disastrous relationships, dysfunctional families, restlessness, and discontent. The truth that proceeds from our true spiritual self redeems us from hell and allows us to enjoy heaven. Thus, our true, divine, spiritual self — wherein lies the truth that sets us free — is our savior.

The following are a few additional comments by the Psalmist: "In my distress I cried unto the Lord, and he heard me. ... I will meditate in thy precepts and have respect unto thy ways. I will delight myself in thy statutes, I will not forget thy word. Make me to understand the way of thy precepts, so shall I talk of thy wondrous works. ... I hate vain thoughts, but thy law do I love. ... Let my heart be sound in thy statutes, that I be not ashamed. ... Thou art my hiding place and my shield. ... Therefore, I esteem all thy precepts concerning all things to be right, and I hate every false way. Thy word is very pure. ... I have more understanding than all my teachers, for thy testimonies are my meditation. I understand more than the ancients, because I keep thy precepts. I have refrained my feet from every evil way, that I might keep thy word. I have not departed from thy judgments, for thou hast taught me. ... Who can understand his errors? Cleanse thou me from secret faults. ... Thy word is true from the beginning, and every one of thy righteous judgments endureth forever. ... Thy righteousness is an everlasting righteousness, and thy law is the truth. ... Turn away mine eyes from beholding vanity, and quicken thou me in thy way. Thou art good and doest good; teach me thy statutes. ... It is good for me that I have been afflicted, that I might learn thy statutes. ... Be still and know that I am God. ... The Lord of hosts is with us. ... Stand in awe and sin not, commune with your own heart ... and be still. ... Quicken us, and we will call upon thy name. Turn us again, O Lord God of hosts, cause thy face to shine; and we shall be saved. ... The Lord is my light and my salvation; whom shall I fear? ... The law of thy mouth is better unto me than thousands of gold and silver. ... I have longed for thy salvation, O Lord; and thy law is my delight. ... He that dwelleth in the secret place of the Most High shall abide under the shadow of the Almighty. I will say of the Lord, he is my refuge and my fortress; my God; in him will I trust."

The Psalmist goes on and on and on praising the Lord: "O Lord my God, I cried unto thee, and thou hast healed me. ... O Lord my God, I will give thanks unto thee forever. ... The Lord hath made known his salvation. ... Know ye that the Lord he is God. ... Create in me a clean heart, O God; and renew a right spirit within me. ... Truly, my soul waiteth upon God; from him cometh my salvation. ... In God is my salvation and my glory; the rock of my strength and my refuge is in God. ... Behold, thou desirest truth in the inward parts; and in the hidden part thou shalt make me to know wisdom. ... Delight is in the law of the Lord."

"Delight" is defined as great joy. And "delight" is "in the law" ... in the truth that rests within our heart. By the "inward parts" and the "hidden part" the Psalmist must have been speaking about the subconscious mind. We gain wisdom and we are saved by doing what the Psalmist said to do: "Commune with your own heart." We realize from what David said that our true spiritual self judges us. He said, "I have not departed from thy righteous judgments ... thy righteous judgments endureth forever" ("thy" alludes to the "Lord," the true spiritual self). And, note the word "forever;" for us individually, it means as long as we live.

Note how the following statements by David take on a new meaning when we realize that he was speaking of communing with the true, spiritual self ... communing with his own heart ... and that we too can commune with our own heart. David said, "I will bless the Lord at all times; his praise shall continually be in my mouth.

The Essential Teachings of Jesus

... The humble shall hear thereof and be glad. ... I sought the Lord, and he heard me and delivered me from all my fears."

Let us not gloss over what David said. In our language, David's true spiritual self delivered him *from all his fears*. Deep inside the soul of us, we insatiably desire to know the truth that frees us from all our fears. Communing with his own heart is the way the Psalmist learned "thy precepts;" it is the way that Moses learned the Ten Commandments. Communing with his true spiritual self is the way that Moses sanctified himself and became holy. Jesus received guidance by going to his Father.

David also said, "The righteous cry, and the Lord heareth and delivereth them out of all their troubles. ... The Lord is nigh unto them that are of a broken heart and saveth such as be of a contrite spirit. ... Many are the afflictions of the righteous; but the Lord delivereth him out of them all. The Lord redeemeth the soul of his servants; and none of them that trust in him shall be desolate."

The following summarizes this section about what David did, what he said, and what he discovered. He was still, he mediated, and he communed with his own heart (the Lord within himself). He discovered the word of God, the truth, the precepts, the redeemer (the same thing that Jeremiah called "thy Saviour"). He found salvation, which is the same thing as being saved. He discovered the truth that freed him of an affliction; by his own understanding he cleansed himself from secret faults. Similarly, Job freed himself from his suffering by understanding that fear was the underlying cause of it.

By understanding what the David said and what he did, we understand how to do some of the things that Jesus told us to do. By communing with our own heart, we can cast out the devils that are lurking in our subconscious mind, we can "clean the inside of the cup and the platter," we can cleanse ourselves from secret faults, we can learn to be as perfect as Jesus told us to be when he said, "Be ye therefore perfect, even as your Father who is in heaven is perfect" ... our Father being our true, perfect self as opposed to our false ego-self. We are as perfect as Jesus told us to be when we have cleansed ourselves from secret faults. We are as perfect as Jesus told us to be when we have obliterated from our heart (from our subconscious mind) those obscure, insidious fears, and deeply held, false beliefs that are the hidden cause of all our mental suffering and all our unhappiness ... that are the hidden cause of all evil and violence.

We know from both the teachings of the Psalmist and from Jesus that truth resides within our heart ... thus, the only place that we can discover it. And the only way that we can discover the truth is by being still and communing with our own heart.

Thus, by doing what the Psalmist did and what he said to do — communing with our own heart — we can find salvation, we can discover the truth that sets us free, we can choose to do the will of the Father, which is a prerequisite for enjoying heaven ... and life does not get any better than heaven. Communing with our own heart is the secret to being our own best teacher, healer, therapist, psychic, astrologer, savior, and guru ... it's all within us.

People would not seek advice and guidance from psychics and astrologers if religious teachers were teaching clearly the gospel of Jesus, which is consistent with the teachings of the writers of the Old Testament. What the people who resort to psychics and astrologers are seeking is what they would experience if they were living in agreement with truth. Thus, to find all the answers we need for finding peace and joy — for finding what will satisfy us and make us happy — we can follow the suggestion of Isaiah and go directly to the source, the God within us. We can do what David, the Psalmist said to do: "Commune with your own heart."

We know from studying "The Psalms" that David found everything he was searching for within himself. And we know that Isaiah raised questions about people seeking advice and guidance from the spirits of the dead, and from wizards, astrologers, stargazers, monthly prognosticators, and the multitudes of sorcerers. He raised the question: Why not just go to the real source, the God within us?

Isaiah said, "And when they shall say unto you, 'seek unto them that have familiar spirits, and unto wizards that peep and mutter,' should not a people seek unto their God? ... If they speak not according to this word [the word of God], it is because there is no light in them" (Isaiah 8: 19-20).

The Essential Teachings of Jesus

Isaiah also said, "Stand now with thine enchantments and with the multitude of thy sorceries ... Thou art wearied in the multitude of thy counsels. Let now the astrologers, the stargazers, the monthly prognosticators stand up and save thee from these things that shall come upon thee. Behold, they shall be as stubble; the fire shall burn them ... they shall wander every one to his quarter; none shall save thee" (Isaiah 47: 12-15).

Note from what Isaiah said that wizards, astrologers, stargazers, monthly prognosticators, and the multitudes of sorcerers will not save us. If they do not speak according to the word of God, it is because there is no light — no truth — in them. The teachings of false teachers will not save us. So, why not follow the advice of Isaiah and "seek unto their God"? The source of our salvation is the God within us. Where did Moses gain the wisdom for being holy, for being sinless (a prerequisite for enjoying heaven), except from within him? The angel of the Lord that appeared unto Moses in a burning bush was a vision, and from this angel — from the vision — Moses gained wisdom and understanding ... all within himself.

There is that place within us (the Psalmist called it "the secret place of the most high") that knows the negative, evil influences that cause us suffering, that create our reality, and that predestines our future. We find peace and joy by abiding by that which is true ... rather than abiding by the false, evil influences that cause us suffering.

In "The Book of Deuteronomy," we find where Moses said something akin to what Isaiah said. Moses said: "If there arise among you a prophet, or a dreamer of dreams, and giveth thee a sign or a wonder, And the sign or the wonder come to pass, whereof he spake unto thee, saying, Let us go after other gods, which thou hast not known, and let us serve them; Thou shalt not hearken unto the words of that prophet ["prophet"is another word for teacher], or that dreamer of dreams; for the Lord your God proveth you, to know whether ye love the Lord your God with all your heart and with all your soul. Ye shall walk after the Lord your God, and fear him, and keep his commandments, and obey his voice, and ye shall serve him, and cleave unto him" (Deuteronomy 13: 1-4).

And again, remember that the Lord your God is your true divine spiritual self. Thus, rather than following the guidance of false teachers, we can do as Isaiah said, "Go to the source, our God." According to Isaiah, this will save us. And, we can do as Moses said and obey our inner voice, the voice of the God within us. Also, we can do as David, the Psalmist said to do: "Commune with your own heart."

The Apostle Paul said, "For there stood by me this night the angel of God, whose I am, and whom I serve ... Saying, Fear not, Paul" (Acts 27:23-24). Note what it is that Paul served: "the angel of God." As explained elsewhere, an "angel" is something within us. Thus, the Apostle Paul (in our language) served his true divine spiritual self ... the same thing as Jesus serving the "Father." Note that Paul spoke of two aspects of himself, "whom I serve;" he served the "the angel of God;" thus, he served his spiritual self.

And, we find: "Teach me to do thy will; for thou art my God; thy spirit is good; lead me into the land of uprightness. Quicken me, O Lord, for thy name's sake; for thy righteousness' sake bring my soul out of trouble. ... for I am thy servant" (Psalms 143:10-12).

Note some significant things about this passage:
- The Psalmist used the words "God" and "Lord" synonymously.
- He said, "Teach me to do thy will; for thou art my God." From Jesus' teachings, we know that only those who do the will of the true spiritual self (what Jesus called the "Father") will enjoy heaven. Doing the will of the "Father" — abiding by that which is true — is the same thing as doing the will of God. And note that the Psalmist said, "for thou art my God." ... speaking of the God within him.
- Speaking of the Lord within him, the Psalmist said, "lead me into the land of uprightness" ... which is honest, honorable and just.
- The Psalmist said (again, speaking of the Lord within himself), "bring my soul out of trouble."
- The Psalmist said, "for I am thy servant." ... the same thing as Jesus worshipping and serving his "Father." Following the guidance of our true spiritual self is the same thing as "being its servant." We

The Essential Teachings of Jesus

either serve our true spiritual self or we serve our false ego-self; we serve either God or Satan ... not both at the same time.

The foregoing comments are consistent with the teachings of Jesus. We free ourselves from the things that trouble our soul by doing the will of — and serving — our true divine spiritual self. Thus, the essential teachings of Jesus (what will save us) are in the Old Testament.

Regardless of what our concept of God is (a mystical being up in the sky, universal God that is in and through everything, a God that is all powerful, all knowing, and everywhere present, God within us), everything we need for our salvation is within us: the law, the truth, wisdom ... "Thy word is a light unto my path." We know from the teachings of the spiritual teachers of the Old Testament — and also from the gospel that Jesus preached — that we find what we are searching for within our own heart. And we find what we are searching for by doing what Jesus did, by doing what the spiritual teachers of the Old Testament did, by doing what the Buddha did, by doing what all great spiritual teachers did. They were still, they meditated; they communed with their own heart.

And we know from the Psalmist that it's better to live in harmony with the truth of our being — "thy law is my delight" — rather than following vain thoughts that evolve from our false ego-self. The Psalmist said, "I hate vain thoughts, but thy law do I love." In our language, the Psalmist hated the false ways of the ego, and he loved the ways of truth ... the ways of his divine, spiritual self. According to the Psalmist, following the guidance of our true, divine self — rather than following the dictates of our false ego-self — is "better unto me than thousands of gold and silver."

Moses left us with the first and the greatest of all commandments several hundred years before the ministry of Jesus. Moses said: "Hear, O Israel; the Lord our God *is* one Lord. And thou shalt love the Lord thy God with all thine heart, and with all thy soul, and with all thy might. And these words, which I command thee this day, shall be in thine heart; And thou shalt teach them diligently unto thy children, and shalt talk of them when thou sittest in thine house, and when thou walkest by the way, and when thou liest down, and when thou risest up" (Deuteronomy" 6: 4-7).

Note in "Deuteronomy" (6:30), Moses said, "And ... to love the Lord thy God with all thine heart, and with all thy soul, that thou mayest live." And in "Deuteronomy" (30:20), Moses said, "That thou mayest love the Lord thy God, and that thou mayest obey his voice, and that thou mayest cleave unto him; for he is *thy life*."

Moses was speaking to people who were already living. And, he said, "for he [the Lord, thy God] is *thy life*." Thus, the words "live" and "life" as used here mean to be fully alive in the spirit of truth ... as opposed to being dead in spirit. "To walk in his ways" is to abide by the guidance of the true spiritual self ... the same thing as "doing the will of the Father," as advocated by Jesus.

Jesus did not say that he was God in human flesh. When he spoke in terms of "thy God," he spoke in terms of something that is within us; for example, "Thou shalt love the *Lord thy God* with all thy heart, and with all thy soul, and with all thy strength, and with all thy mind," and "Thou shalt worship the *Lord thy God,* and him only shalt thou serve" (Luke 4:8), speaking of something within us.

Moses said: "Hear, O Israel; the Lord our God *is* one Lord. And thou shalt love the Lord thy God with all thine heart, and with all thy soul, and with all thy might." Jesus said, "This is the first and great commandment. And the second is like unto it: 'Thou shalt love thy neighbour as thyself.' There is none other commandment greater than these. ... On these two commandments hang all the law and the prophets."

If we abide by these two commandments, we experience the ultimate that life has to offer ... this is it! Life can never — now or ever — get any better than it is when we love like Moses and Jesus commanded us to love.

Can you imagine? Can you comprehend what our lives, our families, and our society — the very world itself — would be like if we loved as both Moses and Jesus commanded us to love? We are *saved* — we enjoy heaven here and now — when we love as commanded by both Moses and Jesus. When we "love thy neighbor as thyself," we naturally "do unto others as we would have others do unto us." Can you imagine how peaceful and joyous life could be when we, as a society, have a loving heart.

The Essential Teachings of Jesus

However, we cannot love anyone until we love ourselves ... until we love the "Lord thy God with all thine heart, and with all thy soul, and with all thy might," which is the same thing as loving ourselves. We cannot love the way that Jesus and Moses commanded us to love with the demons of fear, hate, anger, guilt, shame, jealousy (all the negative stuff that robs us of the "peace that passeth all understanding") simmering in our heart. We cannot love unconditionally until we obliterate the devils from our heart ... until we "clean the inside of the cup and the platter" ... until our heart is as pure as that of little children ... until we are as perfect as Jesus told us to be: "Be ye therefore perfect, even as your Father who is in heaven is perfect." We love freely and unconditionally when we know the truth that sets us free.

Although it seems to have been glossed over, Jesus told us what we would worship when we are truly Christian ... when we have discovered the truth that sets us free and have purified our hearts. Bear in mind that our true spiritual self is the same thing as the "Father." With this in mind, note what we are to love and worship. Both Moses and Jesus said to "love the Lord thy God with all thine heart, and with all thy soul, and with all thy might" ... in our language, love our true divine spiritual self.

When we believe, understand and embody the gospel that Jesus preached, we will worship our true spiritual self. Jesus did not tell us to love, praise, and worship him. Jesus said, "Why callest thou me good? *There is* none good but one; *that is* God" (Matthew 19:17). Jesus also said, "But the hour cometh, and now is, when the true worshippers shall worship the Father [the true spiritual self] in spirit and in truth. ... God is a Spirit, and they that worship him must worship him in spirit and in truth" (John 4:23-24).

Note that Jesus used the words "Father" and "God" synonymously. Similarly, the spiritual teachers of the Old Testament used the words "Lord" and "God" synonymously.

Jesus also said, "Get thee behind me, Satan; for it is written, Thou shalt worship the Lord thy God, and him only shalt thou serve" (Luke 4:8). Translated into our language this means that we will worship — and follow the guidance of — our true spiritual self, rather than worshipping our false ego-self ... thus, "get thee behind me, Satan."

Jesus also said, "No man can serve two masters; for either he will hate the one, and love the other; or else he will hold to the one, and despise the other. Ye cannot serve God and mammon" (Matthew 6:24). We serve either our true spiritual self — the God within us — or we serve our false ego-self ... it's one or the other.

"Mammon" is characterized by a greedy desire for riches ... things that are savored by men (savored by the false ego-self). Things savored by the false ego-self are showy, conceited, worthless, and empty ... are things we can brag about and gloat over ... things that seem to make us appear special and important. These things do not bring us peace, joy, happiness, and contentment.

Isaiah said, "Thou wilt keep him in perfect peace, whose mind is stayed on thee" (Isaiah 26:3). "Thou" and "thee" allude to the true spiritual self. We either "keep our mind stayed on thee" and follow the guidance of our true spiritual self, or we follow the guidance of our false ego-self. When we follow the guidance of our true spiritual self, this is the same thing as "doing the will of the Father," which is a prerequisite for enjoying heaven. Following the whims of our false ego-self brings mental turmoil and suffering ... the "gnashing of teeth."

To worship something is to have love and admiration for it ... to give extreme devotion to it. This is what many Christians have done regarding the man Jesus, rather than understanding — and doing — what Jesus said to do. If we study and assimilate what both the spiritual teachers of the Old Testament said and what Jesus said, we realize that we will worship our true spiritual self when we have discovered the truth that sets us free ... when we have unified with our true spiritual self, the same thing as unifying with God.

Thus, we are not to worship Jesus or anything outside ourselves. We are to worship only our true spiritual self (the God within us) ... the self of us that is perfect, created in the image and likeness of God. We naturally embrace and worship our true, spiritual self when we overcome the false ego-self and are living in harmony with that which is true.

The Essential Teachings of Jesus 285

It's easy to understand why we would worship our true, spiritual self when we realize the benefits derived from doing this ... the benefits derived from living in harmony with truth ... the benefits alluded to by David the Psalmist. Truth proceeds from the true spiritual self ... the self of us that is perfect, created in the image and likeness of God. Truth will save us. Truth will heal us of any psychosomatic illness (illnesses caused by the mind). Truth will resolve relationship, family, and societal problems. Truth will free us from our anger, hate, prejudice, jealousy, anxiety, depression, emotional insecurity, resentment, and the masks we wear, pretending to be something we are not. Truth frees us from our false ego-self (the Satan within us) that always wants to appear special and important ... that always causes suffering and unhappiness.

The ultimate reward of living in harmony with truth — and worshipping our true, spiritual self — is peace, joy, and happiness. Jesus is our example. He said, "I and my Father are one." When we are one with our true divine, spiritual self, we are unified with God ... that is heaven.

When we are alienated from our true divine, spiritual self (the same thing as being alienated from God), that is hell. Hell is characterized by fear, hate, anger, resentment, guilt, anxiety, depression, insecurity, restlessness, discontent, unhappiness ... any state of mind unlike heaven, which is characterized by inner serenity, peace, love, joy, and happiness.

Jesus overcame the world of the ego. We, too, can do this. We must overcome the world of the ego if we are to have joy, peace, and inner serenity; if we are to be genuinely happy, satisfied, and contented ... rather than wearing our mask — keeping up our facade — pretending to be other than the way we really feel ... all the while suffering the torments of a troubled, confused mind ... all the while insatiably desiring to live in harmony with truth, God, and nature. We have overcome the world of the ego when we have discovered the truth that sets us free.

If we study and assimilate what Jesus said rather than glossing over it, we realize that Jesus worshipped the Father within. His life was devoted to doing the will of the Father; his teachings and his guidance came from the Father. Jesus said, "I must be about my Father's business. ... I do always those things that please him."

Similarly, the spiritual teachers of the Old Testament worshipped the Lord ... the same thing as Jesus worshipping the Father ... in our language, the same thing as worshipping our true spiritual self. Thus, to enjoy heaven, we must worship our true, spiritual self, rather than worshipping false gods, rather than following the dictates of our bloated, elephantine ego-self.

Isaiah said: "The Lord was ready to save me; therefore we will sing my songs to the stringed instruments all the days of our life in the house of the Lord" (Isaiah 38:20). And, "Behold, God is my salvation; I will trust, and not be afraid; for the Lord Jehovah is my strength and my song; he also is become my salvation" (Isaiah 12:2). Note that Isaiah used the words "God" and "Lord Jehovah" synonymously. By understanding what Isaiah said here, we realize that — in our language — our true spiritual self is our savior.

Similarly, Micah said, "Therefore I will look unto the Lord; I will wait for the God of my salvation [his savior]; my God will hear me" (Micah 7:7).

The Psalmist knew the benefits derived from abiding by the true, spiritual, divine self several hundred years before the ministry of Jesus. Surely, somewhere, somehow, religious teachers have been led astray from the gospel that Jesus preached, much of which was based on some of the teachings of the writers of the Old Testament.

The famous 23rd Psalm takes on added meaning when we realize that David was speaking of his true, divine spiritual self and the *present life* ... not life after death. He said, "The Lord is my shepherd; I shall not want. ... He restoreth my soul; he leadeth me in the paths of righteousness for his name's sake. Yea, though I walk through the valley of the shadow of death, I will fear no evil; for thou art with me; thy rod and thy staff they comfort me. ... Surely goodness and mercy shall follow me all the days of my life; and I will dwell in the house of the Lord forever" (Psalms 23: 1-6).

The statement, "The Lord is my shepherd; I shall not want," perhaps sums up the ethic of David. Think about it! Our true divine, spiritual self is our shepherd, and by following its guidance we shall not want ... we will have peace and joy. When we are

The Essential Teachings of Jesus 287

living in harmony with truth and have peace and joy, we will naturally embrace and worship our true divine spiritual self.

Job said, "Acquaint now thyself with him, and be at peace; thereby good shall come unto thee. Receive, I pray thee, the law from his mouth, and lay up his words in thine heart" (Job 22: 21-22). And "Neither have I gone back from the commandment of his lips; I have esteemed the words of his mouth more than my necessary food" (Job 23: 12).

Note that Job said, "Acquaint now thyself with him." In our language, this means the same thing as knowing our true spiritual self. This means the same thing that Socrates taught about 500 years BC: "Know thyself." Job esteemed the words he got from his true spiritual self just as Jesus esteemed the words he got from his Father.

In "The Proverbs" we find: "There is a way that seemeth right unto a man, but the end thereof are the ways of death." This alludes to the ways that seem right to the elephantine ego ... the false ways that David the Psalmist hated. We also find in "The Proverbs," "Better it is to be of an humble spirit with the lowly, than to divide the spoil with the proud."

Isaiah said, "Let the wicked forsake his way, and the unrighteous man his thoughts; and let him return unto the Lord ... for he will abundantly pardon" (Isaiah 55:7). In his manner of teaching, Jesus said the same thing: "Come unto me, all ye that labour and are heavy laden, and I will give you rest" (Matthew 11:28). Jesus was speaking to those who were burdened with sin (sinners). Isaiah was speaking to the wicked and unrighteous (sinners). "Return unto the Lord" and "come unto me" mean the same thing. Sinners who believe the gospel and abide by the truth that proceeds from the true spiritual self — those who return to their true spiritual self — will find rest ... will be "abundantly pardoned" ... will be saved.

Realizing that the essential teachings of Jesus (what will save us) are in the Old Testament, we realize that there are ways to be saved had we never heard of Jesus. However, fundamentalists are so adamant about their beliefs about what would save us (things like taking Christ into our heart, believing on the Lord Jesus Christ, accepting Jesus as our savior, believing that we are saved by the blood of Jesus, etc.) that they "strain at a gnat, and swallow a camel" to make the following statement by Luke, author of "The Acts of the Apostles," seem that there is no way to be saved, except by Jesus.

Luke said, "Neither is there salvation in any other; for there is none other name under heaven given among men, whereby we must be saved" (Acts 4:12). In our language, there is no other way that we can be saved, except by truth. Jesus was the personification of truth. However, it is possible to discover truth had we never heard of Jesus. Clearly, we would be saved if we understood and did what the spiritual teachers of the Old Testament taught ... and did. When we have obliterated all the negative impressions from the subconscious mind, our heart is pure, a prerequisite for enjoying heaven. When our heart is pure — regardless of how we achieve this purity — we are unified with God ... the goal of all great religions.

Jesus teachings — in conjunction with what David the Psalmist said — provide one of the most simple and most direct ways of unifying with God; that way is communion with our own heart. If we master the art of calming our mind and communing with our own heart, we would — without fail — become unified with God ... we would be saved.

In summary, the essential teachings of Jesus — what will save us — are in the Old Testament. Jesus and the saints of the Old Testament praised and worshipped — and followed the guidance of — their true divine spiritual self ... what Jesus call the Father and what the saints of the Old Testament called the Lord and the Lord thy God.

Realizing that the essential teachings of Jesus are in the Old Testament helps us shift the focus of our attention from the man Jesus to his message. When the many religious teachers in mainline churches shift the focus of teaching from the man Jesus to the gospel that he preached, the gospel would spread like a sagebrush fire on a dry, windy day. In due time, planet Earth will be a utopia ... like "a new heaven and a new earth." Deep inside the soul of us, every one of us wants to live in harmony with truth, God, and nature ... the way Jesus wanted us to live ... the way of life that brings peace, joy, and happiness.

Chapter 12
When Will Suffering and Violence End?

The solution to suffering, violence, crime, rape, drug abuse, child abuse, and spousal abuse — all that is ugly and deplorable — is simple, and it is what everyone wants. Suffering and violence will end when we correct the cause, rather than devoting so much time, money, and effort trying to alleviate symptoms ... but doing nothing to correct the cause. Jesus and Isaiah told us when suffering and violence will end, but we have glossed over and misinterpreted what they said.

The horrendous, hideous, horrible crimes like the shooting of students and teachers *by students* and crimes like the Oklahoma City tragedy have raised a multitude of questions. Clearly crimes like these are acts of evil. But what is evil? Is evil only something we associate with a major atrocity ... something outrageously evil? What is the cause of evil? When we understand the answer to these questions, we will know the solution to suffering and violence ... the solution to the problems that plague us, our families, and our society.

The Oklahoma City bombing captured attention like nothing else in the history of our nation. One of the factors accounting for so much outrage, anger, heartache, and grief is the death and suffering of innocent children. Nineteen children died and several were injured in this atrocious act of evil.

But what about the suffering of children that is going on around us all the time? We, as a society, do not seem to acknowledge and admit the suffering of children ... we tend to ignore it, evade it, and deny it. The suffering of children in our society takes many forms, including both verbal and physical abuse.

About half a million teenagers attempt suicide annually. The rate of increase is alarming. The suffering associated with suicide is only the tip of the iceberg of the suffering of children and young people in our society. Many children die from neglect and abuse.

In addition to the problems associated with alcohol and various stimulating drugs, we now have another type of drug problem with young people. In an effort to control the behavior of their children, many parents are giving their children prescription drugs. Children as young as two years of age are being given powerful psychiatric drugs. And no one knows the short-term or long-term effects of these drugs on the developing brain.

The cover story of the March 6, 2000, issue of *U.S. News & World Report* is: "Paxil, Prozac, Ritalin ... Are These Drugs Safe for Kids? Many parents are using powerful pills to control behavior."

In the article we find: "According to the surgeon general, almost 21 percent of children ages 9 and up have a mental disorder, including depression, attention deficit hyperactivity disorder, and bipolar disorder."

This is not the say that the remaining 79 percent of young people are mentally and spiritually healthy, happy, satisfied, and contented ... this is not to say they are living in harmony with truth, God, and nature ... the way things are meant to be.

Treating children with psychiatric drugs is an example of treating symptoms, which does not correct the underlying cause of the problem.

Jung, psychologist and psychiatrist said: "If there is anything that we wish to change in the child, we should first examine it and see whether it is something that could better be changed in ourselves."

In 1986, there were slightly more than two million cases of abused children reported to state agencies. In 1994, there were slightly more than three million, an increase of about one million since 1986 (close to a 50 percent increase in 8 years).

It is significant to note that the reported cases include victims of physical and sexual abuse ... not the victims of verbal abuse, which is psychologically destructive. There is no way of knowing the prevalence of verbal abuse; however, in a society with so many dysfunctional families, it is safe to assume that it is extensive.

A child is born into this world in agreement with truth, God, and nature ... free, spontaneous, humble, and pure. The purity with

When Will Suffering and Violence End?

which a child is born is soon corrupted when a child is born into a corrupt environment ... an environment that is inharmonious with truth. Our early childhood environment determines the way we believe and think in our heart, which determines our behavior, what we do and what we do not do.

Within a few years after birth, the minds of most children in our society (a society in which about 90 percent of the families are dysfunctional) are programmed with insidious fears and beliefs that are contrary to truth and that determine the attitude one has toward life. Unwarranted, insidious fears and false beliefs manifest in a myriad of ways that are evil, destructive, and detrimental. They are the underlying cause of one harboring evil, hatred, anger, and jealousy. These unwarranted fears and deeply held beliefs are the cause of one being a cur, of being violent, of being a sexual deviant, of being emotionally insecure ... and on and on and on.

The Apostle Paul said, "For God hath not given us the spirit of fear; but of power, and of love, and of a sound mind" (2 Timothy 1:7). Stop! Notice what the Apostle Paul said. Think about how we came into this world—pure in heart and innocent. Think about how things are now, and how we have gone astray from our true nature ... from being pure in heart.

We do not like to admit it, but for the most part, the cause of evil begins in the family environment. Very simply, a child is not born into this world emotionally scarred, evil, unhappy, restless, and angry. Troubled, intolerable, rebellious children — pitching temper tantrums — is a clue that parents are not giving their children adequate love, mothering, and nurturing ... a clue that parents are not in agreement with truth ... even though they might attend church, pretending and professing to be Christian.

By and large, the deepest emotional scars are those inflicted in the home environment. If a child has adequate love, mothering, and nurturing, the negative encounters outside the family environment are not usually enough to change the inner self ... to change the way a child believes and thinks in his or her heart.

Incidentally, if parents feel guilty or troubled because of anything they read here, it might help to know that the cause is not what they read. They are already troubled and guilty, and the reading only reminds them. If you are living in agreement with truth, you will not feel troubled and guilty because of reading anything in this book.

It might also help to know that the truth that sets you free from fear and deeply held, false beliefs (the source of suffering) is the same truth that will free you from guilt and a troubled mind. Truth is the ultimate end of guilt, repressed anger, all mental suffering, and all unhappiness. Denials of our faults and evading truth only prolong suffering.

Fear is the hidden cause of all negative, undesirable behaviors in children. As children mature, obscure, insidious fears manifest in myriad ways. Obscure, insidious fear is the hidden cause of crime, violence, child abuse, spousal abuse, drug abuse, psychosomatic illnesses, dysfunctional families, divorce ... all that is ugly and deplorable. Where there is insidious fear, there is evil. Evil is associated with all violence and suffering.

Definitions of "evil" include "anything that causes injury or any other undesirable results ... that which causes suffering."

Let us note what Jesus said about evil: "For from within, out of the heart of men, proceed evil thoughts, murders, thefts, wickedness, deceit, pride, foolishness; all these evil things come from within. ... A good man, out of the good treasure of his heart, bringeth forth that which is good; and an evil man, out of the evil treasure of his heart, bringeth forth that which is evil."

Why do some people harbor evil in their hearts, while others harbor love and goodness? All evil, all hate, anger, violence, crime, psychosomatic illness, dysfunctional families, all mental suffering and all unhappiness can be traced to obscure, insidious fear and deeply held, false beliefs.

All negative, destructive subconscious fears and false beliefs can be traced to a lack of adequate love. Love and truth go hand in hand, and they are the solution to all of the social problems in our society. Adequate love will eradicate evil, crime, violence, mental suffering, suffering of children, the breakup of families, restlessness, discontent, unhappiness ... all that is ugly, deplorable, destructive, and detrimental. Adequate love will render families loving, peaceful, happy, harmonious and stable.

While love is the solution to all social problems, we simply cannot love freely and unconditionally with fears influencing our every thought and every action at every turn of the road. Fears and false beliefs propel us to do things we ought not do and hinder us from doing things we ought to do.

How do we learn to love? For the most part, we learn to love by the experience of having been loved ... an experience that comes naturally in a loving, happy, harmonious, functional, stable family. We learn to love primarily by being loved, mothered, and nurtured by a loving mother.

A child who receives the unconditional love of a loving, happy, contented mother — who loves, mothers, and nurtures as nature programmed her to do — is loving, happy, and contented. He or she does not have evil in his or her heart ... does not harbor obscure, insidious fear that is the hidden cause of evil and violence.

On the contrary, the behavior of a child (and its future well-being) is unpredictable if he or she does not get the love, mothering, and nurturing that a child is programmed to expect. Every child inherently desires the love, mothering, and nurturing of a loving, happy, contented mother. And every mother — living in harmony with her true, loving, feminine, spiritual self — inherently desires to stay in the home with her children and give them the love, mothering, and nurturing that children need.

In his book, *Becoming Attached, Unfolding The Mystery Of The Infant-Mother Bond And Its Impact On Later Life,* Robert Karen states: "The struggle to understand the infant-mother bond ranks as one of the great quests of modern psychology, one that touches us deeply because it holds so many clues as to *how we become who we are*" (italics added). "Who we are" is "as we think in our heart." We learn from The Proverbs, "As a man thinketh in his heart so is he."

Certainly the father's influence in the family is important. However, the part of us deep within our psyche that determines who we are — that determines how we think in our heart, that determines how much we love and how much we hate — is influenced most by our bond with our mother.

For those who are interested in the influence of the mother's role on the well-being of a child — for those interested in what the "magical child" is like — they would do well to read the book, *Magical Child,* by Joseph C. Pearce.

In the book, Pearce states: "Bonding is a carefully programmed instinctual response built into us genetically. The mother is genetically programmed to bond to the infant at his or her birth, and the infant is programmed to expect her response. Indeed, without it, the infant is in grave trouble. ... The unbonded person ... will spend his or her life in search for what bonding was designed to give. ... lack of bonding finds no compensation."

And now there is research that suggests that a mother's nurturing stimulates a part of a baby's brain that enhances the baby's ability to learn (August, 2000, issue of Nature Neuroscience).

Psychologist Erich Fromm said, "Mother must not only be a 'good mother,' but a happy person. ... The effect on the child can hardly be exaggerated. Mother's love for life is as infectious as her anxiety. Both attitudes have a deep effect on the child's whole personality. ... There is nothing more conducive to giving a child the experience of what love, joy, and happiness are than being loved by a mother who loves herself. ... Motherly love has been considered the highest kind of love and the most sacred of all emotional bonds."

From the reports that we read and hear about genes, we might make the erroneous assumption that both physical characteristics and mental and emotional traits (including temperament and behavior) are transmitted through the genes. Two simple facts are: (1) If a mother has negative traits (anxious, angry, stressed, depressed), then there is a high degree of probability that her children will acquire these traits. Children are not born with these traits; they acquire them. (2) Mothers (all people) can change negative traits by discovering the truth that sets them free. Medication, although possibly helpful, is not the ultimate answer, and changing genes is not a practical alternative.

A child who gets the unconditional love of a loving, happy, contented mother is saved ... is free from fear. Unwarranted fear does not coexist with perfect love. Beliefs and behavior are learned.

When Will Suffering and Violence End?

A child born into an environment of peace, joy, love and truth would not have evil in his or her heart. He or she would not harbor unwarranted fears that are the root cause of all mental suffering, restlessness, and discontent.

Children are not born into this world spiritually sick, but are made sick — both spiritually and physically — by their environment. Voltaire (historian, essayist, and philosopher), said "Man is not born wicked; he becomes so as he becomes sick."

The Apostle John said, "There is no fear in love, but perfect love casteth out fear, because fear hath torment. He that feareth is not made perfect in love" (1 John 4:18). A child who gets perfect love is made perfect in love. Anyone who is perfect in love naturally adheres to the first commandment: "Thou shalt love the Lord thy God with all thy heart, and with all thy soul, and with all thy mind." Those who love as Jesus told us to love are saved.

Women have demonstrated that they can do almost anything that a man can do. And in many of the chosen professions, women have demonstrated that they are the best of the best. But, what is the significance of all of this?

In his book, *What Life Should Mean to You,* Alfred Adler stated, "Every human being strives for significance; but people always make mistakes if they do not see that their whole significance must consist in their contribution to the lives of others."

The greatest significance — by far the greatest contribution to the lives of others — that anyone will ever make is that of a loving, happy, contented mother. The love and appreciation for loving, dedicated mothers are unsurpassed. A woman may become president of a giant corporation, a celebrity, wealthy, and famous, but what is the significance? What would one give in exchange for his or her soul ... if he or she is basically empty inside, unhappy, restless, and discontented ... if he or she can never get enough material things, recognition, praise, and adulation to be satisfied and enjoy inner serenity, joy, peace, and loving relationships?

The emphasis of a mother's love, care, and nurturing is directed toward the life of our spirit ... toward our spiritual self ... toward the nurturing of our spirit. A mother possesses the unseen influence that impacts the part of us deep within our psyche that determines how we "think in our heart," which determines how loving, peaceful, satisfied, and contented we are.

While the emphasis of the mother's love and care is directed toward our spiritual well being, the emphasis of a father's love and care is directed toward our physical well-being, which is more obvious than the influence of the mother. The emphasis of the father's love and care is directed toward physical things ... toward things such as protection and food and shelter.

Every mother has an innate desire to love her children unconditionally. It's in agreement with her true loving, feminine nature. The impact of a mother on a child depends on the mother's state of mind. If a mother is emotionally insecure, her children will be emotionally insecure. If a mother has repressed anger and is resentful, distrustful, and suspicious, her children will be tainted with these traits. On the other hand, if a mother is loving, happy, satisfied, and contented — living in agreement with truth and nature — her children too will be happy, satisfied, and contented. Similarly, if a mother loves her children unconditionally, they will love unconditionally. When we love unconditionally we are saved, a prerequisite for enjoying heaven.

Although a father has an influence, a mother by far has the most profound influence of anyone on earth in determining our emotional well-being, in determining how emotionally secure we are. There is an old expression, "As a twig is bent, so grows the tree." No one has as much influence on "bending the twig" as the mother ... in determining the way we believe and think in our heart. ... "As a man thinketh in his heart, so is he." By her mothering and nurturing, a mother molds us and shapes us the way we are in our heart. As Emerson said, "Men are what their mothers made them."

Will Rogers said, "It's great to be great, but it's greater to be human." The ultimate of being human is being in harmony with truth and nature ... is being in harmony with God ... deep inside the soul of us what everyone wants.

Can you imagine? Can you comprehend what our lives, our families, and our society would be like if women's feminine energy and their intelligence and capabilities were directed toward their

When Will Suffering and Violence End?

innate desire — the true longing of their heart — to be a loving, mothering, nurturing mother ... the highest of all callings? It's incomprehensible! It's indescribable!

Life was meant to be characterized by love, joy, happiness, peace of mind, inner serenity, and contentment ... not stress, struggle, and strain ... not evil, crime, suffering, and all the deplorable conditions that plague our society. Our society is out of harmony with truth and nature ... out of harmony and rhythm with the way God designed the process to work ... out of harmony with God.

The way life is meant to be is in agreement with truth and nature ... the kind of life Jesus wanted for us ... if only we would believe and comprehend what he said. Life in harmony with truth and nature is natural and normal. Life characterized by depression, anxiety, anger, hate, neurosis, jealousy, loneliness, unhappiness, psychosomatic illnesses, addictions, discontent, crime, and violence is not natural and normal.

We will never solve the problems that plague our society by trying to alleviate symptoms, but doing nothing about the underlying cause. More prisons, more policemen, gun control, the FBI, and V-chips to block violent programs on TV will never stop crime and violence.

When we correct the cause of problems — rather than tinker with symptoms — the problems will vanish. After all the excuses and blame for the social problems in our society (e.g., blaming outrageous TV talk shows and violence on TV for violence in our society), researchers would be hard-pressed to find one criminal, one serial killer, one rapist, one child abuser, one spouse abuser, one drug addict, one Hitler, one person motivated by a violent TV program to commit a violent crime — one person prone to evil and violence — who was reared in a loving, happy, harmonious, stable, functional family and who received the unconditional love of a loving, happy, contented mother.

There is no greater gift that we can possibly give our children than a happy home life in a loving, happy, harmonious family environment—a family in which the parents are unified with God ... expressing life in harmony with truth and nature. This far more important than material wealth.

Some people tend to look at our society (at all the crime, suffering, rape, child abuse, drug abuse, spousal abuse, divorce, dysfunctional families, psychosomatic illnesses, alcoholism, mental illness, and mental retardation [those cases that are environmentally induced], the alarming increase in teenage suicide, crookedness in government, and on and on and on), and brush it aside as "the world in which we live." Let's not forget that the world in which we live is the world we create ... for us individually and collectively as a society and as a nation.

Some people blame many of the deplorable acts of others on human nature, with such expressions as, "It's just old human nature" ... as if human nature is bad; it is not. On the contrary, human nature is perfect ... the way God created it. Only our fearful, false ego-self makes human nature seem bad. All destructive, deplorable, shameful behaviors evolve from the false ego-self. Only good comes from our true spiritual self.

The world in which we live — the condition of our society — does not begin with our schools or with villages; it begins with our families and us. Our schools are no longer a safe place to be. We expect too much from our teachers and our school system. We expect them to teach and to control uncontrollable, troubled, restless students. Some students are troubled with attention deficit hyperactivity disorder and are difficult for teachers to teach and control.

Joseph Pearce, author of *The Bond of Power*, said: "For twentieth-century Western man, anxiety and alienation are commonplace. ... We are each born with a biological blueprint for spiritual maturity, but by the time we leave childhood, our parents and our culture have led us away from the true longings of our hearts and toward the chatter of confused thinking."

Emerson said, "Every violation of truth is not only a sort of suicide in the liar, but is a stab at the health of human society." Violations of truth characterize our fractured, troubled society. Truth is the only thing that will save us individually, and consequently, our society. The whole is no better than the sum of the parts. Our society is a composite of us. Money, materialism, and

When Will Suffering and Violence End?

prestige are not measures of morality and spiritual values ... not a measure of love, joy, happiness, harmony, inner peace, and serenity.

From a simple observation of the many things that men do and have done ... the things that men have invented, designed, constructed, manufactured, produced — the many professions in which they have excelled — and from an observation of the inherent tendency of men (particularly those reared in a reasonably loving, functional family) ... it is clear that men have the power, capability, and the desire to provide and protect.

According to a new study, men have about four billion more brain cells than women. Aristotle said, "Nature does nothing uselessly." Providing and protecting requires more brain cells than loving, mothering, and nurturing. However, loving, mothering, and nurturing add a quality to life that nothing else can replace.

Although not as obvious and clear as the role of men, women have the power and capability to render families — and consequently society — loving, happy and harmonious. Women have the power to restore sanity to an insane, fractured, troubled society ... the power to rule the world.

Contented, happy mothers — living in agreement with their true, loving, feminine nature — have the ability to rear happy, contented children ... it comes naturally ... if only mothers would listen to their inner voice ... if only mothers were abiding by their true, loving, feminine nature. Let's face it! Women are abdicating their role as mother, the type of mother needed to give their children the love, mothering, nurturing, and care that children need to feel genuinely loved, emotionally secure, happy, satisfied, and contented.

About 300 BC, Zeno, Greek Philosopher, said, "The goal of life is living in agreement with nature." Living in agreement with nature is the same thing as living in harmony with love and truth ... the only thing that will ever make us happy, satisfied, and contented.

When women become free to live in agreement with their true, loving, feminine nature, they will be happy, satisfied, and contented ... in due time everyone will be happy, satisfied, and contented. And living in agreement with truth — in agreement with their true feminine nature — is the only thing that will make women genuinely happy, satisfied, and contented.

Regarding the fractured, troubled, dysfunctional families, women are not to blame. If we as a society lived in agreement with truth and nature, women would be happy, satisfied, and contented to fulfill their role as mother ... which is in agreement with her true feminine nature. However, religious teachers are not teaching us how to unify with God, and consequently, how to live in harmony with truth and nature.

Throughout history, most great religious teachers and spiritual leaders (e.g., Jesus, Buddha, Mohammed, Spinoza, Aristotle, Emerson, Gandhi, Plato, Socrates, Confucius, and most of the biblical writers) were men ... which is in agreement with a man's role of providing and protecting. However, religious leaders are not providing the guidance people need in order to enjoy the abundant life that Jesus wanted us to enjoy. Religious teachers are not teaching us how to discover the truth that sets us free; how to unify with God; how to live in harmony with truth, God, and nature ... what everyone wants. In brief, religious teachers are not teaching us the gospel that Jesus preached ... at least not teaching it in a manner we can understand and embody.

Religious teachers are not teaching people the truth about the truth, which is the only solution to reversing the disastrous conditions of our society and the direction in which our society is headed, which is total social collapse. For whatever the explanation, we seem to expect men to be the religious teachers who will lead us in the direction to truth ... who will teach us the gospel that Jesus preached. The gospel of Jesus — if believed, understood and embodied — would reverse the direction in which we are headed, which is toward total destruction.

If we, as a society, understood and embodied the gospel that Jesus preached, we would have peace and joy. If we, as a society, had peace and joy — if we lived in harmony with truth, God, and nature — mothers would be happy and contented mothering and nurturing their children. Families would be loving, happy, harmonious, functional, and they would stay together. The social problems

When Will Suffering and Violence End? 301

that plague our society would vanish. Suffering and violence would end.

Many religious teachers are letting the tail wag the dog, teaching and preaching confusing, soothing-sounding, inspirational stuff that people want to hear, rather than telling people the truth about their faults and how to overcome them; rather than teaching people the truth about the hidden cause of their suffering (which is the Satan within them); rather than teaching people the truth about heaven and how to discover it; rather than teaching people how to discover the truth that will set them free; rather than teaching people the gospel that Jesus commanded his disciples to preach to every creature in all the world.

Aristotle said, "The high-minded man must care more for the truth than for what people think." False teachers do not make it clear to us that the cause of our anger, hate, unhappiness, restlessness, and discontent is the Satan within us ... is our own insidious fears and false beliefs; it's our own ego. False teachers do not make it clear to us that the solution to our suffering is the truth that sets us free and that it is within us.

False teachings have a way of concealing, rather than revealing the message Jesus intended for us. False teachings are a stumbling block in our path to God ... a stumbling block in our path to the discovery of the truth that sets us free ... deep inside the soul of us what everyone wants.

One of the greatest contributions that religious teachers could possibly make to humanity is to teach the gospel that Jesus commanded his disciples to preach to every creature in all the world ... teaching it in a manner that people can understand and believe. Jesus said clearly that those who believe the gospel would be saved.

We cannot expect peace, joy, harmony, happiness, and contentment in a society where 90 percent of the families are dysfunctional. The level of peace, joy, harmony, happiness, and contentment in a society does not rise above the level that is in the family. The level of peace, joy, harmony, and happiness in the family does not rise above the level of the parents.

We "reap what we sow." And we are led astray from that which is true and, consequently, sow thoughts of fear, ignorance, restlessness, and discontent. It's easy enough to observe what we are reaping ... bombings, the shooting in the schools, dysfunctional families, the breakup of families, and violence at every turn of the road.

Jesus told us when suffering and violence will end; however, what he said has been misinterpreted or glossed over. And let's face it! What he said is not matter-of-fact, straightforward and clear. Let's remember that Jesus spoke in proverbs, parables, idioms, metaphors, and descriptive language. To understand what Jesus said, it helps to keep in mind what his basic purpose was and also remember that his basic message is quite simple. As explained in Chapter 5, "Understanding What Jesus Said," Jesus' mission was that we might have peace. He said, "These things I have spoken unto you, that you might have peace" ... meaning in the present time, not after the end of the world.

Jesus' teachings concerned the present, not forecasts of the future as we typically think of foretelling the future. It is a mistake to use the teachings of Jesus to forecast the end of the world, as some people think of the end of the world. Jesus said, "Take therefore no thought for the morrow; for the morrow shall take thought for the things of itself. Sufficient unto the day is the evil thereof" (Matthew 6:34).

Many people wonder about the end of the world, and they think that Jesus forecast some colossal, bizarre ending to the world. There are those who think that Jesus will return to earth ... descending out of the clouds; this is a gross misunderstanding and misinterpretation of the Scriptures.

At least a part of the confusion about the end of the world centers on the answer to a question posed by Jesus' disciples. The disciples asked Jesus, "What shall be the sign of thy coming and of the end of the world?"

In answering, Jesus said, "Take heed that no man deceive you. For many shall come in my name, saying, I am Christ; and shall deceive many. And ye shall hear of wars and rumours of wars ... For nation shall rise against nation, and kingdom against kingdom; and there shall be famines, and pestilences, and earthquakes, in divers places. *All these are the beginning of sorrows.* ... Then shall

When Will Suffering and Violence End?

they deliver you up to be afflicted, and shall kill you; and ye shall be hated of all nations for my name's sake. And then shall many be offended, and shall betray one another, and shall hate one another. And many false prophets shall rise, and shall deceive many. ... But he that shall endure unto the end, the same shall be saved" (Matthew 24: 4-13).

Many of the things to which Jesus alluded have existed both before and since his time; many are rampant in today's society. It's easy to observe the things that he mentioned and especially the part about many false prophets deceiving many people. Clearly, there are many false teachers. One of the false teachings is about the "end of the world."

Part of what Jesus said seems to have been glossed over and misinterpreted: "All these are the beginning of sorrows." "Sorrow" is defined as, "pain or distress of mind." Thus, Jesus was speaking of "all these" being the beginning of suffering, not a sign of the end of the world as we think of the end of the world.

In our language and in view of the way our society has deteriorated, it's safe to add to "all these." In biblical times there were no shootings in the schools, bombing of abortion clinics, drug abuse (at least not like it is today). It's doubtful that the society in biblical times was comparable to our society in terms of violence, stress, anxiety, hatred, jealousy, loneliness, restlessness, discontent, murder, rape, child abuse, spousal abuse, dysfunctional families ... and on and on and on. Let's remember that of all developed nations, America is the most violent.

Let's also note that Jesus said, "But he that shall endure unto the end, the same shall be saved" (Matthew 24:13). This statement could not possibly mean the end of the world as some fundamentalists think about the end of the world ... and those who "endure unto the end shall be saved." No one has endured until the end of the world, as we tend to think of the end of the world. Besides, enduring until the end of the world is not what saves us. Those who persevere and endure until they comprehend and embody the gospel that Jesus preached are saved.

To understand what Jesus said, we must understand his use of the word "world." It's misleading to take verses of Scriptures out of context to support an erroneous belief. For example, fundamentalists have used verse 5, Chapter 17, of the "Gospel According to John," to make it seem that Jesus was a special being ... was God in human flesh: "And now, O Father, glorify thou me with thine own self with the glory that I had with thee before the world was."

One need only to read to verse 19 of that chapter to get some understanding of what Jesus meant by the word "world." He spoke of when he was with his disciples in the world and also of no longer being in the world. He also spoke of his disciples (there is no question about them being human) not being of the world. Jesus said, "They are not of the world, even as I am not of the world."

If we study and assimilate the teachings of Jesus, we realize that he was speaking of the false world of the ego. Jesus was living in the physical world ... not living in the world of the ego. Thus, when Jesus was speaking about the end of the world, he was speaking about the end of the world of the ego, which translates into the end of suffering. Mental suffering, evil, and violence evolve from the false ego-self ... not our true spiritual self.

We might also note in this same passage of Scripture that Jesus said, "These things I speak in the world, that they might have my joy fulfilled in themselves" (John 17:13). Again, this is in agreement with Jesus' mission: That we might have peace and joy ... that we might have life and have it more abundantly. Jesus did not speak of saving people so that they would enjoy heaven after they die ... after the end of the world.

In addition, if we read this same passage (John 17:1-9) carefully, we realize that truth resides in the Father (in the language of our time, truth resides in our true spiritual self), and we are sanctified (saved) by truth. Jesus said, "Sanctify them through thy truth; thy word is truth" ("thy" referring to our true spiritual self).

Also, let's remember that Jesus said, "I must be about my Father's business." His Father's business was saving the lost so that they might have peace. His Father's business was not forecasting such things as pestilence and earthquakes and the ultimate end of the world. Although civilization might be annihilated by nuclear weapons, this is not what Jesus was talking about.

When Will Suffering and Violence End?

Jesus told us when the end would come; however, if we study and assimilate what Jesus said, we realize that he was speaking about the end of suffering ... about the end of the world of the ego, the source of suffering, violence, discontent, and restlessness.

When did Jesus say suffering would end? Jesus said to his disciples, "And this gospel of the kingdom shall be preached in all the world for a witness unto all nations; and then shall the end come." The gospel of the kingdom (the kingdom of God, which is within) that Jesus preached — if taught in a manner that we could understand and embody — would end suffering.

Think about it! If the gospel that Jesus preached and that he commanded his disciples to preach in all the world had been taught during the past 2,000 years (since the death of Jesus), we, our families, our society, our nation — the very world itself — would be characterized by love, peace, and joy. That's the kind of life — that's the kind of world — Jesus wanted for us.

Actually the gospel that Jesus preached is not being preached in mainline churches ... at least, not preached in a manner that we can understand and embody. The gospel of Jesus is hardly preached at all ... much less in the entire world. By observation, we realize how true Jesus statement is: "And many false prophets shall rise, and shall deceive many." Clearly there are many false prophets (teachers), who are not teaching the gospel that Jesus taught.

Jesus' mission was that we might have peace and joy. When we understand and embody what Jesus said, we will have peace and joy ... and that will be the end of suffering.

I am reminded of the statement mentioned previously by Thomas Jefferson, the third president of the United States. Speaking about Jesus and his teachings, Jefferson said, "... my opinion is that if nothing had ever been added to what flowed purely from his lips, the whole world would at this day have been Christian." (*The Gospel According to Jesus* by Stephen Mitchell).

"What flowed purely from his lips" is not the emphasis of the teachings of Christianity. If the world were Christian, we would not have all the chaos, suffering, violence, disintegration of families, and so on. However, the world will not be Christian until religious teachers began teaching clearly the gospel that Jesus taught.

Remember, Jesus told his disciples, "Go ye into all the world, and preach the gospel to every nation. ... He that believeth and is baptized shall be saved; but he that believeth not shall be damned." Suffering ends for us individually — and collectively as a society — when we believe the gospel of Jesus and are saved. ... That is the end of suffering ... the end of the world of the ego.

Those who do not believe will be damned. Many people have been deceived and led astray from the message that Jesus intended for us. Consequently, they do not understand and believe what Jesus said, and they are damned. Suffering and violence are rampant.

If only we study and assimilate what Jesus said, we know that suffering and violence will end when religious teachers teach the gospel of the kingdom of God — the message Jesus intended for us — in a manner we can understand and embody. Suffering and violence will end when we worship and serve our true spiritual self and can say with honesty and understanding, "Get thee behind me, Satan [false ego-self]; thou art an offense unto me."

In his manner of speaking, Isaiah told us when suffering and violence will end. Isaiah said, "Your iniquities have separated you and your God. ... None calleth for justice, nor any pleadeth for truth; they trust in vanity and speak lies; they conceive mischief and bring forth iniquity ... their works are works of iniquity, and the act of violence is in their hands. ... The way of peace they know not, and they have made them crooked paths; whosoever goeth therein shall not know peace. ... In transgressing and lying against the Lord and departing away from our God, speaking oppression and revolt, conceiving and uttering from the heart words of falsehood. ... for truth is fallen in the street and equity cannot enter" (Isaiah 59: 4-14).

Again, the word "peace" surfaces throughout the teachings of the writers of the Old Testament ... and there is nothing about a hell of fire and brimstone after death. In our language, our iniquities (fear, anger, jealousy, violence, selfishness, greed, pride, ignorance, and the desire to do things for ego gratification ... things we can gloat over and that seem to make us appear special and important) have alienated us from our true spiritual self ... have alienated us from God. When we are alienated from our true spiritual self —

When Will Suffering and Violence End?

guided by fear, ignorance, and falsehoods rather than truth — we do not know peace; in one manner or another, we suffer.

Abiding by our true spiritual self is a prerequisite for enjoying peace. Note what Isaiah said: "Arise, shine; for thy light is come, and the glory of the Lord is risen upon thee. For, behold, the darkness shall cover the earth, and gross darkness the people; but the Lord shall arise upon thee, and his glory shall be seen upon thee. ... For the nation and kingdom that will not serve thee shall perish; yea, those nations shall be utterly wasted" (Isaiah 60:1-12). In this passage, "light" is truth, and "darkness" is evil. When we are doing the will of our true spiritual self — when we are unified with God — the "glory of the Lord is upon us." Thus, Isaiah explained when suffering and violence will end: When "the Lord shall arise upon thee, and his glory shall be seen upon thee."

In addition, Isaiah said, "Violence shall no more be heard in thy land, wasting nor destruction within thy borders; but thou shalt call thy walls Salvation, and thy gates Praise. ... the Lord shall be unto thee an everlasting light, and thy God thy glory. ... and the days of thy mourning shall be ended. Thy people also shall be all righteous" (Isaiah 60:18-21).

Think about it! All will be righteous when we are abiding by the truth ("everlasting light") that proceeds from our true spiritual self. ... "Violence shall no more be heard ... the days of thy mourning shall be ended." All will be righteous when we "return unto the Lord" ... in our language, when we return to our true spiritual self, rather than following the dictates of our false ego-self. Surely, suffering and violence will end when all are righteous ... when all believe and comprehend the gospel of the kingdom of God—the message Jesus intended for us.

Jesus said that those who do not believe the gospel would be damned. Note what Isaiah said: "For the nation and kingdom that will not serve thee shall perish; yea, those nations shall be utterly wasted." In our language, to "serve thee" is to abide by the truth that proceeds from our true spiritual self ... in the words of Jesus, the same thing as doing the will of the Father ... a prerequisite for peace and joy ... a prerequisite for enjoying heaven.

Could our nation be on the brink of perishing ... of being "utterly wasted?" Let's face it! If we continue to acquiesce to the dictates of our ego, rather than abiding by the truth that proceeds from our true spiritual self, "we shall perish; we shall be utterly wasted."

We don't think it could happen to America, but could we be on the brink of being under a dictator? Or worse, of being annihilated by nuclear weapons? Unthinkable possibilities! Yet, this might be the direction in which we are headed.

Think about it! Think about all that we are blessed with in this great nation, beginning with God's creation ... many things we take for granted. We are blessed with natural resources, forests, mountains, streams, and the climate and land suitable for producing an abundance of agricultural products, including grains, fruits, and vegetables. In addition, think of all the amenities that have been added to enhance our enjoyment and the freedom and opportunity to pursue whatever it is we wish to pursue. We have our institutions of higher learning, our churches, school systems, our national parks, our transportation network, manufacturing plants, sky scraper buildings, museums, libraries, stadiums, and an abundance of knowledge and scientific inventions, and on and on and on.

In addition, we can be thankful for the contributions of our forefathers, who had the integrity, intelligence, wisdom, and foresight for framing the Declaration of Independence and the Constitution of the U.S. that assure us the freedom and opportunity to pursue peace, joy, and happiness.

Think about it! So many of the things with which we have been blessed — including our lives — could be obliterated in a few minutes by a few people, pushing a few buttons in a few places.

If you do not believe that the risk exists, you would do well to read the book, *The China Threat*, by Bill Gertz (author of the New York Times bestseller *Betrayal*). The following comment appears on the back cover of the subject book: "If you're a fan or horror stories, read this. It will scare the hell out of you," by G. Gordon Liddy.

On the inside of the front cover, we find, "The *China Threat* reveals: An internal Chinese military document exposing how

Beijing is willing to launch a nuclear attack on the United States if American forces attempt to defend Taiwan."

In addition, an article, "China's missile threat growing, report says," appeared in the January 11, 2002, issue of The Knoxville News-Sentinel. The article is based on a report released by the CIA. According to the article, "China is expected to have as many as 100 long-range nuclear missiles aimed at the United States by 2015." The goal is to have an ICBM force capable of striking the U.S. mainline if there is a conflict over Taiwan.

It's doubtful that anyone knows what all the threats are to our nation. We know for certain that there are risks. We know for certain that there are terrorists who are willing to die for the annihilation of America. Think about it! Is it possible that terrorists could destroy America? Let's face it! It might not happen, but it is possible ... especially if terrorists get access to nuclear weapons.

Albert Einstein, physicist and Nobel laureate, said, "If it (the hydrogen bomb) is successful, radioactive poisoning of the atmosphere and hence annihilation of any life on earth has been brought within the range of technical possibilities. ... Peace cannot be kept by force. It can only be achieved by understanding." (*The Great Quotations* compiled by George Seldes).

President John F. Kennedy said, "Unconditional war can no longer lead to unconditional victory. It can no longer serve to settle disputes. ... For a nuclear disaster, spread by winds and waters and fear, could well engulf the great and the small, the rich and the poor, the committed and the uncommitted alike. Mankind must put an end to war or war will put an end to mankind." (*Bartlett's Familiar Quotations* by John Bartlett).

To put an end to war, we must begin from the center of peace within ourselves. Peace begets peace; war begets war. Peace comes from our heart, not from fighting; this is true for both families and for nations. We enjoy peace by getting the wisdom and understanding for knowing the truth that sets us free, the truth that proceeds from our true spiritual self. Wisdom and understanding help us in our personal relationship with ourselves and with God, and consequently, in our relationships with others.

We might learn something from the wisdom of Abraham Lincoln that might help us prevent conflicts with other nations: "The way to destroy our enemies is to make them our friends." The best way to make a friend is to be a friend

Amos, author of the Book of Amos, advocated a return to the Lord to solve the problems confronting the Israelites. Amos posed the question, "Can two walk together, except they be agreed" (Amos 3:3)? Further, Amos said, "Seek ye the Lord, and ye shall live. ... For I know your manifold transgressions and your mighty sins; they afflict the just, they take a bribe ... Seek good, and not evil, that ye may live; and so the Lord, the God of hosts, shall be with you" (Amos 5:6-14). The solution advocated by Amos a few thousand years ago is applicable today: "Seek ye the Lord." When we find the Lord, we follow the guidance of our true spiritual self, and this is the solution to violence and suffering.

In recent years it seems that we have enjoyed the success of a booming economy brought about to a great extent by the technological revolution, and we have lost a sense of true success. Are we really successful — is all well — if we do not have peace and joy? If we really have peace and joy, why are we the most violent nation among the developed nations? Why the acts of terrorism? Why are so many families dysfunctional? Why is the American family disintegrating? Why the bombing of the Alfred P. Murrah Federal Building in Oklahoma City? Why the alarming drug problem? Why the many prisons that are overcrowded? Why are public schools not a safe place to be? ... and on and on and on.

Is all well when there are more than enough nuclear weapons to destroy civilization ... to "utterly waste" every nation on earth? And nations continue to manufacture nuclear weapons.

Remember the wisdom of Isaiah, "the nation and kingdom that will not serve thee shall perish; yea, those nations shall be utterly wasted." We, as a society in which about 90 percent of the families are dysfunctional, do not "serve thee."

We might be closer to being "utterly wasted" than we realize. Although we don't like to admit our errors and to face the facts, we are headed toward destruction, primarily because of our fear, ignorance, greed, and selfishness ... because we are out of harmony

When Will Suffering and Violence End?

with truth, God, and nature. As a noted evangelist stated it, we are a nation bent on self destruction.

Bernard Baruch, consultant to four presidents regarding war, said, "Behind the black portent of the new atomic age lies a hope which, seized upon with faith, can work out salvation. ... Let us not deceive ourselves: we must elect world peace or world destruction" (*Bartlett's Familiar Quotations*).

We are so far alienated from truth, God, and nature that we have chosen the materialistic world of the ego — the things "savored by man" — rather than the spiritual world, things desired of our true spiritual self. We have the power of choice. We have chosen a world of tribulations — of anxiety, depression, hatred, anger, jealousy, revenge, stress, loneliness, emptiness, crime, violence, drug abuse, child abuse, spousal abuse, the breakup of families — a society lacking in peace, joy, and contentment.

Mother Teresa said, "Everybody today seems to be in such a terrible rush, anxious for greater developments and greater riches and so on, so that children have very little time for their parents. Parents have very little time for each other, and in the home begins the disruption of peace of the world."

Typically, we attempt to solve problems by attacking the symptoms, but do not explore the cause of the problems. For example, we blame the drug problem on the countries that supply the drugs without exploring why there is a demand for the drugs. If we did an in-depth study of the messy morass in which we find ourselves, we might discover that we are a part of the problem, not a part of the solution ... the last thing our ego would have us admit. If our families were loving, happy, and stable — in harmony with truth, God, and nature — there would be no demand for drugs.

Let's face it! The American family is disintegrating. As the family goes, so goes the nation. According to Isaiah, a nation inharmonious with truth, God, and nature is sure to perish ... to be "utterly wasted."

William J. Bennett, author of *The Index of Leading Cultural Indicators — American Society at the End of the Twentieth Century*, said: "The nation we live in today is more violent and vulgar, coarse and cynical, rude and remorseless, deviant and depressed, than the one we once inhabited."

We (individually and collectively as a nation) are motivated by greed, selfishness, and evil. Who do you know who does as President John Kennedy said to do? He said: "Ask not what your country can do for you; ask what you can do for your country."

Like an ostrich with its head in the sand, we can easily sit back and declare many things that can make us proud to be an American. Blinded by material comfort, selfishness and greed, and the things desired by the ego — things we can gloat over — we don't see the handwriting on the wall. Peace is more important than wealth. We don't know what genuine peace is. As it is, we are headed toward being "utterly wasted."

We like to think that we are a peaceful nation. Is it logical to think that we are a peaceful nation when we are the most violent nation among the developed nations? How can we be a peaceful nation when many of the decisions made by our elected leaders are rooted in selfishness and greed ... based on what is best for their political party and what is best for special interest groups, rather than what is best for the nation?

Instead of pointing fingers at our leaders and blaming them for the messy morass in which we find ourselves — a nation that is headed toward destruction — let us remember that we elected our leaders. And although we do not like to admit it, our choices for leaders are influenced by our ignorance, greed, and selfishness ... by what we think is best for us ... with no concern about what is best for one and another ... what is best for the nation.

A clever politician knows how to appeal to our selfishness, greed, vanity, and ignorance to muster votes. And regardless of the rhetoric of some of our elected leaders — especially those who are motivated by the lust for power — a high priority is satisfying those who have contributed the most to their election campaign ... with no concern about what is best for the nation. Selfishness, greed, and ignorance will underlie the downfall — the destruction — of this nation.

Regardless of the errors, crookedness, and weaknesses of some of our elected officials, they do not rob us of our freedom to pursue

When Will Suffering and Violence End?

happiness as assured by the Declaration of Independence and the Constitution of the United States of America. We have the freedom to discover the truth that sets us free. And, when we do, we will find true joy, peace, and happiness. If we were guided by the truth that proceeds from our true spiritual self — the only thing that will bring us peace and joy and make us happy — what we desire would be good for the nation. And we would not elect leaders whose lust for power takes precedence over doing what is best for the nation.

We don't really help others find peace, if we do not have peace. The way to have peace within us is by abiding by the truth that proceeds from our true spiritual self. Thus, if we pay attention to the wisdom of Isaiah ("For the nation and kingdom that will not serve thee shall perish; yea, those nations shall be utterly wasted."), we realize that if we continue to follow the dictates of our ego, rather than abiding by the will of our true spiritual self, we "shall be utterly wasted."

C. G. Jung, author of *The Undiscovered Self*, said: "Considering that the evil of our day puts everything that has ever agonized mankind in the deepest shade, one must ask oneself how it is that, for all our progress in the administration of justice, in medicine and in technology, for all our concern for life and health, monstrous engines of destruction have been invented which could easily exterminate the human race. ... *Reason alone does not suffice.* In theory, it lies within the power of reason to desist from experiments of such hellish scope as nuclear fission if only because of the dangerousness. But fear of the evil which one does not see in one's own bosom but always in somebody else's checks reason every time, although one knows that the use of this weapon means the certain end of our present human world."

The one thing that can reverse the direction in which we are headed is being truthful and living in harmony with truth, God, and nature ... the only thing that will make us genuinely joyous, happy, peaceful, and contented. We are naturally honest, truthful, peaceful, and contented when we understand and embody the teachings of Jesus. How many people do you know who are following the true teachings of Jesus? Who are living in harmony with their true spiritual self, rather than following the dictates of their ego?

Anne Frank, German diarist, who died at the age of 16 in a German concentration camp, said, "How wonderful it is that nobody need wait a single moment before starting to improve the world."

Every moment that we express life in agreement with truth and nature, we are improving the world. It cannot be otherwise; that's the way God designed the process to work.

During the 1700s, Benjamin Franklin, scientist, diplomat, and writer, said: "I wish it (Christianity) were productive of good works ... I mean real good works ..." (*The Great Quotations*, compiled by George Seldes). Let us remember that Jesus said, "Blessed are the peacemakers; for they shall be called the children of God." When religious teachers become true peacemakers — teaching the message Jesus intended for us in a manner we can understand and embody — they will be productive of "real good works." We, our families, our nation, the very world itself, will be peaceful and harmonious ... suffering and violence will end.

Suffering and violence will end when we cast the devils from our mind, when we clean the inside of the cup and the platter, when we are converted and are humble as little children, when we are abiding by the truth that evolves from our true spiritual self, rather than being engulfed by the world of the false ego-self (Satan).

We will experience a major transformation when religious teachers teach us the message Jesus intended for us. Suffering and violence will end when we truly worship our true spiritual self and are abiding by the truth within us ... when we are expressing life in harmony with truth, God, and nature ... the only thing that will ever bring us genuine joy, peace, happiness, and contentment.

Can you imagine? Can you comprehend what we, our families, or society, our nation — the very world itself — will be like when we abide by the truth that evolves from our true self ... rather than being caught up in the world of the ego? Can you imagine what it will be like when fathers and mothers are doing the will of their true spiritual self and rear their children in loving, happy, harmonious, peaceful, stable families? We will enjoy heaven ... here and now. Life does not get any better than heaven.

When Will Suffering and Violence End?

Remember the simplicity of Jesus' teachings: Everyone who believes the gospel will be saved. Why complicate the essential teachings of Jesus with something we cannot understand? In all simplicity, suffering and violence — all that is ugly and deplorable — will end when we believe, understand, and embody the message Jesus intended for us. Suffering and violence will end when we are living in harmony with truth, God, and nature ... when we are unified with God ... what everyone insatiably desires.

The challenge for religious teachers for the twenty-first century is to shift from the false, misleading teachings of Christianity to the teachings of Jesus ... to the gospel that Jesus preached and that he commanded his disciples to preach ... teaching in a manner that people believe, understand and embody. This challenge includes teaching people to love, cherish and worship — and abide by — their true divine spiritual self ... the God within us ... the same thing as Jesus worshipping — and abiding by — the Father.

In summary, suffering and violence will end when Jesus said it would: "And this gospel of the kingdom shall be preached in all the world for a witness unto all nations; and then shall the end come." We need only to add a stipulation to what Jesus said. Suffering and violence will end when the gospel of the kingdom is preached in all the world, *preached in a manner we believe, understand and embody.* Suffering and violence will end when we have peace and joy ... the purpose for Jesus preaching the gospel.

Henry David Thoreau, writer, philosopher, and naturalist, said, "There are a thousand hacking at the branches of evil to one who is striking at the root." There are many who are seriously working hard to alleviate the symptoms caused by evil. However, do you know anyone who is seriously trying to correct the root cause of evil? When we correct the cause of evil — rather than tinkering with the symptoms — suffering and violence will cease.

A thought for today: We have a choice. Do we choose heaven or do we choose hell? It's one or the other; we cannot have it both ways. We cannot "serve two masters." We either serve our true spiritual self that brings peace, love, and joy, or we serve our false ego-self (Satan) that causes suffering and violence. If we do not choose peace now, when will we?

Chapter 13
Summary — Life's Greatest Lesson

The sole purpose for Jesus preaching the gospel is that we might have peace and joy ... the same mission of the Buddha about 500 years BC. There will never be anymore peace and joy than that which we have the potential to enjoy this very moment. We experience the ultimate of peace and joy when we are expressing life in harmony with truth ... when we are unified with God.

When we (individually and collectively as a society) believe the gospel that Jesus commanded his disciples to preach to every creature in all the world — when we know the truth that sets us free — we will be loving, happy, peaceful, satisfied, and contented. Families will be loving, happy, harmonious, functional, stable, and they will remain together. Our society will be safe and harmonious ... a utopia ... like "a new heaven and a new earth."

What is being taught in Christianity is based on what fundamentalists believe, which isn't consistent with the gospel that Jesus preached. Christians are captivated by the man Jesus, not by what he taught. Praising and worshipping the man Jesus, Christians gloss over what Jesus said.

Fundamentalists believe and teach such things as: Take Christ into your heart. Accept Jesus as your savior. Believe on Jesus and be saved. Jesus died on the cross to save us from our sins. We are saved by being washed in the blood ... and on and on and on. These things are not the gospel that Jesus preached. And, believing these things does not save us. Believing the gospel that Jesus preached — and doing what he said — would save us.

Fundamentalists believe that the gospel is the good news about Jesus, and that Jesus died on the cross to save us from our sins ... to take away the sins of the world. On the contrary, the gospel is what Jesus preached and what he commanded his disciples to preach to every creature in the entire world. The gospel that Jesus preached is the gospel of the kingdom of God. Jesus said, "the kingdom of God is within you."

Summary

Jesus said to his disciples: "Go ye into all the world and preach the gospel to every creature. ... He that *believeth* [the gospel] and is baptized *shall be saved*, but he that believeth not shall be damned" (Mark 16:16-17).

With the foregoing in mind, here are some of the essentials of the gospel of Jesus—things that would save us:

- Seek ye first the kingdom of God (which is within us).
- You shall know the truth and the truth shall make you free.
- Be ye therefore perfect, even as your Father who is in heaven is perfect.
- Only those who do the will of their Father will enjoy heaven (according to Jesus, the Father and heaven are within us).
- Be converted and become as little children.
- You must be "born again" (meaning the same thing as the previous statement and also meaning the same thing as something that the Apostle Paul said, "Be ye therefore transformed by the renewing of your mind").
- Ask, and it shall be given you; seek, and ye shall find.
- Cast the devils from your heart.
- Clean the inside of the cup and the platter.
- Pray to your Father who is in secret (the same thing as communing with our own heart, as advocated by David the Psalmist).
- You shall love the Lord thy God with all your heart, and with all your soul, and with all your mind.

In addition to what Jesus said, here are a few other things (by others) that would save us:

- Sanctify yourselves. — Moses
- Wash thine heart from wickedness, that thou mayest be saved. — Jeremiah
- Seek ye the Lord while he may be found; call ye upon him while he is near. — Isaiah
- Call upon the name of the Lord (same thing as calling upon and communing with our true spiritual self). — Apostle Paul
- Call upon the Lord in truth. He will hear our cry and will save us (same as what the Apostle Paul said in the previous statement). And, "commune with your own heart." — David the Psalmist

- "Purify your hearts, ye double minded," and "receive with meekness the engrafted word, which is able to save your souls." — James, author of "The Letter of James." (Purifying our hearts is the same thing as "cleaning the inside of the cup and the platter." And, the engrafted word is the *truth* that sets us free.)
- Be ye lamps unto yourselves; seek salvation alone in truth (same thing as communing with our own heart as advocated by David, the Psalmist). — The Buddha
- Know thyself. — Socrates and the Seven Sages of Greece.

All the foregoing boils down to the same thing. When we are pure in heart, we are unified with God ... we are saved. When God and truth reign in our heart, we do the will of our Father (our true spiritual self). According to Jesus, this is a prerequisite for enjoying heaven ... a prerequisite for having peace and joy.

The spiritual teachers of the Old Testament retreated to the Lord within themselves for wisdom and guidance. Similarly, Jesus retreated to the Father within him. Jesus was sent by his Father. The spiritual teachers of the Old Testament were sent by the Lord ... same thing, just different words. Jesus said, "And he that sent me is with me; the Father hath not left me alone" (John 8:29).

From the teachings of the spiritual teachers of the Old Testament and from the teachings of Jesus, we realize that there is something sacred within us: our true spiritual self ... God within us. According to Jesus, truth will save us. Truth is the way and the life of our spirit. We gain wisdom and understanding — we are saved — by communing with our true spiritual self and discovering the truth that sets us free. We are saved by doing what David the Psalmist said to do about 3,000 years ago: "Commune with your own heart."

The message Jesus intended for us is the gospel that he preached about 2,000 years ago, which would save us, if we believed — and did — what Jesus said.

An ending thought: If we do not begin studying and believing the gospel of Jesus *now* — and doing what he said to do — when will we?